Making Peace

Making Peace

THE RECONSTRUCTION
OF GENDER IN
INTERWAR BRITAIN

Susan Kingsley Kent

PRINCETON UNIVERSITY PRESS

PRINCETON, NEW JERSEY

Library of Congress Cataloging-in-Publication Data

Kent, Susan Kingsley.
Making peace : the reconstruction of gender in
interwar Britain / Susan Kingsley Kent.
p.   cm.
Includes bibliographical references and index.
ISBN 0–691–03140–1
1. Sex role—Great Britain—History—20th century.
2. Feminism—Great Britain—History—20th century.
3. War and society.
I. Title.
HQ1075.5.G7K46 1993
305.3'0941'0904--DC20   93–18776

This book has been composed in Adobe Caledonia

Princeton University Press books are printed
on acid-free paper and meet the guidelines for
permanence and durability of the Committee on
Production Guidelines for Book Longevity
of the Council on Library Resources

Printed in the United States of America

1   3   5   7   9   10   8   6   4   2

For Anne

CONTENTS

PREFACE

In 1986, my young niece, Elisa Kent Mendelsohn, was diagnosed with a terminal illness; she died eight months later. As I see now but did not fully grasp at the time, I turned to a study of the Great War in an effort to make sense of the incomprehensible, to learn something about how individuals in the past gave expression to the unspeakable. What resulted was not the analysis of loss and identity that I had intended—that one will come next—but rather a project that derives from my earlier work on gender, sexuality, and politics, yet finds its whole point and purpose in the experiences of war. I am surely not unique in choosing a subject that has enabled me to work out personal issues, but readers should know that *Making Peace* is informed by a sensibility born of my own and my family's pain, an understanding of the extent to which premature and seemingly random death can shatter one's understanding of oneself and others, and an appreciation of the courage, grace, and integrity of which human beings are capable under extreme pressure. In a real and immediate sense, then, this book owes its existence to my relationship with a little girl and her family. More broadly, the experience has reinforced my conviction that no historian is ever detached from her or his subject matter, that we bring to our analyses traces of the cultural and political circumstances in which we operate, and that if we acknowledge these influences, we can use them to enhance our scholarly work.

My scholarly work has been made possible by the generosity of many institutions and individuals. The Susan B. Anthony Center at the University of Rochester and the Division of Sponsored Research at the University of Florida provided me with the resources and time necessary to begin this project; David Colburn, Kermit Hall, Fred Gregory, and Will Harrison at Florida; and Anne Davidson, Jack Kent, and Barbara Kent ensured that I could continue it. The Women's Studies Program at Northeastern University under the leadership of Laura Frader provided welcome material support at the final stage of the project. I also wish to thank David Doughan and his colleagues at the Fawcett Library in London for giving me free and easy access to their wonderful collection, and invaluable advice about its contents.

The Susan B. Anthony Center offered an exciting forum for wide-ranging interdisciplinary discussion, study, and debate; from the associates of the center, especially Mieke Bal, Tom DiPiero, Val Hartouni, Bette London, Constance Penley, Bonnie Smith, and Sharon Willis, I learned much about critical and feminist theory. Jeff Adler, Jim Cronin, Leonore Davidoff, Deborah Gorham, Nicky Gullace, Sandra Holton, Anne Goodwyn Jones, Robin

Kilson, Sheryl Kroen, Tom Laqueur, David Leverenz, Philippa Levine, Jane Lewis, Jim Longenbach, Laura Mayhall, Susan Pedersen, Lou Roberts, Pat Thane, Eldon Turner, Chris Waters, Angela Woollacott, Bert Wyatt-Brown, and my students at the Universities of Rochester and Florida helped out in important ways at various stages of the project, challenging and stimulating my thinking. Special thanks go to Sylvia Freed for helping me to see clearly, and to Michael and Jillian Kinton, Elizabeth and Erika Kent Mendelsohn, Eric Kent, and Joseph Otero for their exuberance and vitality.

My former and current editors at Princeton University Press, Joanna Hitchcock and Lauren Osborne, saw to it that this book would be published. Lauren Lepow edited the manuscript with care, enhancing the narrative considerably. I wish to express my appreciation for their professionalism, judgment, and hard work. Mary Poovey and Hal Smith read the manuscript in its penultimate draft, offering insights and suggestions that strengthened the book in significant ways. While they should not be held liable for the claims I have made here, their criticisms provoked me to sharpen and in some instances to reshape my arguments. I am grateful to them both.

There are, finally, three people without whom this book could not have been conceived or executed. Individually and in combination, Anne Davidson, Joan Scott, and Bonnie Smith have provided the emotional, intellectual, and moral support that has sustained this project from start to finish. Bonnie and Joan read the first draft of the manuscript, pointing out weaknesses and inconsistencies in my arguments and suggesting alternative approaches to the material. Joan's path-breaking work on gender and experience forms the basis of the analysis that follows; more significantly, in her intellectual courage and integrity she has served as a model that one can only hope to emulate. Bonnie has taught me what it means to be a professional. She has given freely of her time, knowledge, and experience, deepening my appreciation of what it takes to be a historian. In ways both subtle and profound, Joan and Bonnie have left their marks on me and on my work. For their friendship, their collegiality, and their example, I offer my heartfelt thanks.

Anne Davidson has stuck by me in the most difficult of circumstances, providing warmth, clarity, humor, and toughness in just the right measure at just the right time. With love and respect, and in recognition of all that she has given me, I dedicate this book to her.

Holliston, Massachusetts
January 1993

ABBREVIATIONS

FANY   First Aid Nursing Yeomanry
NUSEC   National Union of Societies for Equal Citizenship (before 1918, NUWSS)
NUWSS   National Union of Women's Suffrage Societies (after 1918, NUSEC)
VAD   Voluntary Aid Detachment
WAAC   Women's Auxiliary Army Corps
WFL   Women's Freedom League
WSPU   Women's Social and Political Union

Making Peace

INTRODUCTION

THE BROKEN WORLD[1] to which belligerents returned at the end of 1918 offered little solace to societies devastated by four years of unprecedented loss and destruction. Across Europe, soldiers and civilians, men and women, elites and commoners, victors and vanquished alike, faced disorder in every aspect of their lives. The upheavals produced by the First World War provoked responses designed to re-create the social, political, and economic order that had prevailed prior to August 1914. In recasting bourgeois Europe along corporatist economic and political lines, conservative forces sought to reestablish stability and to reassert their status in a world that looked and felt dramatically different from that of the prewar period.[2] In cultural terms, too, attempts to return to what was perceived to have been a quieter, happier, more ordered time were prodigious. Nowhere is this more evident than in the realm of gender identity and relations between men and women. Political and economic restructuring found their counterpart—indeed, their necessary corollary—in the reconstruction of gender after the Great War.

Sensitive and compelling studies detailing the impact of the war on masculinity and male identity have only recently been joined by similar work on femininity and female identity.[3] Historians who have tried to assess the war's impact on the roles and position of women in Britain have generally been restricted by their approaches and methodologies to an exercise in measurement—of employment, wage levels, or rights.[4] Because such indexes of change do not necessarily gauge shifts in the asymmetries of power that marked the relations of men and women in the interwar period, these studies can tell us little about how the Great War transformed the lives of men and women, their relationships with one another, and the cultural understandings of gender and sexuality that informed their consciousness and sense of identity.[5] This book seeks to get at precisely these questions by focusing on feminism—its ideologies and its practices—during and after World War I.

The war's outbreak in August 1914 brought to a halt the activities of both militant and constitutional suffragists in their efforts to gain votes for women. By that time, the suffrage campaign had attained the size and status of a mass movement, commanding the time, energies, and resources of thousands of men and women, and riveting the attention of the British public. In early 1918, in what it defined as a gesture of recognition for women's contribution to the war effort, Parliament granted the vote to women over the age of thirty. This measure, while welcome to feminists as a symbol of the fall of the sex barrier, failed to enfranchise some three million out of eleven million adult women. When war ended, feminists continued to agitate for votes for women on the same terms as they had been granted to men; but organized feminism, despite the fact that a considerable portion of the potential female electorate remained disenfranchised, never regained its prewar status as a mass movement. By the end of the 1920s, feminism as a distinct political and social movement had become insignificant. Feminists' understandings of masculinity and femininity—of gender and sexual identity—became transformed during the war and in the postwar period, until they were virtually indistinguishable from those of antifeminists.

Historians have interpreted the nature of postwar feminism in a variety of ways. Brian Harrison attributes the reticence and discretion of interwar feminists to the requirements of political opportunity, to the sensible decision of feminist leaders to accommodate themselves to the prevailing political culture. His "prudent revolutionaries," moreover, have not lost any of their radicalism; they have simply switched tactics. "Their prudence does not signify mildness of feminist commitment; on the contrary, they envisaged a new society very different from the old—transformed not just in its political system, but in the details of family life." Jane Lewis concurs, seeing in "new" feminism "the potential to develop a radical analysis of women's position. . . . new feminists were asking fundamental questions about the position of women in the family." In their efforts, however, to attract working-class women and feminists in the labor movement who, since the turn of the century, had focused much of their attention on women's demands as mothers, middle-class feminists "failed to make strong enough analytical connections with the position of women in relation to other structures, especially in respect to the workplace and to educational institutions." But as Johanna Alberti has argued, the very success of women in gaining entry to the political process helped to limit the possibilities of their obtaining other, more radical goals such as economic equality with men.

> Differences in political understanding, based to some extent on class, put a considerable strain on feminist solidarity in the 1920s. In order to succeed in the established political structures feminists found that they had to be good party women. . . . Class differences and party allegiances blunted the sharp edge of feminist demands for economic equality, and these demands covered ground which contained the possibility of division between the search for equality and the recognition of women's separate needs.

In an entirely different approach, Sheila Jeffreys lays the blame for feminism's decline at the feet of sexologists, whose sexual ideology "undermine[d] feminism and women's independence. . . . The promotion of the ideology of motherhood and marriage together with the stigmatising of lesbianism helped to reinforce women's dependence upon men." Sexual reform had the effect of sapping women's rage and blunting their criticisms of male behavior.[6]

Harrison, Lewis, Alberti, and Jeffreys have identified the political, socio-economic, and ideological difficulties feminists faced in the crucial period following World War I. Their accounts, however, do not fully explain why the ideology of motherhood and constraining ideas about gender found so ready an acceptance among women who had before the war rejected them. This book will argue that the war proved to be a decisive element in provoking such a shift in thinking. While Harrison has claimed that "it is misleading to place pre-war and post-war history in separate compartments," Alberti believes that "the experience of the war was so crucial" to postwar feminism that she began her investigations into interwar feminists' activities and beliefs in 1914.[7] Alberti is right to see in the war the key to the nature of postwar feminism, but she has not explained the connection between the two. What is missing is an analysis of precisely how war contributed to the shift in the ideologies and attitudes of postwar feminists. This book seeks to demonstrate that the experiences of the Great War—articulated and represented in specific languages of gender and sexuality—forged for many men and women dramatically different ideas about gender and sexual identity from those prevailing in the late Victorian and Edwardian eras, and that these languages and the identities they spawned provide the context within which interwar feminism operated and by which it was constrained.

As I have argued elsewhere, prewar British feminists regarded their movement as an attack on separate sphere ideology and its constructions of masculinity and femininity. They perceived relations between the sexes to be characterized by a state of war in which patriarchal laws, institutions, and attitudes rendered women vulnerable to sexual abuse and depradation, rather than by complementarity and cooperation, as separate sphere ideologists so insistently claimed. For the most part, feminists believed masculinity to be culturally, not biologically, constructed, and attributed women's victimization to a socialization process that encouraged belief in men's natural, biologically determined sex drive. Their demand for the elimination of separate spheres incorporated an attack on the cultural construction of the female as "the Sex," and of the male as the sexual aggressor. Insisting that male behavior could be changed, that masculinity and male sexuality were socially determined and not ordained by God or nature, feminists implied that femininity and female sexuality, too, were products of socialization. Challenging the dominant discourse on sexuality, they aimed finally to create a society in which the positive qualities associated with each sex could be assumed by the other, a society in which the "natural" equality and freedom of both men and women could be achieved.

Antisuffrage women, too, understood men to be inclined toward aggressiveness and destructiveness. They differed from feminists, however, in believing masculine characteristics to be natural, inherent, biologically determined, and, consequently, unchangeable. The antisuffrage campaign of the early twentieth century was informed by the conviction that antagonistic relations between the sexes were natural. Separate spheres, they argued, placed a wall between men and women, protecting women from the most primitive instincts of men. The transformation of existing boundaries between male and female, such as those determining political participation, would not further the interests of women; rather, it would harm them by placing them in direct competition with men, whose anger would be provoked and whose physical superiority and innate brutality would result in women's destruction.[8]

Feminists and antisuffrage women, then, shared the goal of protecting women from men. But because they differed in their understandings of masculinity and femininity, and male and female sexuality, they offered diametrically opposed solutions to the problem of how best to achieve their ends. Feminists envisaged an evolution in male attitudes and behavior. Antisuffragists despaired of any such possibility, believing that women could find security only in the private sphere. Because that private sphere, for feminists, justified oppression and abuse, they sought the elimination of separate spheres altogether and the extension of the positive qualities associated with women to society as a whole.

With the onset of the Great War, many feminists began to modify their understandings of masculinity and femininity. Their insistence upon equality with men, and the acknowledgment of the model of sex war that accompanied that demand, gradually gave way to an ideology which emphasized women's special sphere—a separate sphere, in fact—and carried with it an urgent belief in a complementary relationship between the sexes. Prewar feminists had vigorously attacked the notion of separate spheres and the medical and scientific discourses about gender and sexuality upon which those spheres rested. Many feminists after World War I, by contrast, pursued a program that championed rather than challenged the prevailing ideas about masculinity and femininity appearing in the literature of psychoanalysis and sexology. In embracing radically new—and seemingly liberating— views of women as human beings with sexual identities, many feminists within the mainstream National Union of Societies for Equal Citizenship (NUSEC), the postwar successor to the National Union of Women's Suffrage Societies, accepted theories of sexual difference that helped to advance notions of separate spheres for men and women. This shift did not take place suddenly, and it was resisted throughout the twenties by many other feminists who took themselves off to form such organizations as the Six Point Group and the Open Door Council, but the acceptance of the dominant discourses on sexuality represented a fundamental abandonment of prewar feminist ideology. By the end of the 1920s, "new" feminists found themselves in a conceptual bind that trapped women in "traditional" domestic and maternal roles, and limited their ability to advocate equality and justice for women.

Few historians would share my assessment of feminism's demise in the 1920s and 1930s without qualification. Harold L. Smith, for instance, citing the partial success of the equal pay campaign in keeping the issue of equal pay for men and women in the public eye, denies that feminism in general, as distinct from NUSEC, went into decline. Martin Pugh believes that the "formal decline of feminist organisations" is not incompatible with "the substantial achievements of the women's movement after 1918." He discerns a strategic move on the part of postwar feminists, arguing that they "shrewdly" took advantage of the "somewhat naive male belief in domesticity" to effect change for women. Alberti, for her part, downplays the appeal to domesticity in postwar feminism altogether, arguing instead the centrality of economic independence for women to the 1920s feminist agenda.[9]

These historians are undoubtedly right, and their writings have deepened our understanding of the complexity of this important period. But they do not address the relationship of the way women were represented, by the larger culture and by themselves, to the success or failure of their feminist initiatives. While not discounting the roles played by political opportunity or economic and demographic developments in the shaping of postwar feminism, I want to approach the problem in a slightly different way, one that might enable us to better understand the operations of gender and sexuality in the evolution of feminist politics, and that might offer "new forms of analysis of the construction of sexual difference," as Parveen Adams and Jeff Minson put it. "Once it is recognised that sexual difference is constructed in a variety of practices, it becomes necessary to determine which differences and which practices are oppressive. This is part of the task of setting up objectives for feminism."[10] It should also be the objective for historians of feminism, and it requires a degree of historicizing that has hitherto been missing.

Denise Riley's arguments in *"Am I That Name?" Feminism and the Category of "Women" in History* provide an important starting point for such an undertaking. Riley suggests that the category of "women" is historically constructed and is therefore an unstable entity, an erratic collectivity that cannot be relied upon to hold a constant meaning either synchronically or diachronically. It is always relative to other categories, such as Nature, Class, Reason, and Humanity, which themselves change over time. Just who and what the term "women" is positioned against is of singular importance to the task of defining and articulating a feminism at any historical time and place, for the "unmet needs and sufferings [of women] . . . spring from the ways in which women are positioned, often harshly or stupidly, *as* 'women.'" Riley sees feminism as the "site of the systematic fighting-out of that instability" that is "women." Although a demarcating of the collectivity that is "women" is vital to the establishment of a feminist movement, feminists must both concentrate on *and* refuse the identity of "women."[11]

Prewar feminists demanded an end to the ideological system of sexual difference that produced "women." Their feminism, I submit, as distinct from involvement in a more nebulous "women's movement," lies precisely in their refusal of the sexual discourses that created the category "women," in their transgression of the boundaries and practices that normalized those "women." The activities and ideas we as historians identify as feminist at any given time, then, are contingent on the discourses that construct "women" and on the discourses of resistance that feminists produced in their challenge to society. Such contentions suggest a number of prickly but vital questions for us as historians of feminism and as feminists. For instance, when women do not contest the legitimacy of prescriptions constructing "women"—when they do not challenge the dominant discourses about sexuality but embrace as their own the constructions of masculinity and femininity that delimit their identities and roles, as "new" feminists did in the interwar period—or when they make demands for women that may in fact be quite radical but justify them by traditional separate sphere arguments, as they did after World War I, can we continue to regard their politics as feminist, "new" or otherwise, without an analysis of their strategic considerations and the impact they had on achieving their ends? Or when women explicitly eschew the label feminist, as many did in the interwar period, no matter that they shared the fundamental tenets of what other women were promoting under the banner of feminism, what then? I am not trying to make a case here for a right feminism and a wrong one; rather, I wish to underscore Riley's contentions that the category of "women," and therefore feminism, is always contingent. Because "women" is always relative to other categories, we must be careful in our analyses of movements whose critiques of the gender system necessarily depend upon the definition of "women." We must pay attention to the languages feminists utilized and incorporated in the advocacy of their positions. If we fail to examine feminism in the context of the discursive practices that create the gender system out of which it emerged, then the word can have no real meaning for us or for contemporaries.

For nineteenth- and twentieth-century feminism, Riley identifies the concept of "the social" as the relevant and significant entity against which "women" were defined and articulated. For Victorians and Edwardians, the social was the arena onto which the female—whose whole being had, since the seventeenth century, become increasing sexualized until by the nineteenth century it was "saturated with sex"—could safely be displaced; the concept of "the social" made it possible to consign the sexualized aspects of "women" to the private realm of the family in the case of middle-class women, or, in the case of working-class women, to transfer them onto "new categories of immiseration and delinquency, which then became sociological problems." "Society" became associated with the feminine; "the social" was positioned asymmetrically in relation to "the political."[12] Because sexuality constituted personal—including political—identity, and as female sexuality was said to contain an intrinsic pathology, women's continuing disqualification from the political process was said to rest upon their sexuality and sexual organization. In order to be recognized as individuals qualified to participate in political life, suffragists had, necessarily, to challenge and overturn cultural constructions of femininity and female sexuality. In Riley's terms, feminists utilized the responsibilities attributed to them by this positioning of "women" with "the social" to make their case for their inclusion in politics, expanding the scope of their domestic concerns to the wider society; yet they also had to contest the sexualized connotations of women as "the social" if they were to successfully argue their case for inclusion in the political. They did so by exposing the contradictions of separate sphere ideology, which depended upon the notions of a single (insistent) sexuality for men and the dual nature of sexuality for women—passionlessness and purity for middle-class women, and promiscuity and prostitution for working-class women.[13]

Beginning in August 1914, the "women" of "the social" became placed within the context of war. Metaphors utilized to explain and justify the war drew upon images of women in a variety of ways. Women were depicted variously as the terrain of war in representations that decried the rape of Belgium and France; as the objects of war in propaganda and recruiting posters; as the victims of war in reports of German atrocities; as the parasitic beneficiaries of war in *Punch* cartoons or irate letters to newspaper columns; as the wagers of war in tributes to women's wartime service, particularly that of munitions workers; even as the cause of the war in some accounts of prewar suffrage militancy. In all of these positionings, "women" did not lose its association with the sexual that had characterized prewar representations. Rather, the two concepts, sex and war, became inextricably intertwined in the minds of contemporaries: hysteria mounted concerning "war babies," venereal disease and the reimposition of the Contagious Diseases Acts, women camp followers, and the behavior of women who received separation allowances while their husbands served in the armed forces.[14] In numerous war memoirs and war novels written by women, the war is represented, sometimes even narrated, as a sexual coming of age, as the occasion for sexual maturation.[15] War, in other words, found its most pervasive and vivid representations in metaphors of sex and gender. In the postwar period, sexual conflict and polarization between the sexes provided one of the few adequate means by which the political, economic, and social upheaval occasioned by the Great War could be depicted.[16] This development would have a significant impact upon the thinking of those involved in theorizing about the relations between men and women, particularly physicians, psychiatrists, sexologists, and feminists.

This book constitutes a study of the way gender was utilized to construct war, and of the way war, conceived in gendered terms, then shaped understandings of gender. It will first examine the languages—the systems of meaning—through which the war was experienced and represented, and then analyze the legacy of those experiences and representations for society and feminism. (While the term "feminism" is used throughout the book in a usually unqualified way, it should not be taken to imply a universality across lines of race or class. Interwar feminists, like prewar feminists, were overwhelmingly white and bourgeois, despite the presence of such working-class women as Selina Cooper and Ada Nield Chew, and despite appeals to "global sisterhood" that encompassed Indian women.[17]) Chapters 1 and 2 will explore the experiences of feminists who observed the war from home, and the efforts of feminists to advance their cause against the background of war. Chapter 3 will analyze the experiences of feminists who spent at least some part of the war in the capacity of nurse, VAD (member of a Voluntary Aid Detachment), or physician; who saw action at the front as ambulance drivers, auxiliary soldiers, YMCA or canteen workers; or who were otherwise exposed to the traumas of war directly. This chapter provides a basis for comparative analysis with chapters 1 and 2: the imagined and actual experiences of the war, depicted in languages of gender and sexuality, had much to do with how individual feminists perceived and understood the nature of masculinity, and therefore of femininity. Those different understandings informed the contests about gender that preoccupied feminists; they help to explain the controversies that marked the feminist movement in the 1920s and 1930s. Chapter 4 locates the debates over women's suffrage squarely within the sexualized discourses of war, arguing that the vote was granted, at least in part, because politicians feared a renewal of militant activity on the part of feminists. Such a threat, raising the specter of sex war in the context of the unprecedented destruction of a war depicted in sexual terms, could not be tolerated by either feminists or M.P.'s, who were determined to compromise in order to achieve a peaceful solution. Feminist attitudes of compromise and caution would carry over into the postwar period and in fact characterize the interwar feminist movement. Chapter 5 argues that postwar discourses about gender and sexuality encouraged feminists to compromise their earlier egalitarianism: on the one hand, these discourses promised sexual liberation and a new identity for women; on the other, they referred continually to the threat of discord and, finally, war. Chapter 6 will examine the contests over the meaning of gender between "new" feminists,

whose program came to rely upon an ideology of sexual difference and maternity, and those "old" feminists, or "equalitarians," as they called themselves, who resisted these notions about gender and sexuality, but whose
voices were lost in the cultural cacophony of motherhood.

It will be evident that I am drawing upon poststructuralist theories of
language in my analysis of war, gender, sexuality, and feminism. Such
an approach starts with the assumption that every language act produces
meanings that exceed the author's intention; that all texts create multiple
meanings; that these meanings may contradict one another; and that interpretation of the text does not recover a "true" or original meaning but is itself a part of the play of signification that produces textuality. I do not wish
to imply that the meanings I have attributed to the texts, particularly the
literary ones, quoted throughout this book are the only ones, but rather
to argue that the texts produce *at least* the meanings I identify. For the
purposes of my analysis, the more complex work of textuality has been left
unaddressed.[18]

Chapter 1

THE SEXUAL REPRESENTATION
OF WAR, 1914–1915: REESTABLISHING
SEPARATE SPHERES

IN AUGUST 1914, the story goes, war swept across Europe, shattering the last golden days of Edwardian summer, and ushering in the horrific storms of the twentieth century. But British society in the spring and summer of 1914 was hardly the idyllic scene that has so often been presented with nostalgic longing. Rather, Britain experienced a number of serious conflicts, some of which brought it almost to open warfare. The conflict in Ireland, the conflict with labor, and the conflict with women over suffrage had so intensified that, as George Dangerfield described it, the conflict in Europe appeared almost a welcome means of relieving unbearable tensions. As Samuel Hynes has put it, "A civil war, a sex war, and a class war: in the spring of 1914 these were all foreseen in England's immediate future, and with a kind of relish. Rhetorically speaking, they were already being fought; the language of war had become, by then, the language of public discourse." This language of war "suggests that the antagonists had reached the point at which they desired battle almost for the sake of battle, as a release of the feelings that could find no other resolution."[1]

The outbreak of war in August 1914 was experienced by thousands of men as an ecstatic, liberating moment, a release from the stifling routine and conflicts of industrial bourgeois society. "It was commonly felt," Eric Leed has argued, "that, with the declaration of war, the populations of European nations had left behind an industrial civilization with its problems and conflicts and were entering a sphere of action ruled by authority, discipline, comradeship, and common purpose." The war offered an opportunity to escape from a "world structured by wealth, status, professions, age, and sex," from a world of privacy, "the removal of individuals from a state definable in terms of social, sexual, and political conflict." Moreover, Leed has asserted, "the expectations of change, of community, of an abandonment of privacy were not discarded as 'illusions' in the face of the realities of war." They were lasting motifs of the war experience.[2]

It is difficult to ignore the gendered implications of Britons' reaction to the announcement of war. Privacy is, of course, associated with the home, the private sphere, the domain of women and the feminine. Escape from it meant escape to the world of men, to the domain of the masculine, the army or navy, to the world of discipline, obedience, action; an effacing of the private, the feminine. As Captain Wagstaffe, a character in Ian Hay's *The First Hundred Thousand*, stated, "War is hell, and all that, but it has a good deal to recommend it. It wipes out all the small nuisances of peace-time," first of which he cited as "Suffragism."[3]

H. G. Wells voiced the idea of an effeminate prewar England through Mr. Britling in 1916. "How we had wasted Ireland!" Britling despaired, bewailing the state of things in the summer of 1914. "The rich values that lay in Ireland, the gallantry and gifts, the possible friendliness, all these things were being left to the Ulster politicians and the Tory women to poison and spoil, just as we had left India to the traditions of the chattering army women and the repressive instincts of our mandarins. We were too lazy, we were too negligent. We passed our indolent days leaving everything to somebody else." But with war imminent, Britling exults in the manliness that will prevail. Setting out to visit his mistress, Mrs. Harrowdean, he loses himself in the Essex countryside. "There was little room in the heart of Mr. Britling that night for any love but the love of England. He loved England now as a nation of men. There could be no easy victory. Good for us with our too easy natures that there could be no easy victory." For Wells, women, and the silly, unimportant things they connoted, were upstaged by the serious activities of war. Mr. Britling, who had previously believed his affair to be indispensable to his happiness, found himself, upon the English declaration of war,

> extraordinarily out of love with Mrs. Harrowdean. Never had any affection in the whole history of Mr. Britling's heart collapsed so swiftly and completely. He was left incredulous of ever having cared for her at all. Probably he hadn't. Probably the whole business had been deliberate illusion from first to last. The "dear little thing" business, he felt, was all very well as a game of petting, but times were serious now, and a woman of her intelligence should do something better than wallow in fears and elaborate a winsome feebleness. . . . she passed out of his mind again under the stress of more commanding interests.[4]

In this representation, war promised to destroy prewar effeminacy by delivering men from the domain of domesticity and the concerns of women, to remasculinize them by asserting "more commanding interests" such as troop movements and battles.

Politicians, writers, and critics such as Edmund Gosse, Selwyn Image, and Rupert Brooke viewed the war as an antidote to the diseased and decadent state of Edwardian society, characterized, in part, by a militant feminist movement that challenged and contested traditional roles and behaviors for men and women—as a means to substitute, in effect, a "real" war for "sex war." "We have awakened from an opium-dream of comfort, of ease, of that miserable poltroonery of 'the sheltered life,'" wrote Gosse, in terms usually applied to the lives of privileged women. "Our wish for indulgence of every sort, our laxity of manners, our wretched sensitiveness to personal inconvenience, these are suddenly lifted before us in their true guise as the spectres of national decay; and we have risen from the lethargy of our dillettantism to lay them, before it is to late, by the flashing of the unsheathed sword." He and others believed that England had brought the war upon itself by offering the Germans a soft and tempting target. Unwilling, or unable, to suppress striking laborers, Irish nationalists, or militant suffragists, England looked ripe for conquest. In 1917, debating the issue of votes for women, Lord Sydenham attributed to suffragists responsibility for the war's outbreak in 1914. "When war broke out I think we all believed that this question was practically dead," he complained to the House of Lords in December 1917. "The violence of the suffragists at that time had passed beyond all bounds, and very probably it helped the Germans to believe that a country in which educated women perpetrated outrages on churches and public property was not in a position to wage war." Rebecca West, an ardent feminist, agreed, conceding that "the silly campaign of arson and violence which was in full swing at the beginning of the war, must have contributed to the effect of lawlessness which made Germany think it a propitious moment for the outbreak of hostilities." Such critics, notes Hynes, assumed that "the Germans were right: that Englishmen had abandoned the high austere ideals of conduct that had made the Empire great, and had sunk into a too-comfortable, too-prosperous Edwardian decadence. War became, in this argument, a true English activity, and peace became vaguely foreign."[5] And feminine, we might add, maintaining consistency with the imagery utilized.

Leed has argued that with the outbreak of war, women also experienced "the collapse of those established, traditional distinctions between an 'economic' world of business and a private world of sentiment." One can make such an argument by mid-1915 or so, by which time "nursing service, jobs newly available to women, semimilitary relief organizations, and other wartime activities created by the war for women allowed an enormously expanded range of escape routes from the constraints of the private family," but not for the early days of the war, when, in fact, large numbers of women were thrown out of work by the dislocations the war caused.[6] The sudden and dramatic prospect of a newly masculinized English manhood had its counterpart in the reassertion of women's traditional roles, which included a large measure of passivity, despite feverish attempts on the part of countless women who, to feel useful to the war effort, knitted enough socks and mufflers to outfit half the British Expeditionary Force. As Carolyne Playne described it, "The great era of knitting set in; men should fight but women should knit." Vera Brittain turned, on 6 August 1914, to "the only work it seems possible as yet for women to do—the making of garments for the soldiers. I started knitting sleeping-helmets, and as I have forgotten how to knit, & was never very brilliant when I knew, I seemed to be an object of some amusement. But even when one is not skillful it is better to proceed slowly than to do *nothing* to help." "All day long I knitted away," she recorded the next day, as if she and her compatriots could repair the damage to the social fabric that war might bring. "Various reports kept coming in of battles, different dreadnoughts being sunk, multitudes of Germans being killed." M. M. Sharples recalled in 1915 that "in the first shock caused by the declaration of war, most of us felt stunned. There was an obvious duty before the men. Gallantly they have risen to it, and as we have watched them go, and seen the new expression of strength and purpose dawning in their faces, some of us women have wondered, as we desperately knitted socks and mufflers, what was the use of women in war time at all."[7]

An advertisement for the Adair Ganesh Treatment in the *Lady* of 20 August 1914 suggested one possibility. "Advice to women during the War," read the copy. "Do not neglect your appearance. At times like the present the country should see their women-folk looking their best."[8] A more passive prescription for women is difficult to imagine. But it gave voice to a widespread, seemingly overwhelming desire on the part of British society to take refuge in the apparent comfort and simplicity of separate spheres, and to efface the disruptive and disturbing tensions of the prewar period. Rose Macaulay captured the mood in *Non-Combatants and Others* (1916) in a scene in which Basil, a feminist, artistic type, falls in love with Evie, an unintelligent, uninterested, but beautiful woman. "In some . . . fundamental way," Basil mused, in a construction that Freud's postwar theories would come to reify and naturalize, "she was life itself: life which, like love and hate, is primitive, uncivilised, intellectually unprogressive, but basic and inevitable.

"Basil had once resented the type. In old days he would have called it names, such as Woman. . . . Now he liked Woman, found her satisfactory to some deep need in him; the eternal masculine, roused from slumber by war, cried to its counterpart. . . ." Macaulay saw, too, what such a development might mean for those who had been trying to re-create relationships between men and women along egalitarian lines. When Evie gushed that "'after all, there *is* a difference between men and girls, in the things they should do; I think there's a difference, don't you?'" Basil responded fervently, "'Oh, thank goodness, yes,' . . . not having always thought so."[9]

The reassertion of separate spheres with its implied dichotomies of private and public, of different natures of women and men, of home and front, appeared very early, even among feminists. Merely cursory readings of *Common Cause*, the organ of the National Union of Women's Suffrage Societies (NUWSS), reveal a shift of focus from public, political affairs in July 1914 to more traditional women's concerns in August 1914. The National Union itself, in an unreflective, almost knee-jerk reaction to war, turned to work that emphasized gender divisions. The stage for such a shift in tone and behavior was set during a women's peace meeting held in Kingsway Hall just prior to England's declaration of war, where what Alberti describes as an "almost unbearable sense of powerlessness" prevailed. As Alberti has noted, "for the past ten years rallies such as this had given women a sense of their potential power: the outbreak of war fractured that conviction. The immediate reaction of very many suffragists was to deny responsibility for the war, and of many more to deny their own power." Speaker after speaker pointed out that women without votes could have little impact on foreign affairs. The author of "What War Means" stated in *Common Cause* on 7 August 1914 that "women find themselves in the position of seeing all that they most reverence and treasure, the home, the family, the race, subjected to irreparable injury, which they are powerless to avert."[10] The belief in women's powerlessness contrasted sharply with the outlook of feminists who, just a week earlier, were engaged in a nationwide campaign for the vote, organizing thousands of supporters, canvassing the country, lobbying M.P.'s, and sending deputations to the prime minister.

Indeed, as Alberti has suggested, "it was difficult for women who were accustomed to organising to resist the urge to act immediately in some constructive way." The NUWSS Executive Committee voted "to suspend the ordinary political activities of the N.U. and to recommend the devotion of its organisation to various efforts which have for their object the sustaining of the vital strength of the nation." But by a kind of relentless logic, the sense of powerlessness evoked by the war became transliterated into a conviction that feminists' greatest and most obvious responsibilities in sustaining the vital strength of the nation involved those associated with domesticity. "We . . . very early arrived at the conclusion," Millicent Fawcett, president of the NUWSS, recalled after the war, "that the care of infant life, saving the children, and protecting their welfare was as true a service to the country as that which men were rendering by going into the armies to serve in the field." Indeed, it was the very corollary to men's service. "While the necessary, inevitable work of men as combatants is to spread death, destruction, red ruin, desolation and sorrow untold," she told a Kingsway Hall audience in October 1914, "the work of women is the exact opposite. It is . . . to help, to assuage, to preserve, to build up the desolate home, to bind up the broken lives, to serve the State by saving life rather than destroying it." She asserted in a letter to the *Manchester Guardian* that women's "special duties" of nurturing and succoring were "sufficiently obvious": "doctoring and nursing," "care of the young womanhood of the nation," "care of children," and "care of child-bearing women." *Common Cause* told its readers that women should "care for the home and mind the nation's babies." Paid work—"as far as we are trained and able"—in shops, factories, offices, and schools received only secondary consideration. The paper regularly carried notices on the "Care of

Maternity in Time of War," and articles and appeals for donations "To Save the Babies." The traditional cultural associations of men with war and death and women with home and the giving and preserving of life emerged with virtually no resistance from feminists; indeed, they were often fostered by feminist rhetoric. Even Sylvia Pankhurst, whose work on behalf of women and children derived from her understanding of the poverty they faced in the absence of husbands, sons, brothers, and fathers in the months before separation allowances were allocated, gave symbolic voice to this kind of dichotomizing when she turned a former pub, the Gunmakers' Arms, into a nursery and hospital for babies, which she renamed the Mothers' Arms. As S. Bulan put it in the *Englishwoman*, "at the call of war, the first thought of every man is to fight, of every woman to nurse."[11]

"We want to emphasise the vital part which women have to play in a crisis like the present," intoned *Common Cause* on 14 August 1914, offering schemes for relief forwarded by the local constituent societies in response to the National Union's appeal. In a significant ordering of priorities, it listed the formation of Suffrage Sewing Guilds for the making of maternity outfits, and children's and men's clothing; of committees to distribute clothing; of committees to look after the wives and children of the men who had joined the Reserves; and lastly, of the formation of ambulance classes. Almost as an afterthought the paper reported, "Several Societies suggest that organisations should be established to regulate the food supply, and note any unfair rise in the prices, while a considerable number suggest work in connection with the Red Cross movement and the Voluntary Aid Detachment." The Shetland society reported that "besides sewing parties we are giving three hours' of instruction daily in cooking, bedmaking, etc." While the efficient use of resources and the elimination of waste at home fell largely to women in their role as consumers, the emphasis on domesticity obscured other possible identifications for women. When Sylvia Pankhurst set up a toy factory in the East End to give employment to women there, *Common Cause* responded with one of the more ludicrous representations of women and their work. "All women will rejoice to hear that women are taking up toy-making," it enthused in October 1914. "This meets what will soon be a real need (for nearly all our toys came from Germany) . . . and it is truly 'women's work'!"[12] Virtually nothing was said to contest the legal, economic, and institutional barriers that limited women's abilities to contribute to the war effort in any but the most traditional terms.

"Mothering Our Soldiers" was another activity urged upon readers of *Common Cause*. In September 1914, the paper suggested that women set up laundry and mending stations in every district where Territorials were camped. In November 1914, Dr. Helen Wilson proposed and *Common Cause* endorsed, in what constituted a literal construction of the home front, the formation of a Women's Army to train in and teach the arts of homemaking. "The most precious national service that women can render, whether in peace or war, is the care of the home, the guardianship of the family. On this point Suffragists and Anti-suffragists are agreed. Cannot our young women be induced to 'enlist' for this national service? Can they not be shown that the most practical service they can render to the absent brother, or husband, or sweetheart, is to ensure him a more perfect home when he comes back to it? This means training." The Women's Army she envisaged would be organized along the lines of the Territorial Force. In February 1915, M. M. Sharples suggested, in an article entitled "How to Help," that women train, and train hard, in homemaking practices—in food preparation, sewing, and the making of handicrafts that would help to make life more beautiful. After all, she noted, "we cannot all be Red Cross nurses, nor all distribute relief to soldiers' wives."[13] In these pronouncements, feminists expressed a clear identification with the association between "women" and "the social," but in its most narrow domestic or familial sense.

These efforts to define the nature of women and the terms of their involvement in war did not go uncontested. A number of feminists challenged the impulse of many NUWSS members to give over their lives to knitting and the care of babies. Catherine Marshall told a Newcastle audience in January 1915 that it was a mistake for the National Union simply to close up shop where suffrage was concerned, arguing that women's demand for votes was also made on behalf of the "men who are fighting for us. It is for the sake of the country, and for the sake of men as well as women, that we press it." She also told a March 1915 gathering in Westminster that women shared responsibility for the conditions that had made war possible. At the August Peace Meeting, Helena Swanwick had not responded to the mood of powerlessness that pervaded the meeting with passivity. Rather, she urged suffragists "to think out what the war was about, how it ought to end, and what constructive policy to prepare to prevent its repetition." She initially joined in relief work on behalf of women who had lost their jobs; but soon she was cautioning in a *Common Cause* article that women must raise their daughters not as "the supplementary sex" but as persons of full status. She advised mothers to urge their daughters to use their brains, to become educated, to work usefully for other women and for those of their generation; she exhorted them to instill in their daughters a sense of purposefulness, responsibility, and independence, to teach them to be leaders. Swanwick understood and sympathized with the visceral reaction of those who sought to retreat to home and privacy in the face of war, but she could not countenance it. "Perhaps the greatest sacrifices are asked now of the old," she wrote. "They must not only give their sons to death; they must give their daughters to life, real life. And that may be as hard."[14] She and Marshall, as well as a number of other Executive Committee members, would soon leave the NUWSS in order to work for peace.

While the women who left the National Union to support the peace, rather than the war effort were willing, able, even resolved to counteract the behavior and passivity that consumed so many of their friends and colleagues, they tended to invoke images of women and femininity that reflected the ambivalence of their feelings. Although they did not necessarily believe that women were by their nature peacelike—"women, as women," declared Swanwick, "do not and never will all think one way"—their writings and rhetoric were ambiguous on this point, and often slipped into dichotomizing equations of women with maternity, the giving of life, and peace, and men with aggression, the destruction of life, and war. Swanwick, for instance, as reported in "What War Means," told the Women's Peace Meeting that "the great mass of women were on the side of peace. Woman was the guardian of the race. It was for her to replenish the earth when man had devastated it." In *Women and War*, published in 1915, she argued that "war is waged by men only," while "two pieces of work for the human family are peculiarly the work of women: they are the life-givers and the homemakers." In May 1915, she referred to women as "eternal non-combatants"; the following August, she asserted that "there can be no doubt at all that men get an exhilaration out of war which is denied to most women." In September, a *Common Cause* article argued that the best way to work for peace was in organizations including both sexes in their memberships; it justified its reasoning on the grounds that "no women ever, anywhere, have anything to gain from war; a few men have a great deal to gain from war, and a very large number have the aggressive instinct which most women are without." Catherine Marshall followed the same kind of construction when she described war as, "to women, . . . primarily an outrage on motherhood and all that motherhood means; the destruction of life and the breaking-up of homes is the undoing of women's work as life-givers and home-makers."[15]

These images, while culturally predominant, were by no means the only ones available to feminists. Rose Macaulay offered an alternative way to construct men and women in the process of working for peace. For her protagonist, Alix, the role of "non-combatant" was not to be celebrated, but bemoaned; "bitter and angry" that she cannot fight, Alix describes herself as one of the "sexually unfit" in relation to war. "Oh, I do so want to go and fight," she says. "I want to go and help end it. . . . Oh, it's rotten not being able to; simply rotten. . . . Why *shouldn't* girls? I can't bear the sight of khaki; and I don't know whether it's most because the war's so beastly or because I want to be in it. . . . It's both." She sees in peace work a means of throwing off her enforced passivity and the demoralization it brought in its wake. She tells her brother Nicholas that "as I can't be fighting in the war, I've got to be fighting against it. Otherwise it's like a ghastly nightmare, swallowing one up." Alix explicitly eschews the "sentimental rubbish" which makes people say "that women are the guardians of life, and therefore mind war more than men do." She especially appreciates the fact that her mother, Daphne, "didn't rant or sentimentalise. She could talk of the part to be played by women in the construction of permanent peace without calling them the guardians of the race or the custodians of life. She didn't draw distinctions, beyond the necessary ones, between women and men; she took women as human beings, not as life-producing organisms; she took men as human beings, not as destroying-machines."[16]

From a position diametrically opposite Swanwick's and Marshall's, Emmeline Pankhurst, leader of the Women's Social and Political Union (WSPU), foresaw the war's immediate effect on most feminists. Upon the outbreak of war, the WSPU had promised to cease its militant activities, and McKenna, the home secretary, had agreed to release all suffragette prisoners. "So ends, for the present," Pankhurst noted sardonically in yet another formulation of the substitution of "real" war for "sex war," "the war of women against men. As of old, the women become the nurturing mothers of men, their sisters and uncomplaining helpmates." But, Mrs. Pankhurst later told the *Daily Sketch*, the WSPU would not, as Anne Wiltsher puts it, "nurse soldiers or knit socks, but would continue to work on national lines" on behalf of the recruitment effort. Christabel Pankhurst, as early as September 1914, repudiated the passive prescriptions for women, asserting, "If we are needed in the fighting line, we shall be there. If we are needed to attend to the economic prosperity of the country, we shall be there." Mindful of the need to break down the institutional barriers that limited women's opportunities to fight on the nation's behalf, and of the physical force arguments that were mobilized to deny women the vote *because* they could not fight for their country, she added, "It must be clearly understood that if women do not actually take part in the fighting, that argues no inferiority, that argues no diminution of their claim to political equality. . . . You must remember that if men fight, women are the mothers. Without the mothers you have no nation to defend."[17]

The Women's Freedom League (WFL), a militant suffrage organization led by Charlotte Despard, refused to give up its suffrage work. Despard, too, had claimed that "women are in no way responsible for the appalling situation with which they are faced" when war broke out, and declared women's readiness "to do what is demanded of them for the sake of the nation," but she made it abundantly clear that "no man-made laws shall in future prevent their participation in the rights, as well as the responsibilities, of citizenship." Nina Boyle urged WFL members and "all women who have the real eventual welfare of their country and their race at heart not to let themselves be turned aside at this juncture. . . . Those who, having put their hand to the plough, look back or allow themselves to be lured away now will double the burden and lengthen the struggle for their sisters." In language that defied the linking of women to peace and domesticity by invoking the rhetoric of war, she called upon "all Suffragists to stand to their guns and man their own forts, and not to let themselves be drawn out of their Movement for any purpose whatsoever. In this will be the truest patriotism, the truest service that can be given by any woman."[18]

At an emergency meeting of the National Executive Committee on 10 August, the WFL also formed a relief organization, the Women's Suffrage National Aid Corps, to "render help to the women and children of the nation." Despard's angry editorial of 18 September 1914, "Your Country Needs You," made it clear that this development was not a part of the general scurrying back to home and domesticity; rather, it was a response to the government's failure to provide allowances to the women and children left behind by soldiers gone to the front. It was consistent with the WFL's prewar policy, whose objects, in keeping with the socialist inclinations of many of its members, included the promotion of "the social and industrial well-being of the community." Moreover, the WFL also formed the Women Volunteer Police, so that men might be released for "sterner duties," as Boyle put it, a far cry from sewing, knitting, toy making, or teaching cooking classes. In a formulation that disrupted the construction of man-the-life-destroyer/woman-the-life-giver, Despard entitled a 21 August article "Nature Demands Production Not Destruction."[19] Production and work—not reproduction and maternity—constituted women's functions, as the WFL saw it. The contrast with the NUWSS's emphasis on homemaking and maternity is striking; but the voices of Macaulay, Boyle, and the Pankhursts—at least insofar as women's fighting was concerned—were muffled by the pronouncements of the larger culture.

It would be misleading to suggest that relief work did not have serious purposes, or that the NUWSS did not entertain any other kind of work for women. As *Common Cause* reminded its readers, after a public meeting the National Union organized to discuss women's wartime work in October 1914, "workrooms and menderies may be dull, but if the Union did not employ these women, they would starve." Maternity Centres provided much-needed care for infants and mothers, as the letters of many working-class women attested. Within the National Union, Ray Strachey had come to the conclusion that paid work, not relief work, offered women the greatest opportunities to contribute to the war effort, and she turned the London Society for Women's Suffrage into an employment agency, even as the National Union as a whole continued to advocate and organize for relief activities. In October, *Common Cause* began to solicit funds for support of the Scottish Women's Hospitals, under the leadership of Dr. Elsie Inglis, which would send all-women medical teams to France, Serbia, Romania, and Russia, though the appeal was framed in traditional terms. "There is no service women can pledge themselves to, more worshipful than that of healing," *Common Cause* gushed. By the end of 1914, the National Union's "Women's Interests Committee," in conjunction with Strachey's London

Society, sought to open up nontraditional kinds of work for women, urging that more men might be recruited for the armed forces if women were trained to take their positions in the civil service, in restaurants and shops, and on the railways.[20]

But these initiatives, particularly in the first six months of the war, were always overshadowed by representations and images of women that asserted domesticity—nursing of babies, mothering of soldiers, care of the home—as their proper domain. A solicitation for funds for "Dr. Bernardo's Homes," an orphanage of sorts for motherless children whose fathers were at the front, illustrated what might befall the country if women failed to fulfill their duties correctly. It depicted Private Robinson's wife getting up from her bed "too soon" after the birth of her fourth child and catching a bad chill, necessitating her husband's return from the front. "Nothing can save her and he has to say 'Goodbye.'" reads one frame. "The broken-hearted family. Mother is gone, father must return to duty. What are they to do?" asks the next. Fortunately, Dr. Bernardo's Homes can take over the mother's responsibilities and "give real and happy homes to such motherless little ones—'Till Daddy comes back from the War.'"[21] While these images were marshaled on behalf of Dr. Bernardo's Homes, there is no mistaking another message relayed by the ad. Mrs. Robinson had gotten up too soon from childbed; had she acted more responsibly, her husband would not have been called back from his duties at the front to attend her and make arrangements for his children. Nor would he have had to face the grief that might distract him from fulfilling his obligations in the field.

The NUWSS failed to challenge these images and representations of women; its valorizing of women's fundamental identity as mothers and homemakers constituted an embracing of what Riley calls "the social." In contrast to its prewar stance, however, feminists in the National Union failed to take the next step, to utilize women's association with "the social" in order to make claims for participation in "the political." The organization's rhetoric did not emphasize the needs of women and children whose lives had been disrupted by war, whose survival the absence of soldier husbands rendered problematical and—as it involved contests over resources—political; rather, it asserted that women were especially, exclusively, always, and by nature concerned with mothering and homemaking. This, moreover, from women who had, just a few short months before, been demanding the dismantling of barriers that confined women to a separate sphere.

The reassertion of traditional norms of masculinity and femininity and of separate spheres for men and women[22] found expression in the efforts to legitimate and justify the war itself. Much of the official propaganda presented the war as a fight for and on behalf of Belgium, which was often depicted in the guise of womanhood. For Britons, Trevor Wilson has argued, "the Belgian issue . . . defined the nature of the struggle"—that of a peaceable small country suddenly and without warning overrun by a bullying, great power. "Little Belgium" evoked images of an innocent woman in need of a paternal male's protection. Such chivalric imagery became charged by and infused with sexual implications as accounts of the invasion and rumors of German atrocities reached England and seared the collective British memory. "Very soon the invasion of Belgium became in the popular mind a chronicle of murder, rapine, pillage, arson, and wanton destruction. The image used throughout is unmistakable. In poster and report and appeal, Belgium is the raped and mutilated maiden, left to die."[23]

Much of the atrocity propaganda that circulated throughout Britain focused on outrages committed against women. *Crimes of Germany*, published in 1915, announced, "From the assassination of the archduke's wife at Sarajevo to the shooting of a hospital nurse in Brussels, Prussia and her Allies have concentrated their cruelty upon women." Stories of children with their hands cut off and of women with their breasts amputated appeared regularly in the press—the *Times* and the *Financial News* as well as the *Daily Mail*—and gained wide credence. In September 1914, the *Dumfries Standard*, the *Pall Mall Gazette*, the *Westminster Gazette*, the *Globe*, the *Star*, and the *Evening Standard* carried the story of a girl whose sister, a nurse in Belgium, had written from her deathbed to tell of her mutilation at the hands of the Germans. The *Dumfries Standard* ran what purported to be a facsimile of the letter, which was in fact a hoax. The perpetrator, Kate Hume, was brought to trial, where "her doctor testified she had read so many stories of German cruelties that she actually believed her sister had been killed."[24]

The National Union cited this case in cautioning its members to suspend "judgment upon alleged instances of fiendish cruelty and barbarity on the part of enemies of this country until there has been an opportunity of subjecting these allegations to a careful enquiry."[25] They did not have long to wait. "Some of the most influential documents in the shaping of English war imaginations," Hynes has written, "were those that recorded, in what seemed factual, documentary form, alleged atrocities committed by the German army in the invasion of Belgium and northern France. These accounts appeared very early in the war, and addressed the subject on several levels of authority and sophistication." In May 1915, the government issued the Bryce Report, the findings of a commission charged with investigating stories of German atrocities in Belgium. Chaired by the reputable Lord Bryce, the commission included such respected, distinguished men as the jurist and historian Sir Frederick Pollack; the historian and vice-chancellor of Sheffield University, H.A.L. Fisher; and the editor of the *Edinburgh Review*, Harold Cox. Their stature, combined with "the official and somewhat objective tone of the Bryce report, . . . ensured that it was received favourably both at home and abroad." For one penny, the cost of a daily newspaper, Britons could purchase the "summary of evidence" and an appendix of selected case histories. In what can be described only as a kind of pornographic orgy that fostered voyeurism and made war sexually "exciting," the report told of "the execution of civilians, the torture and mutilation of Belgian women, the bayonetting of small children and just about every conceivable atrocity that could be committed by German soldiers. The appendix contained particularly explicit descriptions of mutilation, rape and murder."[26]

One Belgian refugee reported the case of a family in which the mother and father were shot by the Germans, and "a daughter of 22, having been outraged, died because of the violence she had received." Another related the account of two women he met on the road to Hayne. "I know them both," he attested. "One told me that the Germans had raped her in her house at Hayne near Soumagne and the other told me the same. The women were both together when they were raped. They were raped by a great many Germans." At Micheroux, declared a witness, "from one of the cottages a woman (name given) came out with a baby in her arms, and a German soldier snatched it from her and dashed it to the ground, killing it then and there." A Belgian from Flemalle Grande told of his neighbor, Mrs. D., whose daughter was "driven . . . up into the loft" by two German soldiers, who then raped her. "She was 8 1/2 months gone in pregnancy. . . . The child was born the following day." A Belgian soldier marching along outside Liège came upon

> a woman, apparently of middle age, perhaps 28 to 30 years old, stark naked, tied to a tree. At her feet were two little children about three or four years old. All three were dead. I believe the woman had one of her breasts cut off, but I cannot be sure of this. Her whole bosom was covered with blood and her body was covered with blood and black marks. Both children had been killed by what appeared to be bayonet wounds. The woman's clothes were lying on the grass thrown all about the place.

Another soldier watched Germans

> going into the houses in the Place and bringing out the women and girls. About 20 were brought out. They were marched close to the corpses. Each of them was held by the arms. They tried to get away. They were made to lie on tables which had been brought into the square. About 15 of them were then violated. Each of them was violated by about 12 soldiers. While this was going on about 70 Germans were standing round the women including five officers (young). The officers started it. . . . The ravishing went on for about 1 1/2 hours. I watched the whole time. Many of the women fainted and showed no sign of life.

A refugee from Pepinster stated that he saw

the Germans seize a baby out of the arms of the farmer's wife. . . . The two privates held the baby and the officer took out his sword and cut the baby's head off. The head fell on the floor and the soldiers kicked the body of the child into a corner and kicked the head after it. . . . After the baby had been killed we saw the officer say something to the farmer's wife and saw her push him away. After five or six minutes the two soldiers seized the woman and put her on the ground. She resisted them and they then pulled all her clothes off her until she was quite naked. The officer then violated her while one soldier held her by the shoulders and the other by the arms. After the officer each soldier in turn violated her, the other soldier and the officer holding her down. . . . After the woman had been violated by the three the officer cut off the woman's breasts.

A soldier retreating "saw a woman lying on her back inside a house; her skirt was pulled up over her head. There were no clothes on the lower part of the body. She had a wound extending from between her legs (private parts) to her breast." A Belgian officer testified that "a young girl of about 17 came up to me crying in the village; she was dressed only in a chemise: she told me that 17 girls including herself, had been dragged into a field and stripped quite naked and violated, and that twelve of them had been killed by being ripped up across the stomach with a bayonet." A soldier recounted coming across a girl of fourteen at Weerde: "She was half mad when we found her. Her mother was there, and told us that seven German Red Cross men had violated her one after another." Another found a woman in a convent; she had been "pierced by a bayonet" and was dying. "The woman's stomach had been cut open right across, the wound being some foot or more long. The woman was with child as could clearly be seen from her size." At Eppeghem, Belgian soldiers stated that they "met a woman whose blouse or dress was torn open in front and she was all covered with blood. Her breasts had been cut off, the edges of the wounds being torn and rough. We spoke to the woman. She was with us for 10 minutes, but it was impossible to understand what she was saying as she was 'folle.'" A litany of atrocities committed by German soldiers against women, children, and civilian men continued for some 238 pages.[27]

This kind of imagery linked sex and war in the conscious and unconscious minds of Britons. The Bryce Report, Hynes has argued, "released into English imaginations a style, a language, and an imagery of violence and cruelty that would in time permeate imagined versions of the war, and become part of the record."[28] It needs to be emphasized that the images of violence and cruelty were images, primarily, of acts against women, so that the rape and sexual mutilation of women dominated contemporaries' imaginings and representations of the war. As Wilson has pointed out, propaganda that presented military aims in sexual terms or sought to mobilize the population by means of sexualized imagery required a good deal of distortion on the part of its "authors." When in 1916 a large number of Belgian and French civilians were deported to work for the German war effort, "British propaganda managed, as with the earlier 'atrocities' in Belgium, to convey a sense of sexual outrage. Although most of the deportees were males, a pamphlet dealing with one aspect of the subject was called *The Deportation of Women and Girls from Lille*. Again, a British poster showed a young girl of unquestionable virginity about to be led away by a hulking German soldier." The editor of the *Financial News*, Dr. Ellis Powell, often declared to large gatherings that if the Germans were victorious, "tens of thousands of British girls" would be "removed to human stud-farms in Germany."[29] Demanding, on a conscious level, revenge against the Germans for such acts, these appeals also worked at an unconscious level, spurring the desire to defend women as sexual property.

Recruiting efforts drew explicitly upon images of the rape and sexual mutilation of women to increase the ranks of the army and navy. In February 1915, *The Official Book of the German Atrocities*, preparatory to describing incidents such as those recounted above, made a plea for more men. "It is the duty of every single Englishman who reads these records," it intoned, "and who is fit to take his place in the King's Army, to fight with all the resolution and courage he may, that the stain, of which the following pages are only a slight record, may be wiped out, and the blood of innocent women and children avenged." A poster addressed "To the Women Of Britain" reminded them, "You have read what the Germans have done in Belgium. Have you thought what they would do if they invaded this Country? Do you realise that the safety of your home and children depends on our getting more men *NOW*?" "Mothers!" were exhorted to give up their husbands and sons if they wanted to avoid the fate of Belgian women. "Have you forgotten the Belgian Atrocities? Do you realise what will be the lot of you and your children if the Germans successfully invade England?"[30]

The WSPU drew upon excerpts from the Bryce Report to describe in graphic terms the "horror, lust and pillage" that would follow from a German invasion of England: "the mutilation of women in a hideous fashion," the bayoneting of babies and pregnant women, rape, the cutting off of women's breasts, and "*other cases [that] suggest a perverted form of sexual instinct*," declared the *Suffragette* in May 1915. A report of a speech by Flora Drummond in the same issue demanded to know "how it is that there are to-day men of military age who can calmly sit and read about the atrocities that are being committed and then do nothing."[31]

While the imagery of sexual violation of women served as a means of recruitment and justification for the war, it may well have acted, if only unconsciously, to reinforce the promises of sexual punishment, reward, and release for enlisting that bombarded the British public. Baroness Orczy, the creator of the Scarlet Pimpernel, formed the Women of England's Active

Service League, whose purpose was to persuade men to enlist. Members of the league pledged "never to be seen in public with any man who, being in every way fit and free for service, has refused to respond to his country's call." As a result of her efforts, David Mitchell has claimed, some twenty thousand volunteers joined the colors. Philip Gibbs, a war correspondent, maintained that some soldiers were sent to the front "by the taunt of a girl," while Sir George Young recounts that his chauffeur was threatened by his "lady love" with rejection if he did not enlist, despite the fact that this young man's parents had forbidden him to do so. "What will your best girl say if you're not in khaki?" sneered one recruiting poster; another in the same vein, but addressed to "The Young Women of London," asked them, "Is your 'Best Boy' wearing Khaki? If not don't *YOU THINK* he should be? If he does not think that you and your country are worth fighting for—do you think he is *WORTHY* of you? . . . If your young man neglects his duty to his King and Country, the time may come when he will *NEGLECT YOU*."[32]

Promises of sexual reward for enlisting appeared frequently. An advertisement for Mitchell's "Binnacle" Cigarettes showed a fashionable young woman making eyes at the man in uniform beside her, while pointedly ignoring the man in civilian clothes on her right. In one song that carried unmistakable allusions to prostitution, long the acknowledged avenue by which British men were first initiated in sexual activity, and by means of which they were expected to find relief from pent-up sexual tension, women urged men to "take the King's shilling"—to enlist—with the following:

> On Sunday I walk out with a soldier,
> On Monday I'm taken by a tar,
> On Tuesday I'm out
> With a baby Boy Scout,
> On Wednesday with a Hussar.
> On Thursday I gang oot with a Kiltie,
> On Friday the captain of the crew,
> But on Saturday I'm willing, if only you'll take a shilling,
> To make a man of any one of you.[33]

The representation of the war as unleashed heterosexuality also included women other than prostitutes as actors. Magnus Hirschfeld, in a statement figuring the war as a form of sexual release, asserted that "the great experience of the outbreak of the war, the tremendous emotional excitement that it brought, exercised a stimulating effect upon the women of every land and appears to have raised their need of love considerably. . . . woman reacted to the war with an increase of her libido." Winifred Holtby testified to such an experience, recounting that when the war started, "the first thing it made me do was to fall in love." Lady Randolph Churchill wondered aloud about this phenomenon, asking in 1916, "Why is it that men who have served their

country and us for years in difficult, dangerous, and disagreeable occupations never interested us until we saw them in khaki? Such is the magic of
the trappings of war!"[34]

Historians, echoing contemporaries, frequently comment upon the changes
in sexual behavior that marked the period. "The safest generalization about
the First World War," Arthur Marwick has written, "would be that it was a
time of powerfully heightened emotional activity and responses." Early wartime marriages and increased numbers of divorce cases in the immediate
postwar period are only one measure of significant alteration in behavior.
Premarital sex, at least in the minds of contemporaries, appeared to increase
exponentially. Society responded to such behavior, Marwick has asserted,
with general tolerance. "'Give the boys on leave a good time,'" noted Irene
Clephane, "was the universal sentiment at home." In a letter to *Common
Cause*, "Hugo" urged the government "to make it easy for *every soldier to
become a father* [his emphasis] before going to war. . . . It is well to guard
young men from mere dissipation; but is it well to deprive them of father-
hood, and the women of motherhood, especially when the nation needs the
children?" But not all showed such forbearance and understanding. Rumors
that "printed slips urging men 'to forego no opportunity of paternity' are
being widely distributed in this country" led Maude Royden, a longtime
suffragist and member of the NUWSS, to protest "with all our strength
against this abominable advice," charging that it reduced "women to the
status of mere breeders of the race." Very early on press warnings prolifer-
ated about threats to the chastity of respectable women, of war nymphoma-
nia and the sexual attraction that men in uniform held for women.[35]

As reports of "khaki fever" and dire predictions about "war babies" spread
through the land, women bore the brunt of the anxiety that war produced in
the population. "When quite ordinary men donned khaki," scolded *The
Times History of the World War* in August 1915, "they became in the eyes
of a number of foolish young women objects to be pestered with attention
that very few of them desired." It was not long before such disapproval
manifested itself in governmental policies aimed against women. "War had
barely started," Lucy Bland has argued, "yet already there were moves to
introduce oppressive restrictions on women—in the name of 'protection' of
'our' troops. From numerous sources came claims that multitudes of young
women were infesting military camps, preying upon soldiers, spreading
nasty diseases." In what Hynes describes as part of an ongoing "war against
women," the Plymouth Watch Committee voted in October 1914 to recommend to the Town Council that the Contagious Diseases Acts, repealed
some thirty years earlier after a sustained feminist campaign, be reimposed,
though the government, fearing "the old controversy over the CD Acts,"
resisted the pressure of military commanders and declined to issue the
order. Military authorities sought other ways to keep their soldiers from

women they believed would infect them. In Cardiff in December 1914, Colonel East, invoking the Defense of the Realm Act, imposed a curfew on women "of a certain class"—suspected prostitutes—between the hours of 7:00 P.M. and 8:00 A.M. Acting on the assumption that alcohol consumption encouraged sexual promiscuity, he also banned all women from pubs between the hours of 7:00 P.M. and 6:00 A.M. Other towns quickly followed suit. In Grantham, General Hammersley authorized police and military personnel to enter houses within a six-mile radius of the Army Post Office in order to determine that the curfew was being obeyed and that soldiers were not inside the houses.[36]

Feminists colluded in representing war as a form of unrepressed sexual desire. Much of the news carried by *Common Cause* dealt not with the war effort—casualty lists, battles, or troop movements, for example—but with instances of sexual misconduct on the part of (usually working-class) women. In what it decried as "a national shame," the paper carried a plea "for the protection of our young soldiers, many of them only nineteen, from the solicitations of women. . . . There is no more urgent problem for patriotic women to set the best of their hearts and minds and efforts to solve." The writer, in what may have been an inadvertent but nevertheless quite telling conflation of prostitution and war, argued that the only way to get at the root of "the evil" was to teach women to respect themselves and men to recognize their humanity. "The recognition of it is the one and only hope of making war a less hideous barbarism, and of gradually abolishing it altogether." In October, *Common Cause* declared that the large numbers of women hanging around the training camps, behaving badly and creating "a real scandal," had become "a danger to themselves and others." Various solutions—the utilization of "women's patrols" to police the areas in question, the restriction of alcohol sales, the establishment of recreation facilities for women and girls—were constantly being put forward in the pages of the feminist press. Katherine Harley suggested the formation of an "Active Service Cadet Corps," modeled on the Boy Scouts, to help young girls "face their present difficulties and temptations," a problem of "the most vital importance to the nation." In November 1914, an entire meeting at the Guildhall was devoted to addressing the problem of women's drinking and loitering at the camps, another indication of the near obsession with the display of overt sexuality gripping feminists and the general public.[37]

The sexual imagery utilized to represent the war reflected developments in the prosecution and fortunes of the war and the extent to which the home front was involved. During the first phase, lasting from August 1914 into 1915, the war was often depicted as a remasculinization of English culture, perceived to have become degenerate, effeminate—even homosexual—in the years before the war. This kind of representation relied upon a corresponding imagery of women as refeminized, especially in the aftermath of a widespread feminist movement that had challenged the dominant cultural norms of masculinity and femininity. Thus, an assertion of and emphasis on traditional notions of separate spheres for men and women characterized the first year of the war. It was accompanied by the notion of war as unleashed sexual desire, as gruesome tales of German atrocities committed against Belgian women spread through the land. These representations of war's sexual imperatives were put forward within a framework of traditional gender and sexual relations and did not seriously threaten the bourgeois domestic ideology of separate spheres, an ideology based upon a single model of sexuality for men and a dual model for women. Depictions of khaki fever and stories of war babies offered images of sexual release, of loosening sexual restraints between men and women. While these images hinted at middle-class women's adopting male sexual values and ignoring traditional standards of reticence and chastity, they were nevertheless heavily weighted by class and could thus adequately represent a war that was still thought about and presented in traditional terms. But by mid-1915 or so, as those on the home front began to understand that theirs was not a traditional war, this kind of sexual representation began to change too.

Chapter 2

THE SEXUAL REPRESENTATION
OF WAR, 1915–1918:
SEX, WAR, AND SEX WAR

BY 1916, boundaries between home and front could no longer be drawn with ease. Even before the monstrous casualties of the Somme battles forced Britons to face up to the realities of twentieth-century warfare, the war experience on the home front was changing dramatically. Air raids over London, U-boat attacks on merchant and passenger vessels, the sinking of the *Lusitania*—all resulted in hundreds if not thousands of civilian deaths, bringing the war home in immediate and unprecedented fashion. Britons had to face the fact that this war involved everyone, not just the men who joined the ranks of the armed forces. Wilson has suggested that "the stress on air raids in the press reflected a deeply held conviction among the public: that a clear divide ought to exist between the warrior and the civilian—especially the civilian as woman and child. . . . Clearly, the random bombing of cities violated this conviction."[1] A blurring of identities—of the distinctions between warriors and civilians, between men and women—was taking place, calling forth a different kind of sexual imagery to more adequately represent the war.

Initial responses to the outbreak of war involved a reassertion of separate spheres, of traditional categories of masculine and feminine, and of men's and women's work, from which feminists were not exempt. The bombardments of Scarborough, Whitby, and Hartlepool in December 1914, however, began to persuade many women within the NUWSS that the emphasis on traditional femininity and traditional feminine roles could present a real danger to women in wartime, and created opportunities for voices that had been muffled in previous months to be heard more clearly.[2] An article of 1 January 1915 in *Common Cause* entitled "Women as Non-Combatants" observed that the shelling of the coastal towns "has brought home to us the fact that non-combatants may suffer very severely in war." As a result, the author explained, utilizing images far removed from that of women as homemakers and baby-minders, "women feel acutely that they have a part to play in war . . . as fellows and comrades of men. Women . . . are convinced that schemes for the defence of the non-combatant population would be better carried out with the intelligent co-operation of efficient women, rather than by a summary and unintelligent rounding up of 'women and children.'" The same issue carried an article by Eleanor Rathbone, a prominent National Union Executive Committee member, criticizing the instructions issued by two county lord lieutenants in the event of a German invasion for making no reference to women beyond the need to prevent them from panicking. "No one suggests that women shall take their place as combatants in the fighting line," she hurried to point out. "Whatever some of us may wish in our hearts, public opinion being what it is, such a proposal would be obviously impractical. But in so extreme a national emergency as invasion, if there are any functions which can usefully be performed by women, they have a right to claim those functions, even if it should mean breaking down the masculine tradition that always and under all circumstances the lives of women . . . must be protected." Rathbone suggested that a Women's Volunteer Reserve Army be organized and women be trained in duties that would free men to fight. "Even as auxiliaries of the fighting forces, there are tasks that seem suited to women, if once the idea could be got rid of that they must not be exposed to danger," she argued, citing as examples cooking, washing, mending, and supplying the trenches, and offering as precedent the courage and endurance displayed by the militant suffragists. "I believe that many National Union women would welcome eagerly the opportunity of proving that they are as ready as the militants to face danger," she claimed. "At times of grave national peril, women, if they deliberately choose to do so, have as much right to risk their lives in the service of their country as men."[3]

The following week, another article referring to the threat of invasion noted that "recent experience has shown us all that non-combatants cannot be protected, and must give up all expectation of being protected, if the chance of protecting them conflicts with military tactics or military strategy," and demanded that the authorities "empower [women] to protect themselves. We do not suggest for a moment that non-combatants should attempt to assume the dangerous *rôle* of unauthorised fighters," the paper hastened to add, but it urged that women be asked to organize themselves in units that would be responsible for evacuation, care of the sick or wounded, and the provision of supplies to the forces mobilized to defend the country. Fanny Smart, in an "Open Letter" to the *Englishwoman*, put it more strongly, acknowledging that in wartime, women are a "negligible quantity when it comes to a question of values, and that . . . the saving of a gun is of more importance than the saving of many women." That being the case, she insisted, citing the examples of Belgium and northern France, "this abandonment of women in the present war . . . must be adequately dealt with." She proposed the formation of what amounted to a women's militia, in which women could be organized, drilled, and trained to shoot, to be prepared ahead of time for self-protection on a national basis.

Woman has been told her place is home, that hers should be the sheltered life, that the art of war and self-defence are unwomanly and unnecessary, seeing man is her rightful defender. This is the theory, but the practice now is widely different, and if modern conditions of warfare have changed this practice, it is surely time that women recognised it and organized a scheme for their own protection. That, helpless, inefficient, untrained in self-defence, they should be left suddenly to face unnerving and bewildering conditions—left to the chances of outrage and death, as they have been left in Belgium—is to me horrible and barbarous in the extreme.[4]

Clearly, too, the issues of rape and sexual mutilation played a prominent role in her thinking about women's place in wartime.

Beginning in the spring of 1915, *Common Cause*'s coverage of the war began to shift in tone and in substance. After the Board of Trade issued an appeal for women to register at the Labour Exchanges for war service in March, *Common Cause* carried countless articles about women working in new areas, stressing over and over the need for training. Although stories about toy and doll factories, domestic economy classes, war babies, and maternity continued to be included, they were outnumbered now by such articles as "Votes and the Double Standard," "Women and War Service," "Equal Pay for Equal Work," "Women and the Motor Van," "Women and Economic Conscription," "Sweated Shop Assistants," "War Prisoners in Germany," "War and Free Speech," "Women and Munitions of War." A column entitled "In Parliament" appeared in April and ran regularly. In May, stories entitled "Army Clothing Contracts," "The Cost of War," and "Miners' War Bonus" appeared. By mid-1916 the hysteria about khaki fever and war babies had entirely given way to sober articles about labor and economics: "The Reconstruction of British Industry," "A Suffragist War Savings Association," "Women and Unemployment Insurance," "Maintaining Our Exports," "Wanted—More Chemists." By August 1916, the National Union and *Common Cause* were paying very close attention to the parliamentary debates on franchise reform.[5] The previous emphases upon women's maternal, life-giving instincts had yielded to concerns far more in keeping with prewar feminist attitudes.

While the National Union worked steadily to increase women's opportunities to contribute to the war effort, the WSPU, predictably, took a far more visible role in demanding "women's right to serve." In January 1915, a photograph of Mrs. Pankhurst speaking with a woman bus conductor in France appeared in the *Daily Sketch*, accompanied by a caption that quoted her as "anxious to mobilise the women of Britain . . . to take the place of their husbands." The paper followed this up in March with Mrs. Pankhurst's article "Why Women Should be Mobilised." Christabel Pankhurst urged in the

Suffragette at the beginning of June that "there be universal, obligatory national service for men and women alike." Her call was accompanied by a front-page illustration of a warrior and a woman, she sitting, he standing behind her, but the two of them hand in hand. The woman is armed with a sword, the caption reading "Both for the Country!" The *Times* gave considerable attention to Mrs. Pankhurst's 24 June speech on "the right to serve." As Lisa Tickner has observed, demanding women's "right to serve" in wartime—not just by knitting or providing Belgian relief but by entering munitions factories and joining auxiliary forces—constituted a continuation of prewar feminists' "radical challenge to dominant definitions of femininity, in a context that was no longer subversive."[6]

In this they were aided and abetted by David Lloyd George, then minister of munitions. Already in December 1914 he was searching for ways to increase the nation's munitions output by utilizing a much larger civilian work force, but he realized how much opposition he faced from industrialists and trade unionists who did not wish to surrender jobs to unskilled workers and thereby dilute the wages of the skilled. In late June 1915, at the king's urging, Lloyd George requested that Mrs. Pankhurst mobilize in support of "women's right to serve" a demonstration "like those you used to have for the vote," and provided her with two thousand pounds from the government's coffers. On 17 July thirty thousand women amassed on the Embankment and marched through central London carrying banners that read "For Men Must Fight and Women Must Work," "Down with Sex Prejudice: Let Women Work," and "Shells Made by a Wife May Save a Husband's Life." Some three thousand cinemas throughout Britain showed the newsreel of the march under the heading, "The British Lion is awake, so is the Lioness." As Tickner has pointed out, "women's work in the public spotlight, in the national interest and at the government's behest was . . . both important *and* visible. Suddenly there was an unexpected congruence between [prewar] suffrage representations of an active and capable womanhood and the government's need of it."[7]

Tickner is quite right, but it must be added that the sexualized dimensions of the war and of women as the objects of it continued to be articulated, if in muted form. In April 1915, Christabel Pankhurst had drawn upon the imagery of sexual assault in an article entitled "We Will Not Be Prussianised." She insisted that "the women's cause is one and the same cause as that of the Belgians." In the "women's right to serve" procession, a contingent of women depicting the "Pageant of the Allies" was led by "Belgium," whose "bereaved but unbroken" spirit was identical with "the spirit of British womanhood: the spirit of the March." Given the representations of the "violation of Belgium" and of the atrocity propaganda, the spirit of the march could be seen as that of British womanhood mobilizing to go to war on behalf of sexually violated women. Since the march was directed not at women—who

needed, as Mrs. Pankhurst and Lloyd George were aware, no encourage-
ment to do munitions work—but at the men who owned and worked in the
factories, this mobilization might, given prewar suffrage imagery of sex war,
be construed as one of British women going to war against British men on
behalf of sexually violated women. Indeed, in an October 1915 speech at the
London Pavilion, Mrs. Pankhurst threatened an outbreak of militancy if
women were not permitted to serve. "Women are exercising far more self-
control and self-restraint than perhaps some people give them credit for, but
it is extremely trying to their patience," she warned. "We hear of strikes and
riots amongst men. Well, ladies and gentlemen, what if women lost patience
and began to riot . . . because they were not allowed to work at the time of
their country's need. We hope it won't come to that."[8]

It did not. The nation's need for more soldiers and for women to work in
the positions vacated by men finally overrode any objections to women's
work. As men went off to war, women joined the work force in unprecedented numbers, taking jobs as munitions workers, agricultural laborers,
tram conductors, ambulance drivers, frontline nurses, and, finally, after the
disasters of 1916, auxiliary soldiers. The exigencies of the war after mid-1915
dramatically upset the perceived gender system of the Victorian and Edwardian periods. Mary Somerville exclaimed in the *Women's Liberal Review*,
"Oh! This War! How it is tearing down walls and barriers, and battering in
fast shut doors." The WFL's Nina Boyle could rejoice that "woman's place,
by universal consensus of opinion, is no longer the Home. It is the battlefield, the farm, the factory, the shop." The government's appeal to women
for war service, proclaimed the WFL, was an open acknowledgment that
"woman's place is no longer the home but the nation." For many women, the
opportunity to contribute to national life, to work and to be well paid, was a
rewarding and exhilarating experience. Irene Rathbone, who worked in a
YMCA canteen, confided to her diary that "for years I have not been so
completely free and happy." In 1918, Harriot Stanton Blatch was struck by
"the increased joyfulness of women. They were happy in their work, happy
in the thought of rendering service, so happy that the poignancy of individual loss was carried more easily."[9]

The dismantling of barriers between men's and women's work and the
evident joy women experienced in their new roles fostered a blurring of
distinctions that had helped to form traditional versions of gender identity.
Rebecca West described her visit to a cordite factory in 1916 in terms that
confounded the divisions of home and front. "It is of such vital importance
to the State," she observed in "Hands That War," "that it is ringed with
barbed-wire entanglements and patrolled by sentries, and its products must
have sent tens of thousands of our enemies to their death. And it is inhabited
chiefly by pretty young girls clad in Red-Riding-Hood fancy dress of khaki
and scarlet." Slipping from war imagery to domestic imagery without draw-

ing attention to any sense of incongruence, West highlighted the dramatic changes wrought by the war.

> When one is made to put on rubber over-shoes before entering a hut it might be the precaution of a pernickety housewife concerned about her floors, although actually it is to prevent the grit on one's outdoor shoes igniting a stray scrap of cordite and sending oneself and the hut up to the skies in a column of flame. . . . The girls who stand round the great drums . . . look like millers in their caps and dresses of white waterproof, and the bags containing a white substance . . . might be bags of flour. But, in fact, they are filling the drum with gun-cotton.

The hard work, the long hours, the danger, and, indeed, the deaths of women resulting from munitions explosions led West to declare that "surely, never before in modern history can women have lived a life so completely parallel to that of the regular Army."[10]

Mrs. Alec-Tweedie rejoiced in the fact that "women have become soldiers." Moreover, she predicted, it might not be long before "we may have to have women fighters too. . . . For . . . the war has literally metamorphosed everything and everybody. To-day every man is a soldier, and every woman is a man. Well, no—not quite; but speaking roughly, war has turned the world upside down; and the upshot of the topsy-turveydom is that the world has discovered women, and women have discovered themselves." She argued for the formation of a Woman's Battalion, foreseeing the day when "rather than let the Old Country go under, the women of the Empire would be willing, aye more than willing, to take a place in the firing line. . . . Give them the chance of the trenches . . . and they would step in right royally and loyally again. . . . Women have done more for their country than handle a rifle, and thousands of us are ready to do that, too." As Blatch observed, "The British woman had found herself and her muscles. England was a world of women—women in uniforms." This is a far cry from knitting socks and rolling bandages or providing relief for Belgian refugees; the language of traditional femininity, of separate spheres for women and men, could not adequately articulate the experiences and requirements of a war that failed to respect the boundaries between home and front, between civilian and soldier. Winifred Holtby realized that "so far as modern war is concerned, the old division of interest between combatant and non-combatant decreases, and the qualifications of the combatant lose their dominatingly masculine traits. . . . War ceases to be a masculine occupation."[11]

Many saw in this development a promising future for men and women. "It is difficult adequately to express the confidence, the desire, and the willingness to cooperate that there is now between our men and women," wrote Helen Fraser of the National Union in 1917. "The sexes were meant to work together," argued Alec-Tweedie, "and our factories and public offices have proved how easily they can do it. There is no sex in brains and work. . . . Co-operation is now the password of the sexes, not antagonism." In a formulation that echoed many of the great hopes the war would effect about gender, sexuality, and politics, Blatch noted that "Great Britain is not talking about feminism, it is living it." "The conditions under which large numbers of women then worked carried with them subversive modifications in their clothing, and consequent outlook on themselves and on the world," wrote Mary Agnes Hamilton in 1936. "They learned to move their limbs freely, and to enjoy the action. Those limbs, once the object of lascivious interest to the other sex, were now too freely seen to carry such implications any longer, with the observer or possessor." As a result, a "quite new kind of companionship" between women and men was made possible. "Those who got to know each other in relation to common tasks found that they shared an interest that had nothing to do with sex: that there was a vast new area in existence, i.e., work, in which sex hardly counted, and into which it rarely entered."[12]

For many other people, however, the notion of women's doing men's work created enormous anxiety. Women in uniform were seen disapprovingly to be "aping" men. One woman wrote to the *Morning Post* in July 1916, describing four women dressed in khaki:

> They had either cropped their hair or managed so to hide it under their khaki felt hats that at first sight the younger women looked exactly like men. . . . I noticed that these women assumed mannish attitudes, stood with legs apart while they smote their riding whips, and looked like self-conscious and not very attractive boys. . . . I do not know the corps to which these ladies belong, but if they cannot become nurses or ward maids in hospitals, let them put on sunbonnets and print frocks and go and make hay or pick fruit or make jam, or do the thousand and one things that women can do to help.

Charlotte Haldane wrote scathingly in 1927 of the "'war-working' type of 'woman'—aping the cropped hair, the great booted feet, and grim jaw, the uniform, and if possible the medals of the military men." Caroline Playne remembered seeing, while awaiting a train in the Midlands,

> a sight foreign to anything civilization has ever exhibited before, but typical of the effects of fighting fury. . . . A short local train came in, drew up and disgorged, on the instant, a couple of hundred de-humanized females, Amazonian beings bereft of reason or feeling, judging by the set of their faces, bereft of all charm of appearance, clothed anyhow, skin stained a yellow-brown even to the roots of their dishevelled hair by the awful stuff they handled. . . . Were these really women?[13]

A perception of blurred gender identities appeared at the front as well as at home. Noncommissioned officers in charge of supplying or transporting troops, for instance, might regard their work in maternal terms, as in the case of the sergeant major in Ford Madox Ford's *Parade's End*, whose "motherly heart . . . yearned . . . over his two thousand nine hundred and thirty-four nurslings," and who wished even "to extend the motherliness of his functions" to officers. Front soldiers who had come through battle found themselves reluctant to leave their tents, which "gave them the only privacy they knew, and they wanted to lie hidden until they had recovered their nerve. Among themselves they were unselfish, even gentle; instinctively helping each other." Collecting the wounded, these battle-hardened men carried them "tenderly, soothing [them] with the gentleness of women." The altered lyrics of a sentimental song about Old Blighty explicitly recognized that traditional gender identity had broken down under the extremes of war: "Oh, they've called them up from Weschurch, / And they've called them up from Wen, / And they'll call up all the women, / When they've fucked up all the men."[14]

The war made many men anxious about their masculinity: Captain Mc-Kechnie, in *Parade's End*, agonized, "Why isn't one a beastly girl and privileged to shriek?" Christopher Tietjens, the main character, having seen one of his men die with his face half blown away, immediately turned his thoughts to the woman he loves, thinking that "he himself must be a—eunuch." The unprecedented opportunities made available to women by the Great War—their increased visibility in public life, their release from the private world of domesticity, their greater mobility—contrasted sharply with the conditions imposed on men at the front. Immobilized and rendered passive in a subterranean world of trenches, men found that "the war to which so many [of them] had gone in the hope of becoming heroes ended up emasculating them, depriving them of autonomy, confining them as closely as any Victorian woman had been confined," as Sandra Gilbert has argued. The terrors of the war and the expectations of manliness on the part of the frontsoldier combined to produce in large numbers of men a condition that came to be known as "shell shock." As Elaine Showalter has demonstrated, these cases of shell shock were in fact cases of male hysteria. "When all signs of physical fear were judged as weakness and where alternatives to combat . . . were viewed as unmanly," she has written, "men were silenced and immobilized and forced, like women, to express their conflicts through the body." Robert Graves, testifying on behalf of Siegfried Sassoon, who had been brought up on charges for desertion and whose defense rested upon the claim that he had experienced shell shock, was himself in such a bad "state of nerves" that "I burst into tears three times during my statement."[15]

The terrors of war problematized masculinity, fragmented it, causing men to question their relationship to a universal maleness. On the eve of battle, Frederic Manning reported, "each man became conscious of his own personality as of something very hard, and sharply defined against a background

of other men, who remained merely generalized as 'the others.' The mystery
of his own being increased for him enormously; and he had to explore that
doubtful darkness alone, finding a foothold here, a handhold there, grasping
one support after another and relinquishing it when it yielded, crumbling."[16]

The association of sex and war carried potentially explosive implications for
society when it became clear that this war would require the participation of
all segments of the population; anxiety about the war frequently took shape
as anxiety about sex or was articulated in sexual terms. The charges of khaki
fever and imminent war babies that predominated in 1914 had contained a
kind of patronizing and even good-hearted tone; as the war effort intensified
and casualties worsened, attacks on women's sexuality increased in viru-
lence. "Some women," reported Mrs. Alec-Tweedie, in 1918, "old and
young, became hysterical with war. They went out like cats on the tiles and
shrieked madly. They wanted to mate. Anything would do. . . . Alas, yes,
there are a handful of women who are like festering disease spots in a
healthy body. These women are not all morally bad, but they are temporarily
and temperamentally unbalanced, and they are not playing the game." Making no distinction between prostitutes infected with venereal diseases on the
one hand, and young girls or women infected with khaki fever on the other,
Arthur Conan Doyle wrote to the *Times* in February 1917 of "vile women
. . . who prey upon and poison our soldiers. . . . these harpies carry off the
lonely soldiers to their rooms . . . and finally inoculate them . . . with one of
those diseases." A December 1917 letter to the *Times* referred to women as
"sexual freelances" who "stalked through the land, vampires upon the nation's health, distributing and perpetuating among our young manhood diseases which institute a national calamity." In July 1918, Imperial War Conference attendees heard tales of infected women "lying in wait for clean
young men who came to give their lives for their country." The government,
for its part, introduced regulation 40d of the Defense of the Realm Act in
March 1918, at the height of worries about the German advance, declaring
that "no woman suffering from venereal disease shall have sexual intercourse with any member of His Majesty's Forces, or solicit or invite any
member to have sexual intercourse with her." Clearly, in the minds of many
Britons, sex presented as great a threat to England's survival and existence
as did Germany; the two were, indeed, conflated in many minds. Mrs. Alec-
Tweedie made this connection abundantly clear when she warned that
"every woman who lets herself 'go' is as bad as a German spy, and a traitor,
not only to her sex, but to her country."[17]

   "Unfriendly comment" regarding the behavior of women in munitions
factories and the auxiliary forces began to surface, Wilson has observed.
"The more acerbic wondered what proportion of the factory girl's [*sic*] earn-
ings was derived not from their official employment but from what was

euphemistically called 'the extra shift.'" Siegfried Sassoon's Sherston reported his Aunt Evelyn's complaints about "the disgracefully immoral way
most of the young women were behaving while doing war work." Before
they even reached France, members of the Women's Auxiliary Army Corps
(WAAC) were accused of loose living and of corrupting the morals of "our
poor lads." Upon their arrival, rumors of "immoral conduct" so dogged the
WAACs on the Continent that officials found it necessary to convene a commission of inquiry. Though the commission found the charges of widespread
immorality to be unjustified, "the presumed sexual aspirations of WAACs
towards British soldiers," as Wilson has put it, continued to excite the public
imagination.[18]

It is useful, I think, to regard these chronicles of sexual behavior as more
than sociological observations of the war years. By focusing on sex as one of
the major issues of the war, contemporaries hit upon a means by which they
could imagine, represent, and even narrate—that is, make sense of—the
war, which, according to Fussell and Hynes, defied traditional terms and
habits of thought. As women began to take up jobs previously held exclusively by men, and even to serve as auxiliaries in the armed forces, sexual
representation utilizing traditional heterosexual terms and images was no
longer adequate to the task of giving meaning to a war so completely out of
line with all precedent. Visions of sexuality in which women had become
fully as unrestrained as men, and/or that exposed sex as a drive toward violence, war, and death, began to predominate. Although she understood the
"bacchantic frenzy" that struck "hundreds of reputable women and girls
round every camp" to be "the natural complement to the male frenzy of
killing," drawing an analogy between sex and death that anticipated Freud,
Helena Swanwick "never learnt to tolerate this with an indifferent mind." It
"revolted me almost as much as [the war's] more obvious brutalities," she
recalled, in a remarkably bald illustration of the conflation of war and sex.
Most postwar commentators attributed what contemporaries took for promiscuity to the wastage of life wrought by battle. "Life was less than cheap,"
explained Mary Agnes Hamilton in 1936,

> it was thrown away. The religious teaching that the body was the temple of the
> Holy Ghost could mean little or nothing to those who saw it mutilated and
> destroyed in millions by Christian nations engaged in war. All moral standards
> were held for a short moment and irretrievably lost. Little wonder that the old
> ideals of chastity and self-control in sex were, for many, also lost. . . . The great
> destroyer of the old ideal of female chastity, as accepted by women themselves,
> was here. How and why refuse appeals, backed up by the hot beating of your
> own heart . . . , which were put with passion and even pathos by a hero here
> to-day and gone to-morrow.[19]

"Faced with imminent extinction," wrote Irene Clephane in 1935 of the
millions of young men in the armed forces, "they seized what chances came

of satisfying their sexual impulses. . . . Uprooted from all familiar things, they found their partners among the young women whom, like themselves, the war had detached from the past: girls in the uniforms of the various women's corps, girls who had taken up voluntary nursing, girls newly let loose in offices and factories." Drinking, dancing, drugging, smoking, gambling, and sex, it appeared to commentators looking back upon the war years, were the natural consequences of the stress and strain of total war, with "its dark confusion, its reckless sense of haste and drive, its nervous preoccupation with sex." "These experiences," agreed Clephane, "in an atmosphere of hectic, temporary excitement, seemed the only salvation for the over-wrought minds of serving men and their companions alike." "Brevity of life makes passion more insistent," explained Holtby, in a formulation that drew upon Freud's theories of Eros and Thanatos. "The erotic attraction of death."[20]

Such images threatened traditional gender and sexual arrangements. Moreover, warnings about prostitution and venereal disease were joined now by charges of sexual perversions and of homosexuality, behaviors that dramatically challenged the system of separate spheres and heterosexuality itself in imagery consonant with concerns about the blurring of gender lines. In D. H. Lawrence's "Tickets, Please," women tram conductors, "fearless young hussies," set upon their inspector, John Thomas, whose amorous adventures with a number of women have infuriated them. Their assault is depicted in near-sexual terms, invoking the imagery of rape and castration. "Their blood was thoroughly up. He was their sport now. They were going to have their own back, out of him. . . . His tunic was simply torn off his back, his shirt-sleeves were torn away, his arms were naked. . . . Their faces were flushed, their hair wild, their eyes were all glittering strangely. He lay at last quite still, with face averted, as an animal lies when it is defeated and at the mercy of the captor." "You ought to be *killed*," the ringleader told John Thomas with "a terrifying lust in her voice."

Wells's Mr. Britling distinguished the British war effort from that of the Germans by invoking explicit castration imagery. Coming across a stash of German comic papers in a friend's study, he was overwhelmed by "their amazing hate and their amazing filthiness alike. . . . One incredible craving was manifest in every one of them. The German caricaturist seemed unable to represent his enemies except in extremely tight trousers or in none; he was equally unable to represent them without thrusting a sword or bayonet, sputtering blood, into the more indelicate parts of their persons. . . . This was the *leitmotif* of the war as the German humorists presented it."[21] In depictions of a war that violated the conventional boundaries, the sexual mutilation of women found its counterpart in the sexual mutilation of men.

Male homosexuality, perceived as men's behaving like women, appeared to contemporaries to pose a great danger to the war effort. If the war provided the manly alternative to the prewar threat of effeminacy, then the logical conclusion might easily be drawn, as it was by many, that "setbacks to the British cause" on the battlefield could be attributed to "sexual 'laxity,'" as Wilson has noted. "The sadly unbalanced Lord Alfred Douglas was proclaiming to anyone who would listen—and it seemed a good many would—that Britain's failures in the war were attributable to the 'vice' practised by Oscar Wilde." In 1915, Lord Alfred Douglas wrote in the *Antidote* that "it is just as important to civilization that Literary England should be cleansed of sex-mongers and pedlars of the perverse, as that Flanders should be cleared of Germans." In May 1916, the *English Review* reported on "the moral and spiritual invasion of Britain by German urnings [homosexuals] for the purpose of undermining the patriotism, the stamina, the intellect, and the moral [*sic*] of British Navy and Army men, and of our prominent public leaders." In February 1918 M.P. Noel Pemberton Billing claimed in the House of Commons that the German secret service had the names of forty-seven thousand "English perverts," whom it was blackmailing in order to further its war aims. A few days later, Pemberton Billing's charges appeared in a popular newspaper, the *Referee*, as statements of fact.[22]

Heterosexuality was challenged in other, more pragmatic terms as well—the facts of demography. "Living feminism," as Harriot Stanton Blatch described women's wartime gains, in the war's context could not avoid associations with dismemberment and death, which had created the need for women's participation in the war in the first place. Wells's Mr. Britling inadvertently articulated this thought as he celebrated the difference between northern, Protestant European cultures like England's and that of southern, Catholic countries.

> This new culture [of England et al.] tends to diminish the specialisation of women as women, to let them out from the cell of the home into common citizenship with men. It's a new culture, still in process of development, which will make men more social and co-operative and women bolder, swifter, more responsible and less cloistered. It minimises instead of exaggerating the importance of sex. . . . And . . . it is just all this Northern tendency that this world struggle is going to release. This war is pounding through Europe, smashing up homes, dispersing and mixing homes. . . . it is killing young men by the million, altering the proportions of the sexes for a generation, bringing women into business and office and industry, destroying the accumulated wealth that kept so many of them in refined idleness, flooding the world with strange doubts and novel ideas.[23]

Women's gains could be perceived as being entirely at the expense of men, and of men's lives. The NUWSS's "Weekly Notes" seemed to concede as much in an item about how the appearance of WAACs—marching "sturdily in their low-heeled shoes, heads up, arms swinging together, as only those drilled and trained can march"—was causing people to think very carefully about the future. "There are strange sights to be seen in London streets these days," the Notes continued, "and . . . we speculate as to how much of the old order will be left to return when peace is declared." There may be a typographical error here: I suspect that the editor meant to question how much of the old order would be left to return *to* at the war's conclusion, but the wording printed does give rise to the suggestion that the deaths of thousands of men would ensure permanence for women's gains. Blatch reported of war-working women, "peace will mean an insufficient number of breadwinners to go around and . . . a maimed man may have low earning power. The women I met were not dejected at the prospect; they showed, on the contrary, a spirit not far removed from elation in finding new opportunities of service." Mabel Daggett enthused, "Every time a man drops dead in the trenches, a woman steps permanently into the niche he used to hold in industry, in commerce, in the professions, in world affairs. . . . the ultimate programme toward which the modern Woman Movement to-day is moving is no less than Paradise Regained! It may even, I think, have been worth this war to be there."[24]

It was easy to misinterpret the sentiments of these women, and many did. Hirschfeld reported, in terms that consigned all women to the role of callous warmonger, that with the outbreak of war "women demonstrated the most incredible readiness to part with, nay to send away their beloved ones, husbands and sons," offering up the scenario of a "given man, who had been virtually pushed into the war by his wife or mother." Such an interpretation followed from the way in which propagandists depicted women's duties during the first year of the war. Florence L. Barclay's *My Heart's Right There*, which appeared in December 1914, tells the story of a soldier who goes off to fight, is wounded, and comes home to his wife and child on medical leave. As he prepares to return to his unit, he explains to his wife, "It's a righteous war, my girl; and every man who fears God and honours the King, should be up, and out, and ready to do his share; and every woman who loves her home, must be willing bravely to do her part, by letting her man go." As Wilson has stated, prior to the introduction of conscription, women's "role was to make straight their menfolk's path to enlistment and to ensure that concern for family did not impede husbands and sons from offering their services, and possibly their lives, to their country." But it was a short step from women's facilitating the enlistment of loved ones to their pushing them off to fight. One of the more common recruitment posters declared, "Women of Britain Say—Go!" depicting a woman and her two children, watching from the safety of their home, as her husband marched off to join his regiment. A recruiting poster addressed "To the Women of Britain" asked, "Do you realise that the one word 'GO' from you may send another man to fight for our King and Country? When the War is over and someone asks your husband or your son what he did in the great War, is he to hang his head because you would not let him go? WON'T YOU HELP AND SEND A MAN TO JOIN THE ARMY TO-DAY?"[25] The patient, patriotic woman at home could readily become the agent that would send a man to his death.

As the war wore on and manpower was at a premium, exhortations that women do all they could to get and keep their men in the field became more pointed. "Mothers!" demanded a leaflet in 1915. "Do you expect other Mothers' sons to defend *you and your sons*? Persuade your son to enlist[;] do not hold him back. One word from YOU and he will go. Sweethearts! Has your 'boy' enlisted? If not, why not? Are you selfishly dissuading him? If so the shame of your Country rests upon YOU." Hyperpatriotic women bestowed white feathers—a symbol of cowardice—upon able-bodied men in civilian clothes. Slogans such as "Shells Made by a Wife May Save a Husband's Life" could scarcely conceal the reality that shells made by women also took men's lives, men who had been put on the line by women who took their jobs. As Mrs. Alec-Tweedie put it, "every woman who went into munitions or brick-making set a man free to be a soldier. So over two million extra fighting soldiers were sent to the front by the willing substitution of women themselves."[26]

Men at the front often felt alienated and estranged from those left behind in comparative safety at home; these feelings were exacerbated by the apparent pleasure with which those at home were prosecuting the war. War correspondent Philip Gibbs reported that many soldiers returned from leave "fuming," holding

> the frightful suspicion . . . that at home people liked the war and were not anxious to end it, and did not care a jot for the sufferings of the soldiers. . . . Everybody was having a good time. Munition-workers were earning wonderful wages and spending them on gramophones, pianos, furs, and the "pictures." Everybody was gadding about in a state of joyous exultation. The painted flapper was making herself sick with the sweets of life after office hours in government employ, where she did little work for a lot of pocket-money. The society girl was dancing bare-legged for "war charities," pushing into bazaars for the "poor, dear wounded," getting her pictures into the papers as a "notable war-worker," married for the third time in three years. . . . Millions of girls were in some kind of fancy dress with buttons and shoulder-straps, breeches and puttees, and they seemed to be making a game of the war and enjoying it thoroughly.

"'What are we fighting for?' asked officers back from leave, turning over the pages of the *Sketch* and *Tatler*, with pictures of race-meetings, strike-meetings, bare-backed beauties at war bazaars, and portraits of profiteers in the latest honors list. 'Are we going to die for these swine? These parasites and prostitutes?'" People at home "don't care a fuck what 'appens to 'us'ns,'" exclaimed Madeley in Manning's *Her Privates We*. "When this bloody war's over," chimed in his mate, Glazier, in terms that paired peace with women, but with a twist now, "you'll go back to England an' fin' nought but a lot o' conchies [conscientious objectors] and bloody prostitutes."[27]

The division of front and home, Fussell has asserted, "was as severe and uncompromising as the others generating the adversary atmosphere." Siegfried Sassoon maintained that "the man who really endured the War at its worst was everlastingly differentiated from everyone except his fellow soldiers." The dichotomy of home and front led, finally, to a situation whereby the soldiers on the line felt a greater sense of solidarity with Germans sitting across no-man's-land than with their compatriots at home; indeed, Leed has argued that the bellicosity and rage the frontsoldiers directed against those at home exceeded that aimed at the enemy.[28]

The hostility and anger the frontsoldiery directed against the home— symbolized and epitomized by women— could be intense. In "Glory of Women," Sassoon seethed,

> You love us when we're heroes, home on leave,
> Or wounded in a mentionable place.
> You worship decorations; you believe
> That chivalry redeems the war's disgrace.
> You make us shells. You listen with delight,
> By tales of dirt and danger fondly thrilled.
> You crown our distant ardours while we fight,
> And mourn our laurelled memories when we're killed.
> You can't believe that British troops "retire"
> When hell's last horror breaks them, and they run,
> Trampling the terrible corpses—blind with blood.
>   O German mother dreaming by the fire,
>   While you are knitting socks to send your son
>   His face is trodden deeper in the mud.

"The visiting of violent and if possible painful death upon the complacent, uncomprehending, fatuous civilians at home was a favorite fantasy indulged by the troops," Fussell argues. In "Blighters," Sassoon amuses himself in a music hall with thoughts of "a Tank com[ing] down the stalls, / Lurching to rag-time tunes, or 'Home, sweet Home.'" In "Yellow-Pressmen," victorious soldiers parading through London turn their weapons on the civilians lining the streets; the author later grabs hand grenades, "And with my trusty bombers turned and went / To clear those Junkers out of Parliament."[29]

This hostility was probably intensified by men's identification with characteristics regarded as feminine in a war that seemed to be effacing distinctions between men and women. As Showalter has suggested, "men's quarrels with the feminine element in their own psyches became externalized as quarrels with women." Sandra Gilbert has noted that the antiheroes of post-

war literature, "from Lawrence's paralyzed Clifford Chatterley to Hemingway's sadly emasculated Jake Barnes to Eliot's mysteriously sterile Fisher
King . . . suffer specifically from sexual wounds, as if, having traveled literally or figuratively through No Man's Land, all have become not just No
Men, nobodies, but *not* men, *un*men." Gilbert has seen particularly in Lawrence's poetry the process whereby "the unmanning terrors of combat lead
not just to a generalized sexual anxiety but also to a sexual anger directed
specifically against the female, as if the Great War itself were primarily a
climactic episode in some battle of the sexes that had already been raging for
years." His wartime poem, "Eloi, Eloi, Lama Sabacthani," conveys his sense
of being preyed upon by women: "Why do the women follow us, satisfied,
/Feed on our wounds like bread, receive our blood / Like glittering seed
upon them for fulfilment?" Mrs. Alec-Tweedie confirmed this impression.
"'Ye gods!' the travelling male might exclaim," she wrote, "were this his
first view of the new Britain, 'the women have eliminated us. We shall soon
be as extinct as the dodo.'"[30]

These discrete impressions, in light of the dramatic gains in employment
and freedom women achieved precisely because of the war, coalesced into
a perception that the persistent horrors of the war were, somehow, women's
fault. F. C. Bartlett, a psychologist writing in the 1920s, reported that prolonged stays at the front led soldiers to link thoughts of home—where
women reigned—and death. The telegram that informed Mr. Britling of the
death of his son, Hugh, at the front, was delivered by a girl, not, as should
have been the case in 1915 or 1916, by a boy. Robert Graves believed that
his longevity at the front was a consequence of his maintaining his virginity,
of abstaining from contact with women, clearly linking sex—and women—
with death. This association appears too in the appellations soldiers gave to
German howitzer shells—"grandma" and "aunty"; women usually figured as
beneficent and maternal have become deadly. In *Parade's End*, a private by
the name of O Nine Morgan requested leave to return home to deal with his
wife's infidelity with a prizefighter. His request denied on the grounds that
the boxer would kill him, he was killed instead by a mortar. "This was what
done it, I should say," announced his sergeant major, holding up a piece of
heavy metal. "No, I don't believe that did it," replied Tietjens, who had
made the decision to keep O Nine Morgan at the front. "Something bigger
. . . Say a prize-fighter's fist. . . ." "Oh, I take your meaning, sir," the sergeant
major said. "O Nine Morgan's wife, sir."[31] The cause of death has been displaced from a mortar shell onto a woman.

The prospect of women's waging war against men was raised by Wells's
Mr. Britling Sees It Through in the character of Letty, whose husband Teddy
has been wounded and is missing in action. She proposes to form "The
Women's Association for the Extirpation of the whole breed of War Lords,"
a band of women dedicated to ending all wars by "killing the kind of people
who make them. Rooting them out. By a campaign of pursuit and assassina-

tion that will go on for years and years after the war itself is over." Making
an explicit connection between this group of assassins and the suffragettes,
and raising the specter of sex war, Letty reasons that, after all, "we women
were ready enough a year or so ago to starve and die for the Vote, and that
was quite a little thing in comparison with this business."[32]

For feminists, too, the connection of sex and war could give way to notions
of sex war. In April 1915, Emmeline Pankhurst gave a speech infused and
charged by the imagery of sexual assault. "The men of Belgium, the men of
France, the men of Serbia," she lamented to her Liverpool audience, "however willing they were to protect women from the things that are most horrible—and more horrible to women than death itself—have not been able to
do it. It is only by an accident, or a series of accidents, for which no man has
the right to take credit that British women on British soil are not now enduring the horrors endured by the women of France, the women of Belgium,
and the women of Serbia." According to Mary Lowndes in the *Englishwoman* of October 1914, the belief that men protect women had been
proved false by the events on the Continent. "And, indeed," she added, "we
must remember that it is against themselves, against animal dominance and
brute force, that men must learn to protect their women in days of peace, if
there is to be any hope that in time of war they shall have the same immunity
that (at any rate theoretically) is extended to peaceable non-combatants of
the other sex." The *Vote* continued after August 1914 to carry its regular
column, "The 'Protected' Sex," a compilation of the outrages committed
against women and the lenient sentences imposed on male perpetrators; in
September 1914 it protested vehemently against the policy of supplying the
army with recruits from the ranks of those who had been convicted of assaults against women and children. "With the terrible record of assaults on
women and children achieved by the German soldiers, we should have
thought it a pity to reinforce our army with this particular element," it edito-
rialized. Nina Boyle reported to readers of the *Vote* in February 1915 that
"British officers and officials are treating as gentlemen and soldiers, and not
as criminals, men guilty of the foulest horrors"; she wrote "of a train full of
school-girls . . . who were outraged by officers. The *Lancet* gives a statement
that of a convent of sixty nuns, twenty-nine are expecting to be confined [by
pregnancy] as the result of similar brutal treatment." The line between German soldier and British soldier was not very distinct in the rhetoric of these
women, and Boyle very soon erased it entirely. "Greatest of all dangers to
women," she wrote in August 1915, "is the unbridled passion of men. . . .
even now, in war time, in our own land, from our own men, the danger stalks
undiminished and unchecked."[33]

Mr. Britling Sees It Through was an example of artists' attempts, by 1916,
to represent the war to British society in a newly realistic fashion. (R. H.
Tawney singled it out as the exception to his claim that people at home had

no idea of the nature of the war at the front.) Pacifists had attempted as early as 1915 to bring home to the British public the realities of war by describing "what war does to men's bodies," as Swanwick put it. Quoting Arnold Bennett in the *Daily News and Leader* of 24 March 1915, she told her readership that "the primary object of this war and of all wars is to lacerate human flesh, to break bones, to inflict torture, to paralyse, and to kill. . . . Let us never forget that war is first and last a tearing of human flesh, the shattering of human bones, and the greatest source of human agony, both physical and mental." But these descriptions had little impact on the way the war was taken in by British civilians, for newspaper accounts and official pronouncements continued to tell the story of the war using rhetoric infused with romance and heroism. Until, that is, the Somme battles transformed journalists' understanding of the war and, subsequently, the language and imagery they used to represent it to their readers. As "articulate men experienced the trench world, and tried to record what they had seen there, and women saw the damaged men returning from that world, and experienced loss and grief,"[34] the Rupert Brooke rendition of the war could no longer be sustained. The traditional heroic and romantic rhetoric of the early years did not disappear overnight in the aftermath of the great battles of 1916, but it was overshadowed now by images that defied such high-minded language.

A significant development of 1916—the filming of the war by cameramen sent to the front by the Committee on War Films—altered for good the ways in which the British public would imagine the war. *The Battle of the Somme* appeared in movie theaters in August 1916, attracting record-breaking audiences throughout the country. It depicted

> a version of war that has great, non-traditional symbolic force. In this film, war
> is not a matter of individual voluntary acts, but of masses of men and materials,
> moving randomly through a dead, ruined world towards no identifiable object;
> it is aimless violence and passive suffering, without either a beginning or an
> end—not a crusade, but a terrible destiny. War Office caption-writers tried to
> make it into a narrative of a conventional one-day battle, which the British had
> won, but the visual images deny that story.

Elsie Bowerman, a WSPU member returning home from Russia where she had done hospital work, caught a showing of *The Somme* in Odessa in 1917. "Splendid film," she noted in her diary, "most of it taken actually under fire—but much of it too horribly realistic."[35]

The casualty lists reinforced the gruesome horrors and wastage of life that war correspondents had witnessed. As one contemporary put it, "No one who lived through that time will ever forget the casualty lists of the Somme." In the 31 July 1916 issue of the *Times*, two pages of six columns each, with every line containing three or four names, were given over to the dead. In 1916, Hynes has written, "there could not have been many people in En-

gland, rich or poor, in country or city, who had not been touched by suffering and loss. . . . by mid-war virtually everyone in England had reason to
take the war personally."[36]

The characteristic British manifestation of suffering and loss often appears
to us, from a distance of three-quarters of a century, baffling. Mrs. C. S. Peel
recounted an instance of a woman who was playing bridge with friends at
her club when a servant informed her partner that someone outside wished
to speak with her. "The poor woman went white. Her cards fell out of her
hands. I thought she was going to faint, but she got up and went out of the
room. It was the telegram . . . her son had been killed. One of the proprietors
of the club came in to take her place, and we went on playing." Carolyn
Playne explained that in England

> outward signs of mourning were taboo. . . . It was a relief not to waste time in
> lamentations. The woe was crushed under so that there should be no break in
> the round of their war work. Many a mother, many a wife, after receiving the
> news by telegram or letter that their dearest had perished, went off next morn-
> ing to office or factory, hospital or canteen, looking gayer than usual. The thing
> is incredible, but the miracle happened again and again. . . . Perhaps the chorus
> so often uttered by friends and fellow-workers in war-days: "Isn't she splendid!"
> penetrated to stricken souls with sustaining power.[37]

More likely, the denial of grief, either to oneself or to one's friends or
colleagues, had the effect of distorting both the experiences of war and the
images of the individuals fighting it. Playne suggested that no matter how
determinedly women "crushed down their repulsions, their sorrows and
anxieties, and deadened their souls by ceaseless activities . . . war brought
sorrows that could not be denied or brushed away. So that when the gnaw-
ing of some sudden unbearable grief, some irrefutable blow, struck down
women at home, the tortured mind found refuge, now and again, in real
dementia. Fantastic imaginings were adopted and substituted for obvious
truths." Only now that more realistic accounts and images of the war pervaded the culture, the distorted picture was not that of brave warriors on
horseback fighting chivalrously for the women of the nation, but of massive,
mindless destruction committed by machinelike men. The picture of masculinity conjured up by such imagery was often that of "mechanical dolls who
grin and kill and grin," "a grimacing phantom," "a creature at once ridiculous
and disgusting," as R. H. Tawney described it resentfully in October 1916
while recuperating from wounds received on the Somme in July. He casti-
gated the newspapers for "inventing a kind of conventional soldier" who
revels in the "excitement" of war, finds "'sport' in killing other men," and
hunts "Germans out of dug-outs as a terrier hunts rats." "We are depicted as
merry assassins, rejoicing in the opportunity of a 'scrap' in which we know
that more than three-quarters of our friends will be maimed or killed, care-

less of our own lives, exulting in the duty of turning human beings into lumps of disfigured clay." "The Happy Warrior," Herbert Read's 1916 poem, drips with contempt for those at home who continued to think of the war in chivalric terms: the soldier's "aching jaws grip a hot parched tongue," and his "wide eyes search unconsciously"; a mute automaton, he dribbles bloody saliva down his shirtfront as he stabs and stabs again "a well-killed Boche."[38]

Moreover, the imagery of sexual assault invoked by the Belgian atrocities continued to inform representations of the war. Valentine Wallop, in Ford's *Parade's End*, believed that "all manly men were lust-filled devils, desiring nothing better than to stride over battlefields, stabbing the wounded with long daggers in frenzies of sadism." Ford, having served as a transport officer during the Somme battles, may well have witnessed the training of new drafts of soldiers as they were called up to replace those slaughtered on the front lines, and may have drawn upon it to present Valentine's views. As Robert Graves described those training sessions, drill instructors exhorted Tommies to make "horrible grimaces and utter blood-curdling yells" as they charged at dummies with their bayonets. "Hurt him, now! In at the belly! Tear his guts out!" they screamed, Graves reported; "Now that upper swing at his privates with the butt. Ruin his chances for life! No more little Fritzes! . . . BITE HIM, I SAY! STICK YOUR TEETH IN HIM AND WORRY HIM! EAT HIS HEART OUT!"[39]

Such depictions of masculinity bore little resemblance to the way men at the front perceived themselves or women at the front perceived them, as we shall see in the next chapter; but the power of these bloodthirsty images was lasting and would have significant impact on the way women at home understood the nature of masculinity, femininity, and the relations between the sexes.

In the war's second phase, from about mid-1915 on, the representation of war as unleashed sexual desire gave way to visions of sexual disorder, a blurring of gender lines as women went off to factories and front to do war work and men found themselves immobilized in trenches. Toward the end of the war, sexual disorder came to be portrayed as sexual conflict and polarization between the sexes, or sex war, as men perceived women to be emasculating them, and began, at least rhetorically, to strike back. The use of sexual metaphor—specifically, the images of sexual disorder and then sex war—to give meaning to the experiences of the Great War after 1915, and the notions of masculinity and femininity created thereby, would have a distinct bearing on issues seemingly unrelated to the war, as we shall see in chapters 4, 5, and 6. In the next chapter, we will see a different kind of sexual imagery emerge in the accounts of women who had an immediate, rather than long-distance, relationship to the war.

Chapter 3

FEMINISTS AT THE FRONT:
REINVENTING MASCULINITY

IN 1915, May Sinclair described a series of committee meetings held to decide what program of action her group would offer the military authorities to help the war effort. At one of them, a plan was hatched in which

> we were to have sent out a detachment of stalwart Amazons in khaki breeches who were to dash out on to the battle-field, reconnoitre, and pick up the wounded and carry them away slung over their saddles. The only difficulty was to get the horses. But the author of the scheme—who had brought her breeches—had allowed for that. The horses were to be caught on the battle-field; as the wounded and dead dropped from their saddles the Amazons were to leap into them and ride off. On this system "remounts" were also to be supplied. Whenever a horse was shot dead under its rider, an Amazon was to dash up with another whose rider had been shot dead. It was all perfectly simple and only needed a little "organization." For four weeks the lure of the battle-field kept our volunteers dancing around the War Office and the Red Cross Societies.

Elsie Bowerman, a member of the WSPU, wrote to her mother in July 1916, upon being asked to go to Serbia to do war work, "It is what I've been dying to do, ever since the war started. . . . It is really like a chance to go to the front. . . . It is too thrilling for words." "I am nearly mad with joy," Mary Dexter confided to her journal in September 1914. "I have just today had a letter from the American War Hospital in Devonshire offering me a post." "This was life!" exulted one member of the First Aid Nursing Yeomanry (FANY) upon her arrival in France. "My ears tingled; I breathed in long, deep breaths. Had I spoken, a sort of wild war song would have come from my lips."[1]

At the beginning of the war, women at home who were eager to do their bit at the front visualized a great chivalric adventure, just as their brothers had. Very shortly, however, exultation gave way to sober reflection as this war's realities sank in. The FANY, upon encountering her first soldiers, weary men stumbling along the road, carrying stretchers of wounded and dead, realized immediately that "there was no romance or triumph here, no wild war cry and exaltation—just these men, dirty and muddy and footsore, bringing in their comrades, broken and maimed and moaning . . . or very quiet." "All that war-romancing," Sinclair's Charlotte lamented after a number of weeks at the front. "I see how awful it was. When I think how we went out and got thrills. Fancy getting thrills out of this horror."[2]

Feminists who spent some part of the war in arenas in which the war was actually prosecuted or where the direct consequences of the fighting were manifested experienced the war differently from those whose relationship to the war was mediated by distance and hearsay, and whose battles were parliamentary and political. Nurses, members of the Voluntary Aid Detachments (VADs), and physicians at casualty clearing stations or base hospitals, as well as those who treated and cared for the wounded in hospitals in England; ambulance drivers transporting the wounded from battlefield to operating theater; individuals who served in auxiliary positions at the front or in support areas; YMCA and canteen volunteers in France; and those who underwent the traumas of war as victims of air raids or U-boat attacks—all represented their encounters with and impressions of the war in terms markedly dissimilar to those of their compatriots at home. While many of the images were also sexualized, the tone and content of the imagery conveyed a different understanding of the relations of men and women in wartime. This may help to explain why in the postwar period these individuals—many of them adherents to that wing of the movement derided as "old" feminism—held ideas about the nature of masculinity and femininity, and thus of feminism, that substantially differed from those of their colleagues at home, feminists who would come to be differentiated by the label "new."

A comparison of the language and imagery used by women at home as they contemplated the war with that of women at the front as they reported on their experiences reveals dramatic differences. Direct contact with the war or with its victims was articulated in sober, constrained, sharp, and clear terms. It was as if, in making the transition from home to front, the individual had received a secret knowledge, knowledge that transformed the consciousness, the senses, the very soul of the initiate, who was thereby ushered into a wholly different existence. As May Sinclair put it in describing her attraction to the dangers of the front lines, "it is as if something had been looking for you, waiting for you, from all eternity out here; something that you have been looking for; and, when you are getting nearer, it begins calling to you; it draws your heart out to it all day long. . . . It is something hidden and secret and supremely urgent. Its urgency, indeed, is so great that if you miss it you will have missed reality itself." She finds reality itself in a hospital ward, where "by the clear light and nakedness of the great hall," she sees "rows upon rows of bound and bandaged bodies." "It is utterly removed from and unlike anything that you have experienced before. . . . you are in another world, and under its strange impact you are given new senses and a new soul."[3]

Before acquiring this new knowledge, before, that is, they got to the front or to hospitals where they could witness the agonies of wounded men, women often expressed their perceptions of the war in terms that conveyed mystery, darkness, fantasy, myth, and abstraction. Vera Brittain's diary of the war up until the time she began work as a VAD contains phrases that speak to the obfuscation of reality she and others like her experienced. "One feels as if one were dreaming," she wrote on 4 August 1914, "or reading a chapter out of one of H. G. Wells' books like *The War of the Worlds*. . . . To sum up the situation in any way is impossible, every hour brings fresh & momentous events & one must stand still & await catastrophes each even more terrible than the last." In September, she referred to unknown events on the bat-tlefield causing "an air of mystery to shroud everything"; a month later, she complained that "the war seems enveloped in more of a fog than ever." "Grey mist again," wrote Margery Corbett Ashby, a member and future president of the NUWSS, to her husband Brian at the front in the spring of 1918, when she had gone too long without a letter from him. "What is hap-pening behind it." She described Britons at home as "moving as in an awful dream," and railed against her lack of information about the war, telling him of her "hunger . . . for news, even the poor unreliable news one gets in [the papers]. . . . I notice no casualties have been put in yet. How stupidly we are governed, as if it made things less true because they are not known." When Brittain's fiancé Roland left for the front, she found herself surrounded on every side by "darkness & pain." Roland, she believed, had entered the "Valley of the Shadow of Death," whose ghostlike inhabitants would "hover . . . behind the footsteps of him & [her brother] Edward" and darken her future for all time.[4] Claire Leighton, Roland's sister, referred to the war as "this hideous spectre," while Kate Courtney's diary reveals a lack of con-fidence in her own senses, attributing to fantasy or hallucination some of the sensations she felt. "The bombardment in Flanders is said to be heard in London, and one or two nights I almost felt it throbbing and booming, very muffled, and perhaps my fancy." In October 1915, Brittain confessed that "the war . . . is too gigantic for the mind to grasp," and that Roland, and the hospital to which she had been admitted as a VAD but had not yet worked in "seem both to be growing mythical." Roland had begun to seem less and less real to her, and she could not visualize his features as easily as she had been able to earlier. "He tends to become quite an abstraction," she wrote. Roland admitted the same sense of unreality surrounding his life at home, writing to her from the front asking, "Do I seem very much of a phantom in the void to you? I must. You seem to me rather like a character in a book or someone whom one has dreamt of and never seen."[5]

This sense of the unreality of one another's world—of the disconnection between home and front—caused great anguish to women at home. Mar-gery Corbett Ashby, for example, wrote to her husband that "I am so tor-

tured at all you and the others are enduring & apparently in vain and at the
. . . ghastly helplessness of us all." Feelings of torment, anxiety, suspense,
dread, apprehension, of "fearing the worst," or being afraid of being afraid
accompanied the mystery and remoteness, the shadowy and unknowable
nature of the war for people at home.[6]

Vera Brittain, a prominent "old" feminist during the interwar period, worried that the war "was dividing us as I had so long feared it would, making
real values seem unreal, and causing the qualities which mattered most to
appear unimportant. Was it, I wondered, because Roland had lost interest in
me that this anguish of drifting apart had begun—or was the explanation to
be found in that terrible barrier of knowledge by which War cut off the men
who possessed it from the women who, in spite of the love that they gave and
received, remained in ignorance?" The fear that the war had thrown up "a
barrier of indescribable experience between men and the women whom
they loved" haunted some women, "linking the dread of spiritual death to
the apprehension of physical disaster."[7]

One way to alleviate the anguish and anxiety brought about by experienc-
ing the war from a distance, and to bridge the chasm that was opening up
between those at home and those at the front, was to immerse oneself in the
war effort, to expose oneself to the dangers and horrors of the war that men
at the front were undergoing. Brittain explained that "it is the separation that
is so hard, so bitter. I should not fear the danger for him if I could share
it—much less for myself." She and others set out to find situations that
would enable them to share and even replicate men's experiences. Nursing,
as Lynn Knight has observed, "was one of the nearest approximations to
male experience of battle." Brittain justified her decision to take up nursing
to her parents by explaining that "not being a man and able to go to the front,
I wanted to do the next best thing." Her friend Cora attempted to dissuade
her by asking if she understood what kind of work she was in for. "Of course
I know," she wrote in her journal. "I shall hate it, but I will be all the more
ready to do it on that account. *He* has to face far worse things than any sight
or act I could come across; he can bear it—& so can I." Upon being assigned
to a hospital, she sought out the hardest and worst duties. "My one desire
being to emulate Roland's endurance," she declared, "I seized with avidity
upon all the unpleasant tasks . . . , and took a masochistic delight in empty-
ing bed-pans, washing greasy cups and spoons, and disposing of odoriferous
dressings in the sink-room." Thrush, one of the characters in Irene Rathbone's autobiographical *We That Were Young*, became a nurse because her
fiancé was a soldier. "I felt I had to try and live up to him," she said simply.
"I'm not doing this job out of any high-falutin' patriotic motives like you
people, but just for Ginger's sake—to be more worthy of him."[8]

Coming face to face with war and its victims defused the power of the
horrors imagined by those who were not part of the war effort. In many

cases, the anticipation and dread, the fantasizing about what it must be like, were far more difficult to handle than the situations themselves. Sinclair offers a vivid illustration: "I'll confess now that I dreaded Ostend more than anything. We had been told that there were horrors upon horrors in Ostend. Children were being born in the streets, and the state of the bathing-machines where the refugees lived was unspeakable." Driven to the edge of terror, she endured "those five weeks of frightful anticipation when I knew I must go out to the War; the going to bed, night after night, drugged with horror, black horror that creeps like poison through your nerves; the falling asleep and forgetting it; the waking, morning after morning, with an energetic and lucid brain that throws out a dozen war pictures to the minute like a ghastly cinema show, till horror becomes terror." For five weeks, she explained, "ever since I knew that I must certainly go out with this expedition, I had been living in black funk; in shameful and appalling terror. Every night before I went to sleep I saw an interminable spectacle of horrors: trunks without head, heads without trunks, limbs tangled in intestines, corpses by every roadside, murders, mutilations, my friends shot dead before my eyes. Nothing I shall ever see will be more ghastly than the things I have seen." Indeed, when the ambulance corps to which she belonged actually confronted the reality of Ostend under German attack, "this strange visualizing process ceases, and I see nothing and feel nothing." Again, while Sinclair waited to take her first wounded men from a hospital in Ghent, her dread was palpable, driven by her imagination of what she would encounter. "I confess to a slight, persistent fear of *seeing* these wounded whom I cannot help. It is not very active, it has left off visualizing the horror of bloody bandages and mangled bodies. But it's there; it waits for me in every corridor and at the turn of every stair, and it makes me loathe myself." When she actually comes across her first patient, she finds he is far less frightening than she had imagined. "I have seen one of them," she wrote. "The outline of the wounded body under the blanket, and the head laid back on the pillow. It is impossible, it is inconceivable, that I should have been afraid of seeing this. It is as if the wounded man himself absolved me from the memory and the reproach of fear." When Sinclair was left behind on an ambulance run, the theme of not knowing and being left to fantasize what might be happening recurred. "To stay behind with nothing in the world to do but to devise a variety of dreadful deaths" for her compatriots proved far less tolerable than facing the dangers herself.[9]

Brittain recorded in her journal in August 1915 an experience with a dying patient. "Had anyone told me a month ago that I should sit by a dying man, lift him when he choked and constantly turn him over, I should have been terrified at the idea. Now I do it—not with equanimity, for I cannot think with equanimity of anyone's dying—but with calm." Millicent, duchess of Sutherland, running an ambulance corps in Belgium during the first weeks of the war, confided to her diary in August 1914, "What I thought would be for me an impossible task became absolutely natural: to wash wounds, to drag off rags and clothing soaked in blood, to hold basins equally full of blood, to soothe a soldier's groans, . . . these actions seemed suddenly to become an insistent duty, perfectly easy to carry out."[10]

Clarity, calm, attention to detail, and articulation of the concrete began to enter into the women's language, replacing the mistiness and uncertainty of earlier days, and provided them with an understanding of war's meaning approaching that of the frontsoldiers. Winifred Holtby, a future "old" feminist, experienced at the age of sixteen the bombardment of Scarborough, where she was at school. Just as she and the other students sat down to eat breakfast on 16 December 1914, shells began to fall upon the town. In strong, graphic language that repeatedly contrasted fantasy with reality, Holtby described the experience.

> Crash! Thu-u-d! I sat up, my spoon in the air, all the nerves in my system suddenly strung taut, for the noise was like nothing I had heard before—deafening, clear-cut, not rumbly—as though a heavy piece of furniture had crashed in the room overhead. . . . I was about to speak, when Cr-r-ash—a sound more terrific than the first—and then all the windows danced in their frames; each report was doubled—first a roar, and then an ear-splitting crash as the shell exploded. Then someone whispered "guns." The word, like magic, passed from mouth to mouth as we sat white-faced but undismayed.

The girls were sent out into the countryside, running from shells that "burst quite near." Holtby looked back at the town, over which "hung a mantle of heavy smoke, yellow, unreal, which made the place look like a dream city, far, far away. Only the road was real, and the tight pain that caught us across our breast—it was not fear, but something inexplicable that hurt, and yet in some strange way was not wholly unpleasant." At first "it was all so like a bad dream," but as the shells continued to fall and the road filled up with "refugees," as Holtby put it, the immediacy of the situation—"the Dream that was Real"—could no longer be questioned. But this exposure to the war was short-lived and tended to recede in her memory until it produced an underlying tension and anxiety. Two years later, as she changed the dressings of her beloved friend Bill, as he lay convalescing from wounds at her family's home, the concrete, starkly vivid evidence of the war he provided enabled her to experience "an ecstasy of relief from the half-adult anxiety and suspense which had lain, a dull intermittent ache, beneath the excitement of the Scarborough raid."[11]

Lady Rhondda, future founder of the feminist journal *Time and Tide*, also underwent an exposure to the war that transformed her language from one redolent of darkness and shadow to an idiom of detailed clarity. In 1915, she accompanied her father on a trip to the United States, arriving in "sunlit

April New York, carefree and happy, after being under the heavy cloud of war at home." For the return trip, they boarded the *Lusitania*, the ill-fated vessel torpedoed by a German U-boat. Acutely aware of her surroundings as the ship began to list, she swallowed her fear and ran belowdecks to secure lifebelts for her father and herself. She watched as terror-stricken passengers fought one another for space in the lifeboats, and as a lifeboat tipped and deposited its cargo into the sea. Just then the *Lusitania* righted itself for a moment, and then listed badly again. Water poured over the deck, "the ship sank and I was sucked right down with her," Rhondda recalled. "The next thing I can remember was being deep down under the water. It was very dark, nearly black. I fought to come up. I was terrified of being caught on some part of the ship and kept down. That was the worst moment of terror, the only moment of acute terror, that I knew. . . . At first I swallowed a lot of water; then I remembered that I had read that one should not swallow water, so I shut my mouth." Although she claimed that "everything that happened after I had been submerged was a little misty and vague; I was slightly stupefied from then on," Rhondda's account of the incidents that followed are stunning in their detail. "When I came to the surface," she continued, "I found that I formed part of a large, round, floating island composed of people and debris of all sorts." She grabbed onto a piece of wood floating past.

> A man with a white face and a yellow moustache came and held on to the other end of my board. I did not quite like it, for I felt it was not large enough for two, but I did not feel justified in objecting. Every now and then he would try and move round towards my end of the board. This frightened me. . . . I summoned up my strength—to speak was an effort—and told him to go back to his own end, so that we might keep the board properly balanced. He said nothing and just went meekly back. After a while I noticed that he had disappeared.

She tried to call after some of the lifeboats, but to no avail. She tried to swim by moving her bitterly cold legs, but stopped "because I did not see how I could get along without letting go of my piece of board, which nothing would have induced me to abandon." She did not feel "the sharp agony of fear"; "one was acutely uncomfortable, no more than that. A discomfort mainly due to the intense cold, but further . . . to the fact that . . . when presently a little swell got up, I was seasick. . . . There should be, I thought, a little bottle of chloroform strapped into each [life]belt, so that one could inhale it and lose consciousness when one wished to." Eventually, Rhondda lost consciousness and was picked up by the crew of the *Bluebell*, who, believing her dead, left her on deck, naked, between blankets. When she came to, bruised from head to toe, she was removed to the captain's bunk and ultimately put ashore in Dublin, where she spent three weeks in bed recuperating from bronchial pneumonia. Rhondda's narrative of war—clear, crisp, sharp, and detailed—resembled that of frontsoldiers as they wrote of their participation in battle.[12]

When Brittain's fiancé was killed in France at the end of 1915, she went down to his parents' house, arriving just as Roland's belongings were delivered by the War Department.

> All R.'s things had just been sent back from the front and they were all lying on the floor. I had no idea before of the aftermath of an officer's death, or what the returned kit, about which so many letters have been written in the papers, really meant. It was terrible. . . . There were his clothes—the clothes in which he came home from the front last time—another set rather less worn, and underclothing & accessories of various descriptions. Everything was damp & worn & simply caked with mud. All the sepulchres and catacombs of Rome could not make me realise mortality & decay & corruption as vividly as did the smell of those clothes. I know now what he meant when he used to write "this refuse-heap of a country" or "a trench that is nothing but a charnel-house."

Roland's sister invoked that cold January morning with a slightly different memory. "I am in the garden of our cottage in Sussex," she wrote. "My father is with me. I carry two heavy kettles. They are filled with boiling water, for we are about to bury the tunic—blood-stained and bullet-ridden—in which Roland has been killed. . . . Father watches the windows of the house, for my mother must not see this tunic that Father has hidden from the packages of Roland's effects returned from France. I am to thaw the frozen earth so that it may be buried out of sight." The existence of concrete objects and the palpable smell of the clothing enabled Brittain and Roland's family to realize, "as we have realised since his clothes came back, the meaning of War." The detailed descriptions, the stark clarity of Brittain and Leighton as they wrote of this experience, offer a marked contrast with Brittain's previous writings and mirror the sharpness found in the writing of men at the front. Information, knowledge, certainty provided an antidote to the imaginings that could produce debilitating anxiety and anguish. Brittain testified to the power of detailed information in a February 1916 journal entry. "I had another letter from Mrs. Leighton continuing what Captain Adam told her about Roland's twenty minutes of agony. And Mr. Leighton has drawn up a plan for me, which she has enclosed, showing accurately exactly how Roland was hit, and what followed, & the lie of the land in general—drawn up from Captain Adam's statement. It is very valuable for me—and gives things very accurately."[13]

Women at the front often contrasted their newly active and assertive behavior with the passivity, distance, indirectness, and a sense of slow motion that verged upon paralysis that they had experienced at home. Sinclair described the changes in "Ursula Dearmer"—a young member of her corps—after her exposure to danger at the front. In London, coming before the committee to plead her case for admission to the ambulance corps, "she appeared as a very young girl, docile, diffident, only half-awake." In Belgium after a few weeks, Sinclair recounts, "here she is, wide awake and in full command of the Ostend-Dunkirk expedition." Lady Rhondda reported that the *Lusitania* experience helped "to alter my opinion of myself. I had lacked self-confidence. I knew that I was frightened of many things. If anyone had asked me whether I should behave as I ought in a shipwreck I should have had the gravest doubts. And here I had got through this test without disgracing myself. I had found that when the moment came I could control my fear."[14]

Sharing the experiences of men at the front meant subjecting oneself to harrowing smells, sounds, and sights, which women recorded in extraordinary detail. A WAAC told of "that horrible smell—the battlefield smell" made up of "putrescent water, stale poison gas, and the effluvia of dead bodies" that pervaded the front lines. "It was revolting, sickening. It got into one's inside, so that one remained conscious of it even in one's sleep. It penetrated everything—clothing, blankets; one's very body reeked of it. Nor could one grow accustomed to it as one could to other things." Elsie Bowerman, the WSPU member who had exulted at her good fortune in having been chosen to go out to Serbia with the Scottish Women's Hospitals, confided to her journal the activities of 1 January 1917. "147 wounded arrived," she wrote,

> hospital only equipped for 100—nightmare of a day—one ward just straw— men laid on without taking clothes off. Terrible sights and sounds—lots of very bad cases—gangrene—smell at times almost unbearable—a strange sickly odour quite unlike anything else, which seems to permeate everything and stick in one's nostrils, even when one is out in the fresh air. Operations continuously all day and night till 5 a.m.—nurses up nearly all night.[15]

Dr. Elsie Inglis, director of the NUWSS Scottish Women's Hospitals, listening to the hungry soldiers who could not be fed, "coughing and moaning all night," reported that she and her colleagues "hid our heads under the blanket to shut out the sound." Vera Brittain fainted one night in the ward at the 1st London General Hospital. "Probably the grim, suppurating wounds of the men in the huge ward were partly responsible, although, as I was to learn later in France, they were by no means the worst wounds that a man would receive without immediately qualifying for the mercy of death." In March 1916, hardened by her exposure to ghastly wounds, she noted in her journal two cases so bad that "they make even me almost sick— that of the man with the hand blown off & the stump untrimmed up, & the other man with the arm off, & a great hole in his back one could get one's hand into, & other wounds on his leg & sides & head." Shortly afterward, she transferred to France and helped to nurse the casualties of the Somme battles, and "to dress as best I could the worst wounds that I had ever seen or imagined." In a six-week period that she described as "a regular baptism of blood and pus," she cared for "men without faces, without eyes, without limbs, men almost disembowelled, men with hideous truncated stumps of bodies," in wards that "sweltered beneath their roofs of corrugated iron; the prevailing odour of wounds and stinking streets lingered perpetually in our nostrils, the red-hot hardness of paths and pavements burnt its way through the soles of our shoes." During the spring offensive of 1918, under enormous pressure from the German advance, Brittain found herself alone in a ward transformed into "a newly created circle of hell," dazed by "the dishevelled beds, the stretchers on the floor, the scattered boots and piles of muddy khaki, the brown blankets turned back from smashed limbs bound to splints by filthy blood-stained bandages. Beneath each stinking wad of sodden wool and gauze an obscene horror waited for me—and all the equipment that I had for attacking it . . . was one pair of forceps."[16]

Joan, Irene Rathbone's chief protagonist and the figure drawn from Rathbone's own experiences, "had never seen anything like the wounds" she attended as a VAD in France. "Limbs which shrapnel had torn about and swollen into abnormal shapes, from which yellow pus poured when the bandages were removed, which were caked with brown blood, and in whose gangrenous flesh loose bits of bone had to be sought for painfully with probes." During the first week of her nursing experience, Joan dreamed nightly of the gruesome sights and smells she encountered during the day, finding in her nightmares an outlet for the disgust and horror she had to repress in order to be effective; but soon "she had adjusted herself inwardly and outwardly to the conditions in which her life must now be lived—conditions which, if they could not be accepted as normal, would mean her defeat."[17]

"Normal" life for nurses and VADs like Rathbone and Brittain entailed changing the dressings of patients like McIvor, "the jaw-case, who, when his innumerable and complicated bandages were removed, revealed flat holes plugged with gauze where a nose had been, and pendulous shapeless lips. The stench which rushed forth as the last dressing dropped off was just humanly endurable, and only just. It had an acrid, putrefying quality, unlike that from other wounds." Or attending to O'Leary, who had been "badly burnt by liquid fire. . . . His whole body was a mass of burns; and piece by piece the lint had to be peeled off him while he whimpered like a rabbit, and slow tears ran down his cheeks. . . . the smell here was of yet another order—the stomach-heaving smell of charred flesh." A nurse who volunteered for duty in Belgium upon the war's outbreak described the casualties of an explosion in Antwerp. "The injuries were confined to their faces, heads, and hands," she wrote, "and they were often ghastly. Some were so terribly burned that it was difficult to tell where their faces were; . . . no features seemed left to them. We had sometimes to force an opening where the mouth had been to insert a tube to feed them." In April 1915, during the second battle of Ypres, this nurse and eight others, along with three surgeons, worked day and night for two weeks without stopping as a torrent of wounded poured into the field hospital. "Our hospital soon became a shambles, the [operating] theatre a slaughter house," she recalled. Victims of gas attacks lay about, "fully sensible, choking, suffocating, dying in horrible agonies" as the nurses tried in vain to alleviate their suffering. "As to the theatre, one case was lifted off, a wet cloth mopped the blood onto the floor and another was lifted on. . . . Huge abdominals, one after the other, trephining cases, amputations, ligaturing blood vessels in important places." A FANY in France described an incident with a badly wounded man whom she was trying to hold down as he struggled violently. "He shouted and writhed," she reported, "and at last his head fell back: then, with a mighty effort, he raised himself and opened his mouth to speak; but only a stream of blood rushed forth, and a brave soul had gone to its God!" During the battle for Passchendaele, recalled an anonymous WAAC assigned to a dressing station, "troops came pouring up . . . and as rapidly as they went up they would be brought back—what was left of them—mangled masses of blood, bits of men, limbs missing, groaning bodies with intestines visible, sometimes khaki shapes that screamed like maniacs when the stretchers were lifted out."[18]

Mary Dexter, driving for Dr. Hector Munro's ambulance corps during the spring offensive of 1918 after nursing stints in England and Belgium, described two "bad cases" she had, "one a man with an amputated arm, who screamed at every movement of the car, though I crawled—most nerve-racking, as the road was very bad. And a dying man—the doctors told me he had a bullet in his head, and couldn't live more than a few hours anyhow, and they put him in my car because she has the smoothest springs. It is a dreadful feeling, that a man may be dying in your car at any minute." Evadne Price, writing under the pseudonym Helen Zenna Smith and drawing upon the wartime diaries of Winifred Young, an ambulance driver, reported in excruciating detail the experiences of transporting the wounded from the front to the casualty clearing stations. On her first night out, Smith's protagonist was undone by the "ghastly glimpse of blood and shattered men," "men torn and bleeding and raving." She trained herself not to faint or to vomit at the sight and smell of wounds, which she encountered regularly, and with whose horrible aftermath she had to deal each morning as she cleaned her ambulance after the previous night's runs. "The stench that comes out as we open the doors each morning nearly knocks us down. Pools of stale vomit from the poor wretches we have carried the night before, corners the sitters have turned into temporary lavatories for all purposes, blood and mud and vermin and the stale stench of stinking trench feet and gangrenous wounds."[19]

As Lynn Knight has observed, for women who attended the wounded, "the horrific became commonplace, ... personal testimonies of loss that would seem implausible in fiction, formed the basis of the everyday." Mary Borden's conversation with an orderly about a patient conveys precisely just how matter-of-fact the most gruesome cases might become. "There was a man stretched on the table," she recalled blandly.

> His brain came off in my hands when I lifted the bandage from his head.
> When the dresser came back I said: "His brain came off on the bandage."
> "Where have you put it?"
> "I put it in the pail under the table."
> "It's only half of his brain," he said, looking into the man's skull. "The rest is here."
> I left him to finish the dressing and went about my own business. I had much to do.[20]

So everyday did these horrors become that ordinary habits of eating and drinking went on side by side with them. Brittain recalled, with wonder, that "we were able to drink tea and eat cake in the theatre ... in that foetid stench, ... the saturated dressings and yet more gruesome human remnants heaped on the floor." Borden and her fellow workers drank cocoa in the sterilizing room next to the operating room. "We push back the drums of clean dressings and the litter of soiled bandages, and drink our cocoa standing round the table. Sometimes there isn't much room. Sometimes legs and arms wrapped in cloths have to be pushed out of the way. We throw them on the floor—they belong to no one and are of no interest to anyone—and drink our cocoa. The cocoa tastes very good. It is part of the routine." Such casual living amid blood and guts and amputated limbs speaks volumes about the degree to which nurses, physicians, VADs, orderlies, and ambulance drivers were required to harden themselves if they were to continue their work. The anonymous WAAC recounted that "somehow during the war death did not seem to count. One's sensibilities seemed to be blunted—atrophied. One danced with a man to-night, and a few nights later he would be brought in on a stretcher. Next day he would be dead. Yet one didn't grieve. Perhaps one had not time to grieve. Or one didn't think. The only way to ensure peace of mind during the war was never to think." As Brittain put it, women at the front "quickly developed a defence-mechanism of callousness from perpetual contact with horror."[21]

But, having become accustomed to wartime conditions, frontsoldiers and nurses were startled when intimations of a world beyond the war intruded. Mary Borden recalled how disconcerted she was by the smell of newly mown hay or the whispering of the wind through the grass as she worked in a French field hospital. The smell of the mud on her feet and the blood on her apron, the sound of a dying man whimpering, the pounding of three-inch guns—these, to her, were "natural. It is the whispering of the grass and the scent of new-mown hay that makes me nervous." Mary Dexter, writing from Cugny in December 1917, noted that the sound of the guns had become no more than background noise. "It's strange how I don't mind them here as I do in London—I suppose it's because they 'belong' here." When things did not belong, as when civilians were wounded, the horrors against which individuals had steeled themselves could resurface with great intensity. Dexter confessed to her journal in March 1918 that

> I was dreadfully upset a day or two ago, over two injured civilians. They arrived on a train, and were carried out and put in one of our cars—the man's chest blown to pieces—dying—and the woman legless, hit by an obus, also dying from shock and lack of care. Twenty minutes later I saw the car return. . . . To my horror I found that these two wretched people were still in the car—they had been refused at the hospital, because of being civilians. . . . They were taken in, but it was just about too late—their faces haunted me all that day.

May Sinclair's character Nicholas, in *The Tree of Heaven*, wrote to his brother Michael of his difficulty accepting the death of a small dog run down in the street by a motorcyclist. With sights like bad stretcher cases, he told Michael, "you don't funk at all; you're not shocked, you're not a bit surprised. It's all in the picture, and you're in the picture too. There's a sort of horrible harmony. It's like a certain kind of beastly dream which doesn't frighten you because you're part of it, part of the beastliness." But the dog, hit by a civilian, "made me sick. You see, the little dog wasn't in the picture. I hadn't bargained for him."[22]

Women's sharing the horrors and experiences of men tended to efface the differences demarcating the sexes so vividly at home. For some eighteen months after she went down with the *Lusitania* Lady Rhondda awoke every night at two-thirty in "a sweat of terror." She also experienced during that time what she called "an unreasoning terror of air-raids." As a consequence, she understood and empathized with men at the front. "These things gave me some measure of what a man whose nerves had gone must feel. If four hours' danger and exposure could do all that to me, what must one feel like after months in the trenches? I still cannot understand how any of our soldiers remained sane," she declared.[23]

Women in hospitals and at the front frequently commented upon the identification they felt with the fighting men, evincing a solidarity or comradeship with them that overrode all distinctions of gender. Upon taking up nursing, Brittain constructed herself as in the same camp with fighting men, and as distinct from noncombatants. Her 12 May 1915 diary entry records her thoughts as she justified leaving Oxford to enter hospital training: "I ought not to put the speedy starting of my career forward as an excuse, any more than a man should against enlisting," she wrote. In August 1915, as she saw her brother Edward off at the station to join the war effort, she re-counted the incident in terms that paired herself with her brother, as against her parents, and equated her work with his, "Edward & I, soldier & nurse, & Mother & Daddy." After Roland's death, Brittain put in for foreign service, cognizant of the risks and dangers involved, but all the more deter-mined to go as a consequence. "If I had refused to put down my name I should despise myself as much as I would a regiment that wouldn't volun-teer for foreign service," she explained. Once abroad, she shared with sol-diers the sense of estrangement from the home front, "the uncomprehend-ing remoteness of England from the tragic, profound freemasonry of those who accepted death together overseas," and spoke of those at home as "the uninitiated."[24]

Mary Dexter, describing her uniform to her mother, noted with satisfac-tion the resemblance she and her fellow ambulance drivers had to army officers.

> The uniform is very smart—khaki, of course. Coat like British officers' tunics, with big square pockets and a leather belt—but no leather shoulder strap. Short skirt, coming below the knees, breeches underneath, and big high trench boots, with thick soles. . . . Then I have got a big trench coat (like what the officers wear). . . . My latest acquisition is a silver identity disc with my name, Hackett-Lowther Unit, and my passport number on it. We wear them on our wrists, the same as the soldiers.

She recounted that a poilu had mistaken one of the drivers for a soldier during an air raid. "In her greatcoat and cap and boots he had thought she was a man." In May of 1918, the Hackett-Lowther Unit moved to the front lines, a circumstance that Dexter explained in such a way as to deny gender entirely. "There are three degrees of front work," she wrote, "and we were afraid that being women, we should only get the third kind (which is from here back)—instead of which we are to have the first two degrees. . . . We have numerous new rules to adapt ourselves to. One . . . is that we *must* salute all officers of the army. . . . We are not allowed to go on duty . . . without our tins hats. We are to have gas-mask drill until we can put them on in I forget how few seconds." One war nurse at the front, invited to "have a shot at the Boches" by the major in charge, actually pulled the line that fired a French gun, a .75, at the Germans. "I have often wondered where that shell landed and with what result," she stated.[25]

When Joan, Irene Rathbone's autobiographical protagonist, encountered her prewar beau, Colin, at a base camp in France where she helped out in a canteen, he was taken aback by her appearance. He "saw her differently" now, "not as an adored . . . girl in . . . home surroundings, but as a compan-ion-worker, a sort of 'ancilla domini' among those crowds of soldiers." Cicely Hamilton, a suffragist who would join the ranks of "old" feminists after the

war, in describing hospital routine, conjured up a scene like that of the
trenches, where long periods of quiet and boredom were punctuated by
intense activity. "There would be 'rushes,'" she wrote, "when the ambu-
lances went again and again to the station at Creil, where the trains from the
front discharged their wounded, when every ward was full, and doctors and
nurses were never out of the operating-theatre, and you wondered how they
kept going. And there would be other times—long stretches—when beds
were vacant and operations few, and the staff in general had plenty of lei-
sure." Working as a VAD during the Somme offensive, Rathbone's Joan
elaborated on this theme of identity with the soldiers, noting that nursing
"sisters without their tea were as troops without their rum—they couldn't
function."[26]

VADs, nurses, and WAACs also shared the inconveniences, risks, and
dangers of the fighting men. Helen Zenna Smith's ambulance drivers found
themselves, like their compatriots in the trenches, covered with lice from
their sleeping bags, "our bodies a mass of tiny red bites with the tops
scratched off. We are too hard worked to spare the necessary time to keep
clean," complained the narrator. "It is four weeks since we had a bath all
over, nine days since we had a big wash—we haven't had time." During the
spring offensive of 1918, WAACs, VADs, and nurses faced immediate
threats of death as the Germans moved ever closer to and overran allied
positions. Air raids on Abbeville, where Hamilton was based, necessitated
that she and her co-workers flee their bombed-out hostel and camp in the
hills at night. Brittain recalled the panic and terror she and her colleagues
felt as they tried to handle their duties to the wounded amid air raids and
bombardment from German guns. "For nearly a month," she wrote, "the
camp resembled a Gustave Doré illustration of Dante's *Inferno*. Sisters
flying from the captured Casualty Clearing Stations crowded into our quarters; often completely without belongings, they took possession of our
rooms, our beds, and all our spare uniform [*sic*]. By day a thudding cre-
scendo in the distance, by night sharp flashes in the sky, told us that the War
was already close upon their heels." Days of this kind of strain took their toll,

> and I don't suppose I was the only member of the staff whose teeth chattered
> with sheer terror as we groped our way to our individual huts in response to the
> order to scatter. . . . One young sister, who had previously been shelled at a
> Casualty Clearing Station, lost her nerve and rushed screaming through the
> Mess; two others seized her and forcibly put her to bed, holding her down while
> the raid lasted to prevent her from causing a panic. I knew that I was more
> frightened than I had ever been in my life.[27]

Rathbone's Joan became seriously ill with septic poisoning in the hospital
and mused about dying, discovering that she did not very much mind the
thought of death. "Half of the youth of the world was dead already; she

would be in good company. She thought of the patient soldiers in the war. . . . In a way too she was a soldier. Not much in dying these days. . . . Quite a good thing really to pop off—equal up the sexes a bit." Pamela, another character, who worked in a munitions factory, observed a co-worker as she caught her finger in one of the machines that cut bolts to size and then drilled screw threads into them. "Her finger was slowly wrenched out of its socket, dragging the muscles of the arm behind it. . . . Elsie stood staring at her bleeding stump, the white muscles hanging from it like strings."[28]

Sometimes the blurring of sexual difference became so intense as to elim-inate even the physical markings that distinguished men's and women's bodies, as when Mary Borden described her nursing tour in a base hospital in France. "There are no men here," she wrote of the mangled and broken bodies she attended, "so why should I be a woman?"

> How crowded together we are here. How close we are in this nightmare. The wounded are packed into this place like sardines, and we are so close to them, my old ones [orderlies] and I. I've never been so close before to human beings. We are locked together, the old ones and I, and the wounded men; we are bound together. We all feel it. We all know it. The same thing is throbbing in us, the single thing, the one life. We are one body, suffering and bleeding. It is a kind of bliss to me to feel this.

After the war, Vera Brittain suffered from delusions that her face was chang-ing; when she looked into a mirror, she believed she was "developing a beard."[29]

Women who encountered men at the front, whether they were wounded or not, experienced them in ways and formulated ideas about masculinity that differed markedly from those of the culture at home. In contrast to the image of bloodthirsty soldiers who "grin and kill and grin" (see chapter 2), nurses and VADs described men in terms usually reserved for women and/or children, or in ways that denied them destructive power. An anony-mous WAAC noted that while "people talk about the kindness of women, talk of their sympathy, 'ministering angels,' and the rest of it," the medical officers and orderlies she encountered "were the kindest, noblest, most self-sacrificing beings I had ever met in all my life." She also witnessed, in what she described as "one of the most distressing sights that I beheld during the war," a wounded man in her ambulance who "began crying for his mother— 'Oh, mummy, mummy, come to me—mummy, I want you so . . .' His voice was suddenly like a child's," she wrote.[30] A FANY boasted that under her care "the patients grew fat and rosy-cheeked," and recalled that wounded men would "burst into tears, refuse their food, beg to be allowed to stay," when evacuation orders came for them. Joan, in *We That Were Young*, min-istered to a group of patients "whom she regarded as her special children." In vivid sketches evoking a mother-child relationship, she spoke of men "unable to cut up their own food" who "had to be spoon-fed," the patient to whom she brought a bedpan, "settled him comfortably upon it, wiped him—if he were unable to manage himself—with cotton wool." A man returning from surgery would sometimes "cry like a child from sheer weakness and wretchedness, and she would stay soothing him till he had regained a grip of himself and a sense of his surroundings." With each other, patients were "almost as tender as the nurses." Joan watched a wounded man "become like a frightened child calling for its mother in the dark," and saw men crying as they marched back to the front after a short leave at base camp. Brittain regarded the wounded patients she encountered at Somerville, before she went down to become a VAD, as "pathetic," while the nurses Enid Bagnold worked under referred to them as "boys." Still other women looked upon men as harmless or helpless animals. Helen Zenna Smith described the trainloads of wounded who poured into the base hospital as "a herd of sense-less cattle, . . . a flock of senseless sheep." Mary Borden said of her patients, "Certainly they were men once. But now they are no longer men. . . . Once they were real, splendid, ordinary, normal men. Now they mew like kittens. Once they were fathers and husbands and sons and the lovers of women. Now they scarcely remember."[31]

Often the wounded were referred to not as human beings but as broken objects or body parts. Cicely Hamilton reported that during her stint in France she "grew quite accustomed to hearing human beings spoken of as if they were diseased or damaged portions of their bodies—as fractures or strangulated hernias." Helen Zenna Smith's ambulance driver referred to "these mangled things I drive night after night." Looking back from 1933, Brittain wondered at her ability to "dress unaided and without emotion, the quivering stump of a newly amputated limb." The soldier to whom the stump was attached received no mention. The FANY identified her patients not by name but by their wounds: "a man shot to pieces on one stretcher; a shattered thigh on the stretcher underneath; a broken arm and a shrapnel in the head opposite." Borden did the same, observing of her ward that "there are no men here. . . . There are heads and knees and mangled testicles. There are chests with holes as big as your fist, and pulpy thighs, shapeless; and stumps where legs once were fastened. . . . There are these things, but no men."[32] Of course, this phenomenon of detaching the individual human being from the horrible wounds from which he suffered was a function of the women's need to survive and remain effective, but it also served to separate men from the destructive forces that had occasioned their wounds. Women at the front, unlike women at home, did not equate masculinity with brutal-ity, aggression, and destruction. Rather, they perceived men as very much like children, or, indeed, like themselves.

Because the language used to express the experience of war at the front differed from that utilized to understand the war from the home front, the sexual imagery necessarily differed as well. Neither frightening nor titillating, sex, in the stories offered by the women at the front, provided pleasure, companionship, comfort, and love. Often, women's accounts of their first encounters with the war expressed a sense of exultation, exhilaration, of "the fiercest living," or life "lived so intensely," that carried undertones of sexual initiation. "There is something about the sound of the first near gun of your first battle," wrote Sinclair in her journal, "that, so far from being hateful or dreadful, or in any way abhorrent to you, will make you smile in spite of yourself with a kind of quiet exultation." The anonymous WAAC told of how, when she first heard the rumbling of guns at Amiens, "the sound stirred something in my blood. I detested this war, had detested it from the first, yet when one came within sound of it . . . [ellipsis in source] I can't analyse what it was that . . . made me want to get closer still to the scene of activities. Other nurses told me that the sound of guns affected them like that too. . . . One seemed to become possessed by some sort of restrained excitement; obsessed by what may have been a kind of morbid curiosity."[33]

The language of May Sinclair's journal entries depicts her war experience in unmistakably sexual terms. She found herself irritated with the young Ursula Dearmer and had to ask herself, "Can it be that I was jealous of . . . that innocent girl, because she saw a shell burst and I didn't? I know this is what was the matter with Mrs. Torrence the other day. She even seemed to imply that there was some feminine perfidy in Ursula Dearmer's power of drawing shells to her. (She, poor dear, can't attract even a bullet within a mile of her.)" Later, Sinclair helped to bring a wounded man out of a village, confessing, as if he were her first lover, that "to me he was the most beautiful thing I have ever seen. And I loved him. I do not think it is possible to love, to adore any creature more than I loved and adored that clumsy, ugly Flamand. He was my first wounded man." In *The Romantic*, written in 1920 and incorporating scenes drawn directly from her journal, Sinclair went a step further in representing the war as a kind of sexual initiation, only this time in reverse. The book tells the story of a failure of manhood on the part of John, the romantic, a failure caused by both his cowardice under fire and his careful avoidance of a sexual relationship with Charlotte, with whom he came out to Belgium.[34] The two phenomena—sex and war—are inextricably linked in Sinclair's novel.

Often, women narrated their war experiences as a sexual coming of age, as tales depicting an unfolding of sexual knowledge that led, if not to actual sexual experience, then to positive, relaxed attitudes about or openness toward sexuality. The stories all begin with an expression of more or less conventional Victorian attitudes toward and/or ignorance about sex. Vera Brittain's diary entries before the war's outbreak, for instance, reveal a sense of shame and even disgust about sex, what little she understood of it. When, in March 1913, on their way to play golf, she asked her mother "to disclose a few points on sexual matters which I thought I ought to know," she found the information so "distasteful" and "depressing" that it put her off her game. She did not understand what homosexuality, incest, or sodomy were; and although she had gained "a fairly comprehensive though somewhat Victorian idea of the primitive fashion in which the offspring of even the most civilized parents make their appearance" by reading such works as *David Copperfield, Adam Bede*, and a book entitled *Household Medicine*, she remained "still extremely hazy with regard to the precise nature of the sexual act." "This half-knowledge," she explained, "engendered in me so fierce an antipathy to the idea of physical relationship in so far as this happened to be separable from romance, that when, soon after I left school, I was proposed to by a neighbour of ours, . . . my immediate and only reaction was a sense of intolerable humiliation and disgust." Joan, in *We That Were Young*, was also presented as a conventional middle-class Edwardian girl— earnest, innocent, and entirely ignorant about "that mysterious consummation of love . . . which she had . . . on the whole kept resolutely from her thoughts."[35]

This formulation of female ignorance and prudery depended upon a representation of male sexuality that was its diametric opposite, whose expression we see clearly in the WAAC's account of her wartime experience. Before she set out to work in a hospital, her father, a parson, warned her about men's rapacious behavior. "War changes some men's natures completely," he told her, "makes some of us beasts, at any rate for a time. You have seen little of the world, and nothing of a war world. You most likely think that all gentlemen . . . are underneath what they appear on the surface to be. They most likely are—in peacetime. Yet in a war atmosphere they change—nearly all of them change. Even Henry [his son] I wouldn't trust."[36]

Through contact with men's bodies in the course of their nursing duties the authors became accustomed to and then appreciative of male physicality. Until Brittain began nursing in June 1915, she had "never looked upon the nude body of an adult male." At first she feared she would be overcome with nervousness and embarrassment at the sight of a naked man but found she was not.

> From the constant handling of their lean, muscular bodies, I came to understand the essential cleanliness, the innate nobility, of sexual love on its physical side. Although there was much to shock in Army hospital service, much to terrify, much, even, to disgust, this day-by-day contact with male anatomy was never part of the shame. Since it was always Roland whom I was nursing by proxy, my attitude towards him imperceptibly changed; it became less romantic and more realistic, and thus a new depth was added to my love.[37]

The failure of Sinclair's romantic, John, lay precisely in his inability to get beyond the romanticizing of love—and war—to actually engage with them.

Rathbone was also quite aware of the initiation into sexual knowledge she received from the soldiers under her care, describing the eroticism Joan experienced when she bathed her patients.

> It gave her a peculiar soothing joy to take hold of a long white arm, to soap it, sponge it, and dry it; to wash a muscular young back, listening meanwhile to its owner talking desultorily about his sweetheart, his kids, or his "mates" in the regiment. She was a nurse in uniform, and he was a wounded soldier; the gulf between them was fixed and rigid. And yet across that gulf, unrecognised and certainly unheeded by either, stretched the faint sweet fingers of sex.

Brittain shared that experience of sexual introduction and appreciated it. "Short of actually going to bed with them," she wrote of the wounded she nursed, "there was hardly an intimate service that I did not perform for one or another in the course of four years, and I still have reason to be thankful for the knowledge of masculine functioning which the care of them gave me, and for my early release from the sex-inhibitions that even to-day [in 1933] . . . beset many of my female contemporaries, both married and single."[38]

Nursing Roland by proxy was all Brittain got to do. He was killed before the vicariously sexual pleasures she had through her patients could be acted out with him, though on his last leave home in August 1915 she did experience from his kisses an "agonising joy," "a thrill & a joy," a passion so deep and strong that she feared its power. Rathbone's protagonist Joan did not enter into a sexual relationship with her fiancé Colin, either, before he was killed. Joan, like Brittain, told her tale of sexual initiation through others; both gained a tolerance and broad-mindedness about sexuality through others. In Joan's case, her friend Thrush confided in her about her affair with Ginger, with whom she spent the night before he went out to France. "This information . . . just dropped dryly out, as though of no particular importance and required no comment," but it produced in Joan "a mixture of interest and awe." "A little shaken, a little ashamed" because of what she described as "her own niggardliness in love" with Colin, "subdued and yet exalted, Joan carried on for the rest of the day with the sense of having been let more deeply into life—of having almost herself experienced some new and lovely thing."[39]

The WAAC made the connection between nursing duties and sexual knowledge abundantly clear through a conversation with another nursing sister. "Have you many wounded?" she inquired. "Let me see—about twenty to-day," the sister replied. "Two died yesterday and one this morning. You'll see them all presently." Then, without a break, the sister continued. "Tell me, dear, have you ever had a man?" While the WAAC was shocked by this question, she would soon react to such suggestions with aplomb. When she sought a transfer from her unit, the medical officer urged her not to go, telling her of a "good-looking boy," shot, significantly, in the groin, who was in love with her and who would not recover if she left. The WAAC recalled having changed his bandages: "I had felt him tremble while I dressed his wound, but supposed his trembling to be due to pain." One day, the patient asked her to kiss him; she complied, kissing "him several times—on the lips. I felt his whole body thrill."[40]

Mary Borden utilized the sex/war theme in a somewhat different way, affiliating sex and pain. Pain, "a lascivious monster," is portrayed in imagery usually associated with prostitution. She is "insatiable, greedy, vilely amorous, lustful, obscene—she lusts for the broken bodies we have here. Wherever I go I find her possessing the men in their beds, lying in bed with them."

> She is a harlot in the pay of War, and she amuses herself with the wreckage of men. She consorts with decay, is addicted to blood, cohabits with mutilations, and her delight is the refuse of suffering bodies. . . . You can watch her plying her trade here any day. She is shameless. She lies with the Heads and the Knees and the festering Abdomens. She never leaves them. . . . At any hour of the day or night you can watch her deadly amours, and watch her victims struggling.

This is also the kind of imagery utilized to portray the camp women enflamed by khaki fever at home, those furies preying upon the men in uniform, whose licentious behavior is crippling the war effort and men's abilities to fulfill their masculine destiny. But for Borden the war itself is the whore, feeding on the once healthy bodies of men, rendering them grotesque and unnatural, and unfit for the "tender and lovely love for women" that "clean, normal, real men" seek. Having lost one of those "clean, normal, real men" to the effects of amputation—"she looked around her as if to find the man he had once been"—Borden turned to hospital work.[41]

While the imagery of threatened castration is unmistakable in these stories, it differs from that depicted by Lawrence, Eliot, or Hemingway in being mitigated, not caused, by women. Nurses and VADs, engaged in the battle that "now is going on over the helpless bodies of these men," "we who are doing the fighting now, with their real enemies," are arrayed on the side of mutual, tender, loving, participatory sexual activity against a sexuality that is aggressive, predatory, diseased, and pecuniary. They do not usually win this fight, but even Borden's story of her experience is nonetheless articulated in the same positive sexual terms as Brittain's, Rathbone's, and the WAAC's. The WAAC justified her kissing of the wounded man whom she did not love by equating sex with life giving. "From that day onward he was quite a different person," she explained. "He told me that now he had something to live for."[42]

Sinclair illustrated a similar contrasting of the negative, predatory, destructive sex madness obsessing the home front with the positive, healing, life-giving sexuality experienced at the front in *The Tree of Heaven*. Her hero, Nicholas, denounced the belief that "this gorgeous fight-feeling" he experienced at the front "is nothing but a form of sex-madness," calling such an idea "rotten" and misconceived. The ecstasy he felt in battle, and which his brother Michael also experienced when he came out, turned not on killing other people but on the "chance of being killed. . . . You're bang up against reality—you're going clean into it—and the sense of it's exquisite." In Sinclair's formulations, sex, death, and reality are intimately linked with one another, if not in fact interchangeable. War is ecstasy, reality, knowledge. As Michael put it in a letter home, "Doesn't it look as if danger were the point of contact with reality, and death the closest point?" "You get the same ecstasy, the same shock of recognition, and the same utter satisfaction when you see a beautiful thing," he asserted.[43]

The war, in these stories of a sexual coming of age, served as a fount of information, a source of (sexual) knowledge that provided its beneficiaries with an access to war denied those at home. Inescapably, the experiences of war involved death in millions of instances, but it was death brought about not by sex, as might be portrayed at home, but by the "real," as opposed to the romantic, nature of war. Knowledge about sex and about war equipped its holders with a clear-sighted, concrete, detailed comprehension of life at the front and of the human beings who lived there, in contrast to the romanticizing and fantasizing of the war, and the distortion of the men who fought it, that took place at home. Mystification, lack of knowledge, and dread anticipation characterize many of the accounts of the home experience, whereas clarity, directness, immediacy, and the acquisition of knowledge characterize the accounts of front experience.

Women at the front or in positions that approximated those of the frontsoldiers shared with the men experiences denied to those at home. Rather than construe men in fantastic terms, derived from a different construction of war given in patriotic journalism, government propaganda, and sanitized letters home, feminists at the front had an understanding of men's experiences and of men that was far more in keeping with those of the men themselves. We have seen that the sexual violation and mutilation of women by men served as one of the chief means by which the war was represented at home. Women at the front, by contrast, saw not the mutilation of women by men but the mutilation of men by weapons of mass destruction produced by industrial societies. Their familiarity with what men suffered led them to think of the male of the species not as some barbaric, destructive creature who could not control his most violent instincts, but as a hurt, pathetic, vulnerable, patient, childlike victim of circumstances far beyond his control. The sexual imagery utilized to depict or represent the war, consequently, involved a much greater sense of partnership, of participation on equal terms, of fellowship with men, than did that of the home front. Whereas aggression and conflict characterized the sexual relations that were mobilized to depict the war at home, stories of sexual initiation, of awakening, of a sexual coming of age, predominated among the women at the front. These were described as affirming encounters with life lived at its fullest, though passion was often invoked. Comfort, caring, and giving, as opposed to conflict, violence, and destruction, characterized the relations of men and women who shared the horrors and exigencies of war. These differing understandings, particularly about the nature of masculinity (and thus, given the dichotomies of male/female, of femininity) and the relationship between men and women, had, as we will see in the following chapters, important consequences as feminists began to formulate policies that turned on their conceptions of gender and sexuality. As Elizabeth Robins—who did not go to the front during the war—explained it, before the war, she had perceived the "woman question" clearly; in the postwar period, she discovered "that clearness breathed upon, till one lost sight for a while of what one had seen and learned." In contrast, a writer for *Time and Tide* reported on "those women who have had their minds widened and their knowledge of life increased by their war service. . . . They are much better fitted for clear thinking than they were."[44]

The divergent views about men and women occasioned by differing experiences of the war showed up most pointedly in postwar debates about the nature and scope of feminism; but already, in 1916, the representation of the war as conflict between the sexes informed and colored not only the discourses surrounding Parliament's decision to grant women the vote, but also feminists' acceptance of limitations on suffrage that flew in the face of their fifty-year commitment to votes for women on the same terms as they were or would be granted to men.

Chapter 4

THE VOTE: SEX AND SUFFRAGE IN
BRITAIN, 1916–1918

REFERENCES to the relationship among sex, suffrage, and war began immediately upon the outbreak of hostilities. A direct and immediate association
between suffrage and war emerged from proclamations of the Pankhursts as
they turned their energies away from fighting the government and toward
fighting the Germans. The Pankhursts viewed the war in France as an inten-
sification of the conflict that had been raging at home between men and
women, and articulated their feelings about the international war in explicit
suffragist terms. The 7 August 1914 edition of the *Suffragette* carried a front-
page drawing of men fighting at close range, some engaged in hand-to-hand
combat. The caption read, "Worse than *Women's* Militancy," implying that
the two struggles—for the vote and for victory against Germany—differed
only in degree. Emmeline Pankhurst wrote in a pamphlet circulated to
WSPU members regarding the suspension of suffragette militancy, "It is
obvious that even the most vigorous militancy of the W.S.P.U. is for the time
being rendered less effective by contrast with the infinitely greater violence
done in the present war not to mere property and economic prosperity
alone, but to human life."[1]

Christabel Pankhurst, upon returning from Paris where she had been in
hiding from British authorities, explained that the suspension of militancy
was necessitated by "the danger in which the country stands, and . . . the
terrible cost in suffering and in life that the war imposes." She insisted,
however, that "the public must not forget, how closely related is the question of women's votes with the war, and with the national safety." She accused the government of neglecting the defense of the country, charging
that "if the time and energy that of late years have been devoted to fighting
against the Suffragettes had been devoted to preparing to fight against the
Germans, it would have been better for the country." She compared WSPU
members to "other war-worn, wounded soldiers" and suggested that "as
militant women, we may perhaps be able to do something to rouse the spirit
of militancy in men." "There are none who more fully understand, none
who more wholly admire the bravery of the soldiers who have faced fear-
ful odds in battle, than do the militant women, who themselves know something of the discipline of warfare." "To fight for Belgium!" she exclaimed.
"That to a Suffragette seems indeed a great cause, because this little country

has withstood and has fought an enemy infinitely stronger than itself in the physical sense. . . . that is the spirit in which some of your own citizens, the militant women, have been fighting for a long time." She urged out-and-out support for the war effort, reminding her followers that "the world domination that Germany seeks to win would mean the abasement of women, would mean a disastrous check to women's progress towards equal citizenship. Obviously, the might-is-right principle upon which German policy is now based is altogether contrary to the principle upon which women's claim to citizenship depends." In October 1914, Pankhurst told a Carnegie Hall audience that "we call Belgium the Suffragette country," while Germany was "a Male Nation." By that time, rumors of German atrocities had reached British shores, so that Pankhurst's identification with Belgium carried clear sexual implications. "Bismarck boasted that Germany is a male nation," she reminded the crowd. "We do not want male nations. . . . A nation exclusively dominated by the male and by the ideas of the male, is a nation governed unnaturally. . . . The more you have the man's and woman's point of view balanced, the more sane will be the nation. Therefore we will not allow a male nation to dominate." She entitled a speech delivered at Carnegie Hall in January 1915 "International Militancy," describing the Great War in terms of an enlarged and expanded suffragette militancy. As the *Suffragette* put it bluntly in May 1915, "all true Suffragettes are standing by those who at the risk of death are resisting the leader of the Anti-Suffragists—William II."[2]

It was not simply the Pankhurst faction that conflated the cause of suffrage and that of the war. Nina Boyle of the WFL, the only suffrage organization to continue its agitation for votes for women after the war broke out, urged, in the language and imagery of war, "all Suffragists to stand to their guns and man their own forts," and not to be drawn away from their cause. Rebecca West, no friend of militancy, nevertheless believed that

> the very round-and-tumble of the movement had its merits; in Palace Yard or at the street corners they acquired a courage which now they use in the service of their country. . . . one doubts that women would have gone into the dangerous high explosive factories, the engineering shops and the fields, and worked with quite such fidelity and enthusiasm if it had not been so vigorously affirmed by the suffragists in the last few years that women ought to be independent and courageous and capable.

Beatrice Harraden's fictional munitions worker, Alice Somers, announced as she left to take up her position in the factory, "I go to fight militarism, tyranny in the world—yes, and in the home." Helen Fraser, a member of the NUWSS Executive Committee after the resignations in March 1915, wrote in 1918, "The forces we women fight in the enemy are the forces that have left women out in world affairs. Germany is the Fatherland, never, it is significant, the Motherland as our little Islands are, and its mad dream of militarism and *Weltmacht* is the dream of men who deny any constructive part to women in the great affairs of life." The *Vote*, the publication of the WFL, carried an article in January 1915 entitled "The War and Women." It described the unofficial Christmas truce that had broken out on the western front, during which the British fraternized with the Germans and exchanged gifts. "All grasped the big Saxon's meaning when he shouted, 'Ve vants to know if you vas as fed up mit dis var as ve vas,'" the paper declared, "and another German shed tears and said it was not war but murder, and that he wanted to go home to his wife and child." In a remarkable leap from the truce between combatants on the western front to a future truce between the combatants on the home front, the writer predicted, "It is certain that before very long men will ask what on earth caused them to take up arms against women and resist a most just, rational and thrice necessary claim to citizenship."[3]

Suffrage became rhetorically bound up with the war in another quarter as well, that of the NUWSS. On 4 August 1914, a meeting sponsored by the International Women's Suffrage Alliance (IWSA) convened in Kingsway Hall, London. It had been called a day earlier, before Britain's declaration of war, in order to urge the government to remain neutral and to mediate the conflict between the warring nations of Europe. Millicent Garrett Fawcett, president of the National Union, reluctantly and with "very grave doubts," chaired the meeting. She decried war as "insensate devilry" but called upon her followers to suspend their feminist activities—"the highest and most precious of national and international aspirations and hopes"—in favor of war relief work, to recognize that "we as citizens have now our duty to perform." The next day, Germany having rejected Britain's ultimatum to retreat from Belgium and Britain having therefore declared war on Germany, Fawcett received a letter from Lord Robert Cecil, the leading Unionist supporter of the women's cause. "Permit me to express my great regret," he wrote,

> that you should have thought it right not only to take part in the "peace" meeting last night but also to have allowed the organisation of the National Union to be used for its promotion. Action of the kind will undoubtedly make it very difficult for the friends of Women's Suffrage in both the Unionist and Ministerial parties. Even to me the action seems so unreasonable under the circumstances as to shake my belief in the fitness of women to deal with great Imperial questions and I can only console myself by the belief that in this matter the National Union do not represent the opinions of their fellow country women.[4]

While Fawcett wholeheartedly embraced Britain's war effort, she nonetheless let stand Cecil's characterization of the National Union's participation in a "peace meeting," thereby necessitating her explicit distancing of the organization from any association with "peace" if it was to retain parliamentary support.

A stark dichotomization of war and peace, and the requirement that suffragists make an uncompromising declaration for one or the other, emerged from debates within the National Union over two related issues: whether the group should undertake or participate in an educational campaign about peace, and whether it should support a women's peace conference held in The Hague in April 1915. Throughout the fall of 1914, Fawcett successfully forestalled any split in the National Union over support for the war by directing the organization's energies and efforts to relief work. She was not able, however, to keep Executive Committee members from debating the issues, debates that became so bitter, in fact, that those who took what has been called the "pacifist" side—Helena Swanwick, Isabella Ford, Margaret Ashton, Catherine Marshall, Maude Royden, Kathleen Courtney, and Chrystal Macmillan—have been omitted from official accounts of the National Union written by Fawcett and by Ray Strachey. Strachey privately referred to these women as "the lunatic section," "the wild women of theory," and "poisonous pacifists." Some members, such as Swanwick and Ford, argued that the organization should campaign against the war, seeing in peace work the very principles of women's suffrage. "In militarist states," wrote Swanwick,

> women must always, to a greater or less degree, be deprived of liberty, security, scope, and initiative. For militarism is the enthronement of physical force as the arbiter of nations, and under such an arbitrament [*sic*] women must always go under. . . . If destructive force is to continue to dominate the world, then man must continue to dominate woman, to his and her lasting injury. The sanction of brute force by which a strong nation "hacks its way" through a weak one,

she insisted, explicitly referring to the sexual assaults on Belgian women by German soldiers,

> is precisely the same as that by which the stronger male dictates to the weaker female. Not till the idea of public right has been accepted by the great nations will there be freedom and security for small nations; not till the idea of moral law has been accepted by the majority of men will there be freedom and security for women. . . . People who desire the enfranchisement of women will only be effective workers if they work for pacifism, or the control of physical by moral force. Pacifists will only be effective if they admit that women's claim to freedom is based on the same principle as the claim of small nations.

"If our NU hangs back," wrote Isabella Ford to Catherine Marshall in October 1914, "the cause of W. Suff. will be irrevocably damaged in the future." Maude Royden recognized that "there was no question of opposition to the war itself within the great Suffrage organizations, since the vast majority of their members believed that the war had been forced upon us and was, on our part, a battle against a militarist ideal." She insisted, however, that militarism and feminism "must be in eternal opposition.... The Women's Movement in all its aspects . . . is an assertion of moral force as the supreme governing force in the world."[5]

These women soon became lumped in with those—such as Marshall, Courtney, and Ashton—who sought middle ground between the antiwar group's position and Fawcett's, Strachey's, and Lady Frances Balfour's refusal to entertain any talk of peace. "The time to discuss proposals of peace is when peace is nearer," Lady Balfour told the Executive Committee in November 1914. "We can have no peace until Germany is beaten." Anything short of wholehearted support for the war effort would harm the suffrage cause. "What would statecraft think of a body sitting in the middle of a war and affirming its belief in arbitration and conciliation as opposed to war?" she demanded. The compromise group chose not to proactively oppose Britain's involvement in war; it sought through the National Union to educate the public about the causes and prevention of war so as to avoid future wars. But as the controversy increased in the latter months of 1914, the parties to it began to refer to one another as the "pro-Hun" or the "pro-war" faction, "two equally wounding forms of misrepresentation," Marshall pointed out to Fawcett in a letter dated 28 November 1914.[6] A hardening of positions attended this kind of rhetorical practice.

Fawcett attempted to institutionalize her patriotic feelings as NUWSS policy, proposing to include on the agenda of the organization's first annual council meeting since the war's outbreak a resolution stating that "the British Empire is fighting the battle of representative government and progressive democracy all over the world and therefore the aim of the National Union as part of the general democratic movement is involved in it." The antiwar forces combined to defeat this agenda item, substituting instead one that resolved,

> This Council of the N.U.W.S.S. adopts as a fundamental consideration which should govern the settlement after the war the principle laid down by the Prime Minister in his speech in Dublin on Sept. 26th, 1914, viz.:—
>
> The substitution for force, and for the theory of the Balance of Power, of a real partnership between nations based on the recognition of equal right and established and enforced by a common will.[7]

This resolution articulated a vision of international relations very like that of marital relations espoused by feminists throughout the prewar period. The council approved another resolution that explicitly made this connection.

> Since the Women's Movement is based on the principle that social relations should be governed not by physical force but by recognition of mutual rights, this council of the N.U.W.S.S. declares its belief in arbitration as opposed to

war, and urges the Government to do its utmost to ensure that in future International disputes shall be submitted to arbitration or conciliation before recourse is had to military force. . . . Further, this Council of the N.U.W.S.S. calls upon the organized women of the world to combine in agitation for political freedom, in the belief that the enfranchisement of women would facilitate the settlement of International disputes by arbitration and hasten the establishment of a lasting peace.

As Marshall put it, "This question is for some of us such an integral part of the whole question of women's political duties."[8]

The council voted to support the sentiment expressed by the resolution, but not to empower the National Union to undertake an educational campaign to promote such principles. It did resolve to continue the policy set by the Executive Committee in August 1914, that is "to suspend the ordinary political activities of the N.U. and to recommend the devotion of its organisation to various efforts which have for their object the sustaining of the vital strength of the nation," creating ambiguity about the future course of the NUWSS. When Fawcett took the chair on the last day of the meeting, she did not hesitate to clarify her position, at least. Speaking for herself, she told the delegates, she believed that the greatest national duty was to drive the Germans from French and Belgian soil. "Until that is done," she declared, "I believe it is akin to treason to talk of peace."[9]

Stunned by such accusations and questioning of their good faith, Swanwick, Marshall, and Courtney resigned from the Executive Committee in March 1915. (Maude Royden had resigned the editorship of *Common Cause* two weeks earlier.) Courtney's letter to the Executive Committee summed up their reasoning. "To my mind," she explained, "this refusal on the part of the Council ["to build up public opinion on lines likely to promote a permanent peace"] is not only a refusal to do the work which the moment demands, it is also a refusal to recognise one of the fundamental principles of the Suffrage Movement."[10]

The debate over whether the NUWSS ought to participate in the Hague Peace Conference in April 1915 completed the organization's division into polarized factions of war and peace, with the result of blurring the contours of feminism and laying the groundwork for another, more fatal split in the National Union in the 1920s. In December 1914, Fawcett had written to Carrie Chapman Catt, president of the IWSA and one of the organizers of the peace conference, opposing any call for an international peace congress on the grounds that women are "as subject as men to *national* prepossessions and susceptibilities." She felt certain that anger and dispute would ensue, and that the women's cause would "then run the risk of the scandal of a PEACE conference disturbed and perhaps broken up by violent quarrels. . . . a *Peace Congress of Women* dissolved by violent quarrels would be the laughing stock of the world." In March 1915, the Executive Committee discussed an invitation to cooperate with the International Congress of Women meeting in The Hague to discuss ways of mediating the international conflict. Fawcett "considered that it would be injurious to the reputation of the National Union for common sense to send delegates to the Congress and it would also be injurious for it to do so as indicating a total aloofness from national sentiment." She cited a passage in the *New Statesman* of 13 March 1915, in which the author had asserted,

> In sympathy as we are with many of its objects, we think that the holding of such a conference just now is a very grave mistake, and we particularly regret that the most powerful Suffrage organisation in this country should be so closely associated with the scheme. . . . we cannot help feeling that the mere ability to discuss a resolution calling for an immediate truce whilst the German armies are in occupation of Belgium and a large district of France implies an aloofness from national sentiment which must, to say the least, profoundly restrict the influence of those who feel and exhibit it. It is quite certain that the vast majority of women in this country, whether Suffragists or "anti-s" are not capable of such detachment. And that the Conference should be in any sense representative is therefore inconceivable.

Lady Balfour added that "participation in such a Congress would cast dishonour on our Sons who were fighting at the front," and she threatened to "leave the Union and head a campaign in the country against the women who acted in this way" if the NUWSS agreed to send delegates to the conference. Mrs. Tuke supported Balfour, but Isabella Ford argued that "the question of the settlement after the War had everything to do with Suffrage. She was of the opinion that it was extremely important that the Suffrage point of view should be put at the Congress. The Suffragist Cause was opposed to Militarism." The Executive Committee, however, voted 11–5 against sending delegates to the International Congress. Its position, articulated by Oliver Strachey in an article in the *Englishwoman* in April 1915, was that suffragism, or the demand for "equal political power for men and women [,] does not imply either democracy or pacifism." "It would be quite absurd to say," Strachey argued, positioning the National Union in the war camp, "that the abolition of war is one of the fundamental principles implied in the suffrage movement when the facts only are that the abolition of war and the equal treatment of men and women with regard to votes are two distinct principles."[11]

More resignations from the Executive Committee ensued. Margaret Ashton wrote that "the attitude of the majority of the Executive Committee on the question of women's responsibility in national and international affairs appears to me to be an entire negation of the principles for which our long fight has been waged, and a shirking of the essential duty of women suffragists to uphold the ideal of moral force in human affairs." Cary Schuster charged that the Executive Committee's decision ran counter to the will of the National Union as a whole as it had been expressed at the council meeting. It "is absolutely subversive of the democratic principle," she wrote to the Executive Committee, "and introduces into the Suffrage movement methods reminiscent of those by which the Imperial Chancellor controls the Reichstag." Mrs. P. Stanbury's belated letter of resignation explained that "to me the most important thing *for suffragists* to do was to work against militarism, and to work quickly, because the reliance on physical force makes the rightful position of women in human Society impossible." But what made her resignation "inevitable," she said, was the view that "the action we proposed seemed 'akin to treachery to our country.'"[12]

In response, Lady Balfour denied but nevertheless articulated the affiliation of the National Union, and of suffrage generally, with the cause of war. "By implication," she said, "those who resigned put those who remained in a position of not associating themselves with a desire for peace. The point was that those who remained did not consider that this was the right moment for peace. The very word 'peace' put the Country in the wrong. Any work for peace at the present time was 'inopportune' & implied disloyalty to our soldiers." She moved that the resignations from the Executive Committee be accepted.[13]

In its refusal to talk of peace, the National Union thus became within the dichotomization of war and peace a "war" organization. But it did not do so simply by default. In an attempt to counter pacifist arguments that equated feminism with peace, the *Englishwoman*, under the editorial direction of Frances Balfour, Mary Lowndes, Edith Palliser, J. M. Strachey, and E. M. Goodman, published an article justifying the apparently anomalous case of

> a woman's journal . . . almost entirely devoted to problems of war. War is brutal, barbarous, materialistic, whereas women's influence in the world is of the spirit. And yet, as applied to the War in which we are now engaged, there is no real inconsistency. For this War is really a war on our part for the maintenance of moral principle as against brute force. It is, therefore, a war in the support of which all our spiritual as well as material forces are, rightly, being mobilised.

Helen Fraser explicitly identified the feminist cause with that of the men at the front, arguing that "the men who in this war fight all that is meant by militarism and material force . . . are one with the women who reach out to greater and nobler spheres of work—one in their reaching out from the primitive barbaric and savage to that more splendid battleground where spiritual forces, the eternal verities, are ranged."[14]

Martin Pugh has observed that the National Union's ability to remain untainted by any peace movement for the duration of the war contributed mightily to its success in securing the suffrage in 1918. As Anne Wiltsher has argued,

It is highly likely that if the National Union had made a wholesale effort at communication with "enemy" women, or openly and persistently debated the foundations of a permanent peace amongst its members, female suffrage would not have come as soon as it did. Conscientious objectors were disenfranchised for five years after the war and women might have been kept voteless as a punishment, if pacifism amongst suffragists had been overt and widespread. It would have been a brave step indeed to risk half a century of women's struggle.[15]

Parliament granted the vote to women over the age of thirty in 1918. Contemporary observers in the suffrage and antisuffrage camps attributed the government's willingness to enfranchise women to its appreciation of the work women performed during the war. Fawcett noted in 1925 that "there was not a paper in Great Britain that by 1916–17 was not ringing with praise of the courage and devotion of British women in carrying out war work of various kinds, and on its highly effective character from the national point of view." Minister of Munitions Edwin Montagu proclaimed to the House of Commons in August 1916, "It is not too much to say that our Armies have been saved and victory assured by the women in the munition factories where they helped to produce aeroplanes, howitzer bombs, shrapnel bullets, shells, machine tools, mines, and have taken part in shipbuilding." Winston Churchill, for his part, declared that "without the work of women it would have been impossible to win the war." Herbert Asquith, an inveterate foe of women's suffrage, announced his conversion to the enfranchisement of women on precisely these grounds. "I think that some years ago I ventured to use the expression, 'Let the women work out their own salvation,'" he recalled in March of 1917.

> Well, Sir, they have worked it out during this War. How could we have carried on the War without them? Short of actually bearing arms in the field, there is hardly a service which has contributed, or is contributing, to the maintenance of our cause in which women have not been at least as active and as efficient as men, and wherever we turn we see them doing . . . work which three years ago would have been regarded as falling exclusively within the province of men.[16]

Historians have, for the most part, accepted this explanation, adding that the cessation of militancy during the war years enabled politicians to back down from their opposition with their dignity intact. Pugh goes one step further, arguing that "the virtual disappearance of the woman's campaign" as a whole, and not simply the militant movement, "paved the way for woman suffrage," while the fall of Asquith and the advent of a coalition government dominated by Conservatives provided an opportunity for the Tories to swell their ranks with newly enfranchised older women. Sandra Stanley Holton takes exception to this view, which ignores or at least minimizes the work of suffragists both before and during the war. She believes that women would have won the vote by 1918 without the war's intervention; indeed, that the war may even have postponed the victory. "Women's war work may have been important in converting some former opponents," she concedes, "or providing others with a face-saving excuse to alter their positions. But even before this, the political alliances the democratic suffragists had formed in support of their demand had ensured that women would have to be included in any future reform bill." She cites in support of her claim the negotiations taking place among David Lloyd George, Sylvia Pankhurst, and George Lansbury over women's suffrage in the weeks just prior to the war's outbreak. "The evidence suggests," she argues, "that with a general election in view the Liberal leadership had at last made up its mind to tackle women's suffrage in the context of an adult suffrage bill." The NUWSS leadership were probably not involved in these negotiations, she adds.[17]

But the outbreak of war in August 1914 halted the activities of both militant and constitutional suffragists in their efforts to gain votes for women,[18] and squelched the government's interest in pursuing any kind of reform bill. It was only in 1916, when the government became concerned about the need to call a new election, that franchise reform became an issue. On the basis of the old franchise—occupation of residence for a twelve-month period prior to 15 July of an election year—the men of the armed forces and those serving in related industries would no longer be eligible to vote. Various schemes for the amelioration of this injustice were advanced, but Parliament finally agreed on the need for a new franchise. At this point, the NUWSS stepped in, demanding that women be included in any reform that enfranchised new male voters on the basis of service to the country, claiming that women's contributions to and sacrifices for the war effort entitled them, no less than men, to full citizenship. Moreover, the suffrage societies, according to Mary Stocks, "announced that any proposal to tamper with the franchise would bring their period of war quiescence to an end. . . . As Mrs. Henry Fawcett said, they had buried the hatchet, but they had marked the place where it was buried and were prepared if occasion arose to dig it up." There can be no doubt, as Holton insists, that because "suffrage organisation [had been] maintained to a remarkable degree during the first years of the war, . . . suffragist participation was . . . a significant factor in the debates and campaigning that preceded the Representation of the People Bill of 1917."[19]

While contemporaries emphasized women's war service, they did so within a framework of past and current understandings about sex, war, and sex war that colored their proceedings and heightened the urgency of reaching a satisfactory conclusion. M.P.'s and suffragists worked out their compromise over women's suffrage on the basis of three widely held assumptions: that, prior to August 1914, a sex war had been raging throughout the land; that it had been subsumed in the larger international conflagration;

and that failure to resolve the suffrage issue would result in its flaring up again. As Andrew Rosen has observed, several M.P.'s hinted that the militancy of the prewar years might very well resurface after the war if women were not enfranchised; this contingency persuaded many former antisuffragists in Parliament to reverse their position. Lord Hugh Cecil reminded the Commons of

> the strong feeling which animates a certain number of women in order to obtain the franchise. That is a very important consideration. I believe it to be a very serious matter that any important body of opinion should be discontented and dissatisfied, and it always ought to weigh heavily on Parliament in extending the franchise that there is a body of citizens who very much wish to have it and who wish it so keenly that it produces a disordering and disturbing effect on them. . . . it seems to me that to give women suffrage . . . is to adopt a conservative measure which is likely to allay discontent, to promote justice, and to maintain the efficiency of representative institutions in Parliament.

Walter Long cautioned his fellow M.P.s that "a renewal of those bitter controversies over which we have wasted so much time in the past" must be avoided, and he urged antisuffragists "to think twice and thrice before they commit themselves to this policy of destruction. I implore them to join with the Government in a policy of construction and progress" by voting for women's suffrage.[20] Long never changed his conviction *against* women's suffrage; he voted for it only to avoid the "bitter controversies" of the past.

Brian Harrison, on the other hand, dismisses the idea, put forth by Christabel Pankhurst, that "it was politicians' fear of resumed militancy that really won women the vote in 1916–18." Militancy, he argues,

> was little discussed in the parliamentary debates. It is Lord Crewe's speech of January 1918 that furnishes Christabel with her sole piece of evidence. . . . She offers no evidence that this speech influenced a single vote in the House of Lords, by which time the Bill had passed through the assembly which mattered most, the House of Commons. The speeches which do mention militancy— Crewe's, Law's, and Cochrane's—all discuss it in the context of welcoming its absence.

Harrison fails to comprehend that in welcoming its absence, M.P.'s demonstrated a near obsession with the possibility of another round of militancy. Les Garner also downplays the threat of renewed militancy, on the grounds that the WSPU was not in any position to bring it about.[21]

Harrison and Garner acknowledge that the threat of *general* postwar disorder did have an impact on M.P.'s. Harrison argues that "if fear of militancy influenced politicians at all at this time, it was the fear that Britain would witness post-war militancy on the grander scale experienced by Russia during 1917: a mass violence for which franchise extension in 1918 was . . . seen

as the cure." Garner has argued that "the War . . . heightened political instability and furthered militant class struggle. . . . Revolution was in the air and,
if women were to remain loyal to the state, their wartime effort and sacrifice
had to be acknowledged." Moreover, he suggests, the age restriction placed
on women voters might well have stemmed from "the hope that older
women would be less rebellious." The Speaker of the conference appointed
to draw up the Reform Bill, James Lowther, was "convinced of the great
desirability of amicably settling this thorny question, and of finding a solution for issues fraught with the possibility of engendering grave domestic
friction and internal friction." Ramsay MacDonald warned of revolution if a
new, far more representative franchise was not introduced before the war's
end.[22]

By the time the House of Lords took up the measure for deliberation, the
Bolshevik revolution had taken place, coloring almost the entire debate.
M.P.'s could not avoid drawing parallels between one international move-
ment, socialism, and another—women's suffrage. Earl Russell asserted in
December 1917 that

> we do not grant the vote for fitness; we grant it . . . for the protection of the
> State, in order that through the ballot-box the State may learn, from the organ-
> ised opinion of those who have grievances and who desire their remedy, what
> those grievances are. I suggest that the vote is granted nowadays on no kind of
> fitness, but as a substitute for riot, revolution, and the rifle. We grant the suf-
> frage in order that we may learn in an orderly and civilised manner what the
> people who are governed want.

The earl of Lytton, responding to Lord Bryce's and Lord Sydenham's linking
of women's suffrage and anarchy in Russia, countered, "What is it in the
example of Russia that we should not imitate? Not the fact that she has
introduced manhood and womanhood suffrage, but that she did not do it in
time. 'Too late,' is a motto which may be found written over the victims of
every revolution. We do not intend that it shall be found written over the
ruins of this House."[23]

Lord Curzon, the leader of the antisuffragist forces in the House of Lords,
dropped his opposition to the women's suffrage clause of the Reform Act for
exactly this reason. Back in January 1917, even before the Russian Revolution, Lord Islington, undersecretary of state for India, had written to Curzon
urging him to take cognizance of "the grave situation which might arise" if
women's suffrage were to be rejected. "One hardly dares contemplate what
might happen in the country," he lamented, "if the Franchise Bill was
dropped which would certainly be the case if the woman's vote was eliminated. . . . the line now between order and revolution is as thin as it can be,
and action of this character, at this moment, would tend to reducing that line
to vanishing point. . . . [The Reform Bill] stands out as the one hopeful buffer

between Govt by Constitutional method and revolution." Walter Long also cautioned Curzon, in a letter dated 20 December 1917, that failure to en-franchise the masses would bring them "very near to a rebellion." Curzon heeded their advice, telling the House of Lords in December 1917 that "peace abroad, whenever we attain it, will not mean repose at home. . . . if the epoch which we are closing has been darkened by all the horrors and tragedies of warfare, the epoch that is coming will be disturbed by convul-sions and agitations, not less remarkable and very likely destined to shake even more profoundly the whole machinery of State."[24] When the women's suffrage clause came up for a division, Curzon abstained, seconding the earl of Selborne's assessment that if the Lords killed the women's suffrage clause, the Commons would not pass the bill. Then, as Selborne predicted, "in the climax of this war you will split the nation from top to bottom. You will have against you not only those of the women who have desired the franchise; you will have against you the men who desired the franchise, and the seamen and soldiers who are looking forward to the franchise." As Harri-son has remarked, "it was indeed hardly surprising that Curzon . . . should subordinate his distaste for woman suffrage to his fear of social revolution."[25]

Fear of renewed militancy, then, if only in the guise of postwar domestic disorder, clearly helped to bring about women's suffrage. But why, at this time, should it carry such weight? After all, the political situation in Great Britain prior to the war's outbreak—with intense labor unrest and the immi-nent threat of civil war in Belfast—could hardly have inspired confidence in the nation's stability. Certainly, as Harrison and Garner point out, the Rus-sian Revolution provided a graphic example of the dangers of social strife, but more was at stake for members of Parliament, as well as for suffragists. In reading the debates literally, and in failing to situate them in the larger context in which they took place, these historians have missed an opportu-nity to understand just what they meant to contemporaries. If one takes a critical approach to the debaters' language, one will find that it was not militancy itself that had so significant and visceral an impact on politicians, but what it represented. "Votes for women," in the war's context and as a result of the terms of the discourses surrounding the issue as it was debated within and without suffrage ranks, carried a heavy symbolic load, reflecting and exciting unprecedented anxieties about gender, power, and conflict. In order to understand both the victory of women's suffrage and the willingness of feminists to accept what was in fact a half measure one must never lose sight of the backdrop against which both took place: the war. As Lloyd George put it in March 1917, "the women's question has become very largely a war question." "This Bill which we are discussing," the earl of Lytton advised the House of Lords in December 1917, "is vitally connected with the war; it is wholly wrapped up in the war, and it is certainly and strictly war legislation."[26]

The connection between suffrage and war informed all the arguments about women's suffrage, both pro and con; the debates over votes for women were embedded in reflections on the war. Some antisuffragists, for instance, denied that women had made any contribution to the war effort, or linked them with pacifism, and based their continued opposition to votes for women on these grounds. Arnold Ward, one of the leaders of the National League for Opposing Woman Suffrage, having gotten "leave from his military duties to fight the battle at Westminster," as Brian Harrison put it so tellingly, told the House of Commons that

> the case against women's suffrage, so far from having been weakened by the events of the War, has been immeasurably strengthened. . . . we have drawn from the lessons of the War an entirely new series of overwhelming facts and illustrations of the principles on which our case was founded before the War. . . . the women of this country have not fought, and have not asked to fight. . . . in all the operations connected with the War the work of men has been decisive and the work of women has been auxiliary. . . . The position of women in politics ought to be an auxiliary one . . . and . . . the men, who decided the issue during the War, should continue to be the masters in time of peace.

"Is it wise," he asked, "to place upon the register a mass of necessarily inexperienced voters liable to be swayed by the arguments of hysterical agitators and consequently liable to use the vote to the detriment of the interests of our soldiers and sailors?" The lord chancellor agreed. "Would not there be," he asked, "a vast amount of material for agitation, by those who are called pacifists, who are in favour of a hurried peace, among the millions of women who without political experience it is proposed to enfranchise by the Bill? . . . is it not necessary to bear in mind what might be on them the possible effect of war weariness—loss of sons, husbands, brothers, and it might be scarcity and privation . . . for the children whom they love more than they do their own souls." Their susceptibility to pleas for peace might leave Prussian militarism intact, he argued, invoking the connection between women and peace espoused by many feminists. The *Anti-Suffrage Review* in March 1917 proclaimed that "it is safe to infer that every Pacifist and every No-Conscriptionist is a Suffragist."[27] The enfranchisement of women, in this version of events, might very well mean the defeat of Great Britain.

By contrast, speakers in favor of women's suffrage often viewed the vote as a reward for those surrogate warriors who helped to make victory possible. W. H. Dickinson, a leading suffragist M.P., advanced the case for women's enfranchisement by comparing women's service and sacrifice to those of men. "The Prime Minister says that men have sacrificed and lost their lives in the trenches. Whose death was it that sounded like a clarion cry throughout the Empire more than any other? It was the death of a woman— Miss [Edith] Cavell. Who have sacrificed their lives in the same way as men through fever, in the wards of hospitals, and elsewhere? Women." Lloyd George recounted to Parliament in March 1917,

> When I was Minister of Munitions we had very dangerous work. It involved a special alteration in one element of our shells. . . . [It was] a very dangerous operation, and there were several fatal accidents. It was all amongst the women workers in the munition factories. There was never a panic. They stuck to their work. They knew the peril. They never ran away from it. I remember that when the first Zeppelin raids were made, when bombs were dropped outside important munition factories—I do not want to say too much about the men: we had some difficulty for two or three days afterwards with some of them getting them to work at night in the munition factories, but we never had any difficulty with regard to the women.[28]

The debates comparing women's service with men's, as Lloyd George's remarks indicate, sometimes polarized men and women or suggested conflict between them; they were informed by the idea that women's inclusion in the franchise would come, somehow, at the expense of men, or at least of men's interests. This theme emerged as early as 14 August 1916, when Asquith used the threat of women's agitating for inclusion in any new franchise reform as a means of sinking the proposal to enfranchise soldiers and sailors. "The moment you begin a general enfranchisement on these lines of State service," he warned,

> you are brought face to face with another most formidable proposition: What are you to do with the women? . . . They say they are perfectly content, if we do not change the qualification of the franchise, to abide by the existing state of things, but that if we are going to bring in a new class of electors, on whatever ground of State service, they point out—and we cannot possibly deny their claim—that during this War the women of this country have rendered as effective service in the prosecution of the War as any other class of the community. It is true they cannot fight, in the gross material sense of going out with rifles and so forth, but they fill our munition factories, they are doing the work which the men who are fighting had to perform before. . . . What is more, . . . they say when the War comes to an end, and when these abnormal and, of course, to a large extent transient, conditions have to be revised, and when the process of industrial reconstruction has to be set on foot, have not the women a special claim to be heard on the many questions which will arise directly affecting their interests, and possibly meaning for them large displacements of labour? . . . I say quite frankly that I cannot deny that claim. It seems to me, and it seems to all my colleagues, . . . that nothing could be more injurious to the best interests of the country, nothing more damaging to the prosecution of the War, nothing more fatal to the concentration of the national effort, than that the floodgates should be opened on all those vast complicated questions of the franchise, with

an infinite multiplicity of claimants, each of whom can make a perfectly plausible if not irresistible case for themselves.[29]

Sir Edward Carson responded to Asquith's threat with one of his own.

I say that as regards these various classes of voters who are held up . . . as a bogey to try and prevent us from putting forward this claim on behalf of the soldiers and sailors, that you can draw no comparisons between any person claiming the franchise and the man who is risking his life and health in the trenches, and who is daily rendering himself liable to be shot on behalf of this country. I do not believe there is any comparison between that and, say, the women's franchise question. . . . if anybody tells me that you are forwarding the cause of women . . . by suggesting that they are coming forward and saying, "We will not allow the sailors and soldiers who are fighting for us to be enfranchised because we cannot be considered at the same time," I say that they are putting a bar to their own cause which they will find will have considerable influence upon the question.[30]

Commander Bellairs hurried to inform the House of Commons that "I have been authorised on the part of the Women's Social and Political Union . . . to say that they repudiate that statement altogether made by the Prime Minister. They express the utmost anxiety that the soldiers and sailors should be given the vote. . . . They authorise me to say that they will not allow themselves to be used to prevent soldiers and sailors from being given the vote." Emmeline Pankhurst, in a startling editorial in *Britannia*, the successor to the *Suffragette*, accused Asquith of using women's suffrage as "an excuse for disenfranchising the Sailors and Soldiers. . . . Mr. Asquith insults as well as injures women when he tries to use them as catspaws to prevent the best men of the country from recording a vote, while any and every crank, coward or traitor, is to be free to vote as usual."[31]

In the context of a war represented in sexual terms, and of debates that pitted women's claims against those of soldiers and sailors, renewed militancy meant conflict between the sexes, or sex war. Debates about women's suffrage often implied that sex war threatened to break out at any time and was in abeyance only because it had been subsumed in the larger, but not dissimilar, international conflict. A number of M.P.'s referred to the truce in the sex war made possible by the war with Germany. Sir John Simon told the House of Commons that in order to solve such controversial problems as whether women should participate, through enfranchisement, in the post-war reconstruction of the country, "you need atmosphere and temper in which they can be solved, and it would appear to me that there are an atmosphere and a temper both in the House of Commons and in the country now which are favourable to considering problems of this sort. Are we, therefore, really acting wisely if we proceed on the assumption that the atmosphere and the temper will be better and more hopeful for the solution of such problems when the anxiety of the War is over." J. R. Clynes believed that "a period of compromise is, after all, possible to us in this country, that while War is being waged in other lands we here, in . . . a state of peace, can use that condition . . . to settle on lines of compromise those highly controversial questions." The marquess of Crewe described the war years as "the present general truce" in the war between men and women. The NUWSS publication, "Weekly Notes," in January 1916 quoted an article that had appeared in the *Herald* conflating the suffrage movement with war. "We owe a debt to the past and to the present, . . . to the women who laid down their lives for the Cause, and to the men who are laying down their lives for what they conceive to be a similar Cause in the European War."[32]

The prospect of renewed sex war once the war in Europe came to an end created anxiety for M.P.'s, helping to persuade many of them to support votes for women as a means of forestalling its recurrence. Lord Hugh Cecil explicitly cautioned in May 1917, "The controversy about women's suffrage is a miserable one. The argument is increasingly used as to the controversy between the two sexes; it is the most intolerable we can conceive, and a question of that kind is much better brought to a close as soon as possible." The marquess of Crewe shared his concerns about postwar conflict between the sexes, raising the threat of danger another degree by referring to the possibility of physical combat, and arguing in favor of votes for women as a deterrent:

> The atmosphere after the conclusion of the war . . . cannot be in the political sense calm. It may be very much the contrary. . . . I recall the political position on this subject as it existed just before the war. We all know how high feelings ran. . . . it would have been no surprise to us, the members of the Government of that day, if any one of our colleagues in the House of Commons who had taken a prominent line either for or against the grant of the vote to women had been assassinated in the street. . . . That is an atmosphere, if the grant of the vote is refused, which will undoubtedly be recreated, one of these days.

"The existence of those passions in the past and the probability of their recurrence in the future" led him to ask "whether it is not wiser to attempt to settle this question during the present general truce than to await the reopening of the struggle, perhaps in even more violent forms than before, for it will certainly be renewed"—if, as he stressed, women's suffrage was scuttled.[33]

Andrew Bonar Law told a National Union deputation in August 1916 that "the clashing of interests of the sexes after the war was a very strong argument in favour of enfranchising women." Millicent Garrett Fawcett, in a February 1917 conversation with Bonar Law, told him "she was very much afraid that if Electoral Reform were again shelved, militancy would begin

again and that this would be a disaster to woman suffrage and to England."
Bonar Law, she reported to the Executive Committee of the NUWSS, had
replied that "he believed that the militants would be killed and that this
might lead to riots of every kind. He thought the situation very uneasy."[34]

While making a different connection between women's suffrage and war,
the antisuffragists nevertheless invoked the same specter of sex war as did
the proponents of women's suffrage. While the latter urged women's suffrage as a means of avoiding conflict, Arnold Ward warned his colleagues in
the Commons that the women's suffrage measure "is bound to lead to the
most bitter conflict both in and outside this House." "The evil will not cease
with the passing of the Bill, because for years suspicion and resentment
must dog the footsteps of the enfranchised women, and in the years to come,
whenever any unpopular measure or thing is passed or done, which may be
traced to the influence of the female voters, men's minds will recur with
indignation and wrath to the circumstances of their enfranchisement."[35]

The conflation of feminism with sex war was not, of course, new, but the
context in which the equation was made was entirely different now. In the
aftermath of the Somme, of Loos, of Passchendaele, a conflict between
the sexes could not be tolerated; it conjured up images of the battlefield
horrors that so gripped the country's imagination. Feminism soon became
linked in the public mind not merely with sex war, a somewhat familiar
concept, but with armed conflict, death, and destruction. It raised the specter of combat in the streets of England—combat between men and women.
The imagery of warfare between men and women, moreover, gained valida-
tion and a new and terrifying meaning from the atrocity propaganda that
circulated throughout Britain, much of which, as we have seen in chapter 1,
focused on outrages committed against women.

Fear of renewal of the sex war, raised now to intolerable levels, also
helped to determine the terms under which women would be admitted to
the franchise. While the Representation of the People Act gave men the vote
on the basis of residence of premises, a grant of virtual universal manhood
suffrage, it restricted the women's vote to those who were householders or
the wives of householders, and who had attained the age of thirty. The age
requirement ensured that women would not enjoy a majority over men,
whose numbers had been greatly reduced in the slaughter of war. It also
ensured that those eligible to vote were likely to be wives and mothers; those
excluded were largely single, working-class women who had made so significant a contribution to the war effort, who might, as Martin Pugh has put
it, see in the vote an opportunity to maintain their "footing in industry and
to retreat further from marriage and motherhood."[36]

In consenting to the age qualification, suffragists abandoned their long-
held principle of sex equality: votes for women on the same lines as it was or
should be granted to men. Fawcett and other NUWSS leaders earnestly

explained to their unhappy Labour followers, most of whom would not be eligible to vote because they were underage, that "meticulous criticism"— efforts to eliminate the age restriction—might result in the bill's failure, and that they did not want to "risk their prospects for partial success by standing out for more." While welcome to feminists as a symbol of the fall of the sex barrier, the provisions of the Reform Act, as Brian Harrison has noted, "would have shocked pre-war feminists." In fact, it shocked wartime and postwar feminists as well. Dora Montefiore, articulating the outrage felt by many working-class women, decried the "treachery" and "betrayal" of the suffrage societies, "which had collected several thousands of pounds on the pledge of 'obtaining the vote for women on the same terms as it is *or may be* granted to men.' Immediately the men obtained Manhood Suffrage the Women Suffrage Societies backed down, betrayed their subscribers, and agreed to take a limited measure." Pugh has observed that in light of the fact that the Reform Act enfranchised men of nineteen if they had served in the armed forces, "the limit on women was almost an insult."[37]

Fawcett's strategic capitulation on so major an issue was not simply a reflection of her cautious nature, though caution was certainly an ever-present feature of organized feminism during the war, exacerbated, perhaps, by the movement's weakened position after the 1915 resignations of some of the National Union's most conspicuous and energetic members, and by Emmeline and Christabel Pankhurst's defection from suffrage ranks.[38] Her explanation elides an important, yet unaddressed, problem within suffrage historiography. As Pugh has noted, with the Representation of the People Act, "the women were made to swallow the very mixture that had been considered so unpalatable when offered to them in 1912—a large dose of male suffrage in combination with a limited franchise for women. In 1917, however, nearly all the women's organizations meekly accepted what was offered them, and this was the most noticeable effect of the War upon their cause." Neither Pugh nor any other historian has pursued this last point, but it is one that positively cries out for explanation. We must consider the acceptance of the age restriction—just as we must regard Parliament's decision to grant women the vote in the first place—in the context of the war, as at least partially a consequence of categorical "women's" implication in a war represented in sexual terms. "The advancement of 'women' must always take its tone from the differing backgrounds out of which their candidacy is to be prised," Riley argues. "It is never possible for 'women' to be amassed as completely unshadowed subjects. . . . Feminism never has the option of putting forward its own uncontaminated, self-generated understandings of 'women': its 'women' too, is always thoroughly implicated in the discursive world."[39] And this discursive world, in the years 1914–1918, was wholly one of war, informed by and thoroughly immersed in sexuality. Thus "women" became contaminated by the terms against which it was defined, and women's claims were made in and constrained by this context.

The National Union's discursive complicity with the war, both literally through relief work and metonymically within the terms of the debate about war and peace, had a distinct bearing on the group's cautious stance in the debates over suffrage in 1916 and 1917. For if the National Union identified itself as a war organization mobilized in the conflict between nations, might this not imply—especially after 1915 when women were actively taking on soldierlike roles, and given the discourses that equated or conflated the international war with sex war—that it also (or potentially) constituted a war organization mobilized in the conflict between men and women? If so, Fawcett and the other members of the group's Executive Committee could be held responsible, in holding out for more, for perpetuating the war between the sexes. Compromise on the issue of age limitations, by contrast, could reduce the tensions between men and women and help to bring sex war to a halt for good. Maud Selborne inadvertently pointed to the prevention of sex war by shifting the subjects of female citizenship from "women" (and warriors) to "mothers." She believed the compromise on women by means of an age restriction to be "thoroughly illogical," but went on to undercut this sentiment by conceding, "Yet if you are to enfranchise women gradually (surely a prudent choice if their great numbers are taken into consideration), a wiser choice of those to first shoulder the responsibility of citizenship could hardly have been made. The great mass of the mothers of the nation will be able to vote." As Pugh has observed, the Representation of the People Act tied most women's rights to their husbands', reflecting "the long-standing preference expressed by Liberal and Labour reformers for including the wives of workingmen in whatever changes might be made, and the traditional hostility towards bestowing the vote upon spinsters." "Wives," presumably, could be counted upon to follow their husbands' leads, and to obviate the radical potential of mere "women." To politicians, "the woman over 30 . . . appeared to be a stable element in a changing world, one who was unlikely to seek to promote radical, feminist issues in parliament if enfranchised."[40]

A careful reading of the National Union's arguments about suffrage reveals a current of fear permeating feminist ranks during the war, the nagging concern that the gains women had made during the war were only for the duration, and that any misbehavior on their part would bring down ruin upon their heads. Certainly, in a war for national survival, demands for women's suffrage could as easily be construed as anti-British as they had been construed as antiman in the years before 1914. Most suffrage societies had recognized this danger when they suspended their political activities in favor of relief work, hoping to demonstrate that support for the nation overrode a potentially selfish and divisive campaign aimed at changing Britain's gender system. Nor would such an identification of priorities after 1914 have been inconsistent with most prewar feminists' conceptions of their relationship to the nation. As Vron Ware and Antoinette Burton have shown in separate studies, Victorian and Edwardian feminist identity, ideology, and practice were intricately wrapped up in concepts of British superiority— ethnic, racial, and moral; while they frequently sought to represent their movement as international, British feminists also laid claim to women's part in shouldering the "white man's burden" as a means of justifying their demands for participation in the political order.[41]

The fear of being perceived as antipatriotic haunted the National Union and influenced its behavior. Fawcett suggested as much early in December 1916, in response to a letter from Lord Northcliffe urging her to organize "some great meeting or united deputation" to persuade the government to include women in a new franchise act after David Lloyd George replaced Asquith as prime minister. She opted for the private deputation rather than the public meeting, explaining,

> I believe that as a consequence of the experience of the last twenty-nine months, Women's Suffrage has obtained a new and far stronger position than ever before; and that this is due not only to the good work done by women, but to the good spirit in which it has been done, the spirit of whole-hearted love of our country and reverence for its aims in this war. It is this, if I mistake not, which has made such an impression on the public mind. We must beware of acting in any way calculated to weaken this position.[42]

Maintaining the nation's hard-won unity became an obsession of both M.P.'s and suffragists as they sought to produce a franchise bill: the all-party Speaker's Conference met twenty-six times between 12 October 1916 and 26 January 1917 in order to reach an agreement that the House of Commons as a whole could accept. Compromise and conciliation characterized these sessions; as Pugh put it so poignantly, "in the third bitter winter of trench warfare this group of thirty-two middle-aged and elderly politicians found in the Conference one of the few ways open to them of making a personal contribution to the cause of national unity." Fawcett wrote in December 1916, "The War has been one of the great events of the world; . . . Before the War the nation was torn by faction: deadly quarrels were going on between class and class, in some quarters between sex and sex, between party and party. Hatred and disdain within each camp for the other were preached as if they were a sort of devil's gospel." The war changed that, giving all Britons, men as well as women, a new sense of priorities, a new conception of the value of things. "We want to see the War Conscience transplanted to the conditions of Peace," Fawcett urged. "We want to see an England where the old enmities and suspicions shall be assuaged and supplanted by a better mutual understanding between class and class, party and party, employers and employed, sex and sex, Irish Nationalists and Irish Unionists."

As the Easter Rebellion had erupted and been put down by armed force only some eight months prior, the positioning of sex conflict alongside that

of the Irish conflict is significant. Her emphasis on unity elided her conviction that if suffragists refused to accept the vote on the terms set forth by the
Speaker's Conference, the cohesion of the country would break down, and
women could be held responsible for renewing and perpetuating the conflict
between the sexes. She raised the possibility of sex war, ostensibly to deny
it, but cautioning that it was the nation's wartime unity that offered the
antidote to such a specter. "Some Labour leaders have gone so far as to
predict the outbreak of a serious sex-war in this country when the war with
the Germans is over," Fawcett went on,

> because they say that the men who will then get their discharge from the Army
> will find the work to which they were accustomed before the war being done by
> women for less than half the wages which the men had received. . . . I do not
> myself believe in the possibility of a sex-war. We should have had one long ago
> if it had been a possibility; there have been evils great enough to provoke it, the
> cruel injustice of many of the laws relating to women; the measureless ocean of
> contempt for women expressed in nearly all classical literature in which the
> youth of many men is steeped; unlimited political authority on the one side and
> unlimited subjection on the other. But there have always been the real things
> to keep us straight: the love of husband and wife, of father and daughter, of
> mother and son: the causes that we have worked for together, a common patri-
> otism, a common agony in hours of national disaster and strain, a common uplift
> at the signs of national greatness and unity.[43]

Fawcett feared that to stand out for more on the suffrage question would
be disastrous. "The [Speaker's] report is a result of a carefully balanced compromise," she told her followers. "There had to be give and take on both
sides: the suffragists got the abolition of the sex disqualification, but had to
yield on the question of equality of qualification. . . . it might be fatal for us
to come in from the outside and say we won't have this and we won't have
that. Such a course might very well bring the whole delicately balanced
structure about our ears."[44]

Fawcett was referring here to the compromise on women's suffrage ham-
mered out by the Speaker's Conference, but her warning about toppling
"the whole delicately balanced structure" carried another, more portentous,
meaning about the delicate balance of male-female relations during wartime. In June 1916 Nina Boyle had given voice to this concern, contesting
the prevailing optimism about relations between men and women. "War has
not in any way altered or abolished the shocking injustice with which
women are habitually treated," she insisted. "Murder, and brutal assault of
women are of incessant occurrence. Men who have not gone to the trenches,
and men who come back from them, vie with each other in this pleasing
pastime." She made an explicit appeal for votes for women on precisely
these grounds. "This, then, being the position of women in war," she de-

clared, "it behooves us to turn our thoughts seriously towards what their position will be in peace. . . . in view of the tragedy of their position we can only look with uncomprehending wonder on the meanness of the men who would withhold from them their meed of citizenship." Moreover, she claimed, the "extraordinary bitterness shown by the women of all nationalities," a "natural result of the impotence imposed on the sex," posed "the worst and most real danger to the peace of the world in the future."[45]

Charges of brutal murders of women and children, of rape and mutilation by German soldiers, were, as we have seen, reinforced and given credence by the atrocity propaganda designed to facilitate recruitment and stiffen British resolve. The reports of sexual assaults, mutilations, and rape committed by Germans against Belgian and French women and children resonated with prewar suffragette and suffragist charges of sexual assaults on British women by British men, part and parcel of the sex war that suffrage, it was expected, would terminate. The connection between suffrage and war could easily lead to one between sex and war, and finally to sex war, even when that connection was denied by individuals like Fawcett. Such discursive linkages made it possible to conceive of a scenario in which British women were not safe from British men. To stand out for more, in such imaginative circumstances, risked exposing women, men, and Britain to a species of warfare that could not be contemplated.

The capitulation of suffragists on so vital an issue as the age restriction, then, resulted in part from the terms in which the debates over suffrage were framed and conducted between 1914 and 1918: at one level, M.P.'s and suffragists asserted women's right to vote as a function of wartime service, defining them, at least in part, as warriors; on another, feminists within the NUWSS carried on a heated debate about the relationship of women and feminism to war that ultimately placed their organization, and thus the question of suffrage, squarely within the camp of war. As the war had become steeped in sexual imagery, the National Union's involvement in it could be construed as participation in sex war, especially if feminists were to sink the Reform Bill by rejecting its provisions for women. The terms of the discourses about suffrage, infused with representations of war, sex, and sex war, helped to circumscribe feminists' abilities to achieve the goals of their sixty-year struggle. As we shall see in the next chapter, fears of sex war continued unabated; they were exacerbated by popular accounts of and scientific explanations for the behavior of men returning home from the war.

Chapter 5

POSTWAR DISORDER AND THE
SALVATION OF SEX

IN MAY SINCLAIR's *The Tree of Heaven*, Nicholas objected that the poet who had written "this gorgeous fight-feeling . . . is nothing but a form of sex-madness" knew little about "war, or love either"; yet he also conceded that "there's a clever chap in my battalion who thinks the same thing. He says he feels the ecstasy, or whatever it is, all right, just the same as I do; but that it's simply submerged savagery bobbing up to the top—a hidden lust for killing, and the hidden memory of having killed, he called it. He's always ashamed of it the next day." The connection between sex and war that permeated representations of the war both at home and at the front, as this passage illustrates, produced in many Britons' minds a belief in a naturalized relationship between sex and war, giving rise to misgivings about the return of soldiers following the Armistice. "With the conclusion of conflict," Leed asserts, "the notion that war had been the playing field of insubordinate libido was a crucial feature in the anxieties which surrounded the figure of the returning veteran."[1]

The hostility and anger frontsoldiers directed toward the home—symbolized and epitomized by women—seemingly got played out after the war. Hamilton described the postwar era as "an ugly epoch," when "the passion of enmity, fanned through four years, was not extinguished by the mere act of signing an armistice; it took time to burn itself out, and so long as it burned we had need to hate, and our hatred, deprived of an outward object, turned inward. . . . The war mood seemed to have become a habit with us; instead of hating by nation we hated by party and by class." Though she did not mention hatred by sex, in keeping with an almost total postwar feminist silence on sex war, she did relate an incident that occurred in 1919. "I remember asking a conductor to stop his bus for me in the Fulham Road; as he made no movement, I thought he had not heard and pulled the cord myself—whereupon the man turned and struck me." Frontsoldiers returned home in a violent frame of mind. Philip Gibbs wrote in 1920 of the veterans,

> All was not right with the spirit of the men who came back. Something was wrong. They put on civilian clothes again, looked to their mothers and wives very much like the young men who had gone to business in the peaceful days before August of '14. But they had not come back the same men. Something had

altered in them. They were subject to queer moods, queer tempers, fits of profound depression alternating with a restless desire for pleasure. Many of them were easily moved to passion when they lost control of themselves. Many were bitter in their speech, violent in opinion, frightening.[2]

In January 1919, returning soldiers rioted all over England; in June 1919, soldiers waiting to be demobilized attacked the Epsom police station and killed the station sergeant; in July, ex-servicemen protesting against having been excluded from the ceremonies that marked "Peace Day" in Luton destroyed the town hall, and one hundred casualties resulted. Rathbone's Joan, who went to work in a War Pensions Committee office after the war ended, observed that "to refuse a man his claim was a detestable task, and was often to provoke his fury. . . . All the men seemed to be nervy, and some definitely unhinged. Doubtless they would settle down in time, but their release from the military machine was not, at the moment, beneficial to them." The *Vote* reported in May 1919 that "certain disquieting features marked the demonstration of the Discharged Soldiers and Sailors last Monday afternoon." It especially noted, with deep concern, "the animus . . . displayed against the women conductors on the omnibuses as they passed the procession," and the attempt by "a party of demonstrators" to drag "a young woman off a service car in which she was driving an officer who, by the way, did nothing to assist her." In 1920, an article in *Time and Tide* entitled "Child Assault" lamented that as a result of the Great War "many people have become . . . mentally and morally unstable, and . . . in consequence crimes of a certain class are to-day alarmingly common over the entire country. Among these crimes is that of child outrage."[3]

Newspapers carried innumerable accounts of sexual attacks upon women. Gibbs reported that "the daily newspapers for many months have been filled with the record of dreadful crimes, of violence and passion. Most of them have been done by soldiers or ex-soldiers." He was struck by the "brutality of passion, a murderous instinct, which have been manifested again and again in . . . riots and street rows and solitary crimes. These last are the worst because they are not inspired by a sense of injustice, however false, or any mob passion, but by homicidal mania and secret lust. The murders of young women, the outrages upon little girls, the violent robberies that have happened since the demobilizing of the armies have appalled decent-minded people." The *Vote*, explaining "Why Carriages Reserved for Women Are Needed," reported that "a young soldier, described in court as a desperate and dangerous man, was charged with assaulting a girl, aged 16, a domestic servant, in a railway carriage. . . . he sprang at her and caught her by the throat. . . . the accused said . . . he would have 'done her in.'" The version of masculinity fashioned by these media stories of criminal acts and sexual assaults recalled and played upon the images of rapacious, lustful soldiers circulating during the war; they informed interwar fears of postwar disorder and the solutions that would be put forward to allay them.

Gibbs blamed the war for producing these violent acts against women. "Our armies," he explained,

> established an intensive culture of brutality. They were schools of slaughter. It was the duty of officers . . . to inspire blood-lust in the brains of gentle boys who instinctively disliked butcher's work. By an ingenious system of psychology [officers] played upon their nature, calling out the primitive barbarism which has been overlaid by civilized restraints, liberating the brute which has been long chained up by law and the social code of gentle life, but lurks always in the secret lairs of the human heart. It is difficult when the brute has been un-chained, for the purpose of killing Germans, to get it into the collar again with a cry of "Down, dog, down." . . . Our men, living in holes in the earth like ape-men, were taught the ancient code of the jungle law. . . . The code of the ape-man is bad for some temperaments. It is apt to become a habit of mind. It may surge up when there are no Germans present, but some old woman behind an open till, or some policeman . . . or in a street riot where fellow-citizens are for the time being "the enemy."

Gibbs blamed "the seeds of insanity in the brains of men" on the "abnormal life of war" and on women who gave them venereal disease. In this version, the war and women were enmeshed. "Sexually [the men] were starved," he argued. "For months they lived out of the sight and presence of women. But they came back into villages or towns where they were tempted by any poor slut who winked at them and infected them with illness. Men went to hospital with venereal disease in appalling numbers. Boys were ruined and poisoned for life."[4]

Whatever the explanation, contemporaries could readily believe, on the basis of immediate past experience, that aggression, destructiveness, and violence were inherent characteristics of masculinity, and that social peace and order would depend upon minimizing the provocations of men to anger. The antidote to disorder following a war that had been represented in sexual imagery and sexual metaphor would itself be depicted in sexual terms.

The perceived blurring of gender lines occasioned by war's upheaval led many in British society to see in a reestablishment of sexual difference the means to re-create a semblance of order. As Eric Leed has pointed out, "war experience is nothing if not a transgression of categories. . . . war offered numerous occasions for the shattering of distinctions that were central to orderly thought, communicable experience, and normal human relations." Britons sought to return to the "traditional" order of the prewar world, an order based on natural biological categories of which sexual differences were a familiar and readily available expression. As Holtby remarked, for many years prior to and during the war, "the position of women radically altered.

A new attitude recognised their common humanity as of greater importance than their sexual difference. . . . But that again is changing—indeed, has already changed." As early as 1916, in fact, the *Factory Times* urged that "we must get the women back into the home as soon as possible. That they ever left is one of the evil results of the war."[5]

After the partial enfranchisement of women in 1918, public anxiety about women's place in society centered on work. Removing women from their wartime jobs to eliminate competition with men for work was regarded as one way to assure, as Ray Strachey put it, "that everything could be as it had been before." Where once women had received accolades of the highest order for their service to the country during wartime, by 1918 they were being vilified and excoriated for their efforts. Irene Clephane, writing in 1935, believed that press attitudes toward women workers began to change between 1918 and 1919. "From being the saviours of the nation," she wrote, "women in employment were degraded in the public press to the position of ruthless self-seekers depriving men and their dependents of a livelihood. The woman who had no one to support her, the woman who herself had dependents, the woman who had no necessity, save that of the urge to per-sonal independence and integrity, to earn: all of them became, in many peo-ple's minds, objects of opprobrium." Nina Boyle noticed the shift in attitude as early as September 1916, warning feminists who "see in the period 'after the war' a hatching-ground for ideals of brotherhood and sisterhood and democratic goodwill" that their optimism was entirely misplaced. Writing at a time when the need for a franchise bill including women was being recog-nized, she observed, "Even the slavish, adulating Press, appearing to realise that its fulsome panegyrics may add strength to the women's claims, are beginning to play on another string. *The Daily Mail*, an old offender, has turned its attention from women workers to women shirkers; and we may now expect the streams of praise to be converted into torrents of abuse."[6]

Philip Gibbs returned from the front and reported that ex-soldiers could not find employment because "the girls were clinging to their jobs, would not let go of the pocket-money which they had spent on frocks." E. Austin Hinton, in a letter to the *Saturday Review* in December 1918, attempted to trivialize and invalidate women's war efforts, insisting that the woman who took up "what she calls 'war work'" did so "for the sake of a love or flirtation and associated giddiness, which the freer and more licensed life has made it possible to indulge." A correspondent for the Leeds *Mercury* wrote in April 1919 of his "unfeigned pleasure" that women bus conductors and under-ground drivers would no longer be holding their positions. "Their record of duty well done," he complained, "is seriously blemished by their habitual and aggressive incivility, and a callous disregard for the welfare of passen-gers. Their shrewish behaviour will remain one of the unpleasant memories of the war's vicissitudes." Given the nature of the war's real vicissitudes, this is a profound statement of hostility. As W. Keith pointed out in the *Daily News* in March 1921, in an article titled "Dislike of Women," "the attitude of the public towards women is more full of contempt and bitterness than has been the case since the suffragette outbreaks." The pressures on women to leave their jobs and return to the domestic sphere were intense—and successful. By 1921, fewer women were "gainfully employed," according to the census of that year, than in 1911. In 1927, Oxford University limited the number of students permitted to attend the women's colleges.[7]

For many Britons, feminist insistence on equality and women's right to participate in the public realm of work and politics threatened a return to normalcy and raised the specter of continued conflict after the Armistice. This fear of continued conflict derived from the unprecedented nature of the war itself. Fussell has reminded us that during the war "one did not have to be a lunatic or a particularly despondent visionary to conceive quite seriously that the war would literally never end and would become the permanent condition of mankind." Robert Graves and Edmund Blunden, for instance, were convinced that the war would be endless. Mary Borden, nursing at the front, was overwhelmed by such a vision. "There is War on the earth," she wrote, "nothing but War, War let loose in the world, War—nothing left in the whole world but War—War without end, amen." Cicely Hamilton's faith in progress and in the future was destroyed by the air raids she endured while stationed in Abbeville during the German spring offensive of 1918. "On one of these nights," she recalled later,

> the worst that I remember, the invaders scored a hit on an ammunition dump in the Somme valley; and it was while I lay and watched the glare in the sky that the world suddenly changed for me. Up till then the war, hideous as it was, had been something that would end, as other wars had ended, leaving the world to lick its wounds and heal; now there flashed into my mind the meaning and truth of the Eden legend. . . . on that red, evil night on the hillside it came without warning, seemed to crash into my brain. . . . I know I was terrified enough that night, as plane after plane came over from the east; but above and beyond my personal fear was fear and horror of the future.[8]

Many contemporaries remarked upon the persistence of the war long after the Armistice had ended actual combat. Ray Strachey, who stayed at home during the hostilities, wrote to her mother of the prospect of the war's end. "You would be astonished, Mother, and probably incredulous, to find how little excited anyone is about peace. . . . we had all settled down to war as a permanent condition and so don't believe it. And perhaps we are a little afraid of peace," she added, cognizant, perhaps, of the kinds of difficulties the postwar period would hold for Britain.[9]

With the cessation of hostilities in November 1918, frontsoldiers continued to experience the anxieties of the trenches in nightmares: Sassoon dreamed that the war was still going on "every two or three months" at least through 1936. Carl Jung's dreaming about the war in 1926 led him to conclude that "the war, which in the outer world had taken place some years before, was not yet over, but was continuing to be fought within the psyche." Irene Rathbone's Joan discovered that "the war—officially over—still lingered on. The results of it were all around, distressingly, insistent; and the men who for so many years had been heroes were now 'returned soldiers,' a problem to their country." In Christabel Pankhurst's *Pressing Problems of the Closing Age*, published in 1924, the war is everywhere, exciting her prophecies of the world's end. In her view, people were asking or secretly thinking, "When will be the next war?" "For we all know, even if we do not admit it, that more war is coming. Indeed, we even wonder why it has not broken out before now."[10]

Leed has argued that "it is not an overstatement to say that many combatants came to understand everything in the terms of their war experience." Dichotomization, polarization, and conflict became the models through which political, social, literary, artistic, sexual, and psychological experience was lived. The notion of "the enemy," Fussell has contended, provides "the most indispensable concept underlying the energies of modern writing." Indeed, as Hynes has shown, the pivotal role of the enemy was not limited to writing; it pervaded British culture. The "wars after the war," as he has called the wartime-created divisions between men and women, older and younger generations, and pro- and antiwar groups, "gave English culture of the Twenties its characteristic tone. . . . The war was a presence in imaginations, even those that had not experienced the war directly; and it was a presence in society, dividing, separating, imposing oppositions." As Modris Eksteins has claimed, the years of the 1920s were indelibly marked by the war, "a motif that recurs again and again. . . . a motif that no one discussed at length at the time, but that runs through the entire cultural landscape like a black thread." "The imagery and vocabulary of war permeated all forms of culture in the twenties," Eksteins has argued; because the British public did not wish to be reminded of the war so recently fought, the war "took care to camouflage itself."[11] One of the cloaks it wore was that of sexual antagonism, of warlike relations between men and women. The linking of war and eroticism in wartime and postwar writings made it possible to represent sexual relations between men and women as war, just as war had been represented as a form of sexual relations between men and women.

Sexual conflict provided one of the few adequate means by which the political, economic, and social upheaval occasioned by the Great War could ultimately be represented.[12] The introduction and popularization of Freudian theory in the early 1920s offered both language and explanation for what had gripped the nation between 1914 and 1918; indeed, Freud himself was persuaded by the war's unprecedented violence to define the tendency toward aggression as an instinct rivaling the libido. In "Reflections upon War and Death," written in 1915, Freud noted "the brutality in behaviour shown by individuals, whom, as partakers in the highest form of human civilization, one would not have credited with such a thing." What contemporaries believed to be "evil tendencies" capable of being eradicated from society were, he explained, "elemental instincts . . . common to all men" that "aim[ed] at the satisfaction of certain primal needs." Individuals who behaved well in society, following the dictates of civilized culture, did not necessarily do so according to the "dictates of their own natures." Rather, in submitting to society's ideals and standards, they were vigorously suppressing their primitive instincts. The transformation of instincts demanded by culture was not necessarily permanent and could be "undone by the experiences of life. Undoubtedly," Freud warned, "the influences of war are among the forces that can bring about such regression."[13] In *Beyond the Pleasure Principle* and *The Ego and the Id*, published respectively in 1920 and 1923, Freud's preoccupation with war and aggression culminated in his formulating the notion of a death instinct that did battle with its opposite drive, Eros; he thus abandoned his earlier dichotomous pairing of drives— that of libido and ego. Aggression, Peter Gay observes, "to which Freud had earlier devoted a measure of attention that he now deemed inadequate, became from 1920 on the equal adversary of Eros."[14]

The pairing of Eros and Thanatos, of life and death, intimately linked sex and aggression. "The aim of all life is death," Freud declared, but the rush toward death is countered by the sexual instincts, "the true life instincts." When the drive toward death nears its completion, the drive toward life jerks it back and forces it to start anew. The opposition between the two resembled that between love (or affection) and hate (or aggression), what Freud had earlier called "ambivalence of feeling." "If only we could succeed in relating these two polarities to each other and in deriving one from the other!" Freud exclaimed, and he proceeded to do so through the example of sadism. "From the very first," he explained,

> we recognized the presence of a sadistic component in the sexual instinct. . . . But how can the sadistic instinct, whose aim it is to injure the object, be derived from Eros, the preserver of life? Is it not plausible to suppose that this sadism is in fact a death instinct, which, under the influence of the narcissistic libido, has been forced away from the ego and has consequently only emerged in relation to the [love] object? It now enters the service of the sexual function.[15]

By 1923, with the publication of *The Ego and the Id*, Freud had come to believe that the two classes of instinct, the sexual instinct, or Eros, and the death instinct, represented by sadism, were "fused, blended, and alloyed with each other," ineradicably intertwined. "The sadistic component of the sexual instinct would be a classical example of a serviceable instinctual fusion" of the life and death instincts, he argued. "The instinct of destruction is habitually brought into the service of Eros." Moreover, "some degree of communication exists between the component instincts," so that "an instinct deriving from one particular erotogenic source can make over its intensity to reinforce another component instinct originating from another source," and "the satisfaction of one instinct can take the place of the satisfaction of another." In fact, Freud claimed, it does not much matter which instinct is satisfied, "so long as it takes place somehow,"[16] laying the groundwork for sexologists who would see in the satisfaction of the sexual impulse the solution to threats of war.

Freud extended his theories about the interrelatedness of sexual instincts and death drives, widening the focus from individuals to whole societies in *Civilization and Its Discontents*, published in 1930. Men, he insisted, drawing upon "the horrors of the recent World War" in support of his claim, "are not gentle creatures who want to be loved." Rather they are characterized by aggressiveness and cruelty, capable of, indeed only prevented by civilization from regularly demonstrating, extremes in rapine and murder. Drawing upon thoughts first expressed in "Reflections upon War and Death," Freud announced that "civilization is built up upon a renunciation of instinct. . . . it presupposes precisely the non-satisfaction (by suppression, repression, or some other means?) of powerful instincts." Depriving an instinct of satisfaction was both difficult and dangerous; if such deprivation is not alleviated by the satisfaction of another instinct, "one can be certain that serious disorders will ensue." The threat of serious disorders in Europe, in 1930, was not without foundation, either in domestic arenas or on the international stage. Indeed, Freud ended his book with an appeal of sorts for world peace. "The fateful question for the human species," he wrote,

> seems to me to be whether and to what extent their cultural development will succeed in mastering the disturbance of their communal life by the human instinct of aggression and self-destruction. It may be that in this respect precisely the present time deserves a special interest. Men have gained control over the forces of nature to such an extent that with their help they would have no difficulty in exterminating one another to the last man. . . . And now it is to be expected that the other of the two "Heavenly Powers," eternal Eros, will make an effort to assert himself in the struggle with his equally immortal adversary.[17]

A comprehensive collection of Freud's theories of psychoanalysis appeared in translation in Britain in 1922. Derived from lectures Freud delivered at the University of Vienna between 1915 and 1917, the volume offered a complete introduction to the fundamental tenets of psychoanalysis—the psychopathology of everyday life, dreams, and neuroses—to interested readers and students. In a lecture on the censorship of dreams, Freud concluded by inquiring of the audience, "Do you not know how uncontrolled and unreliable the average human being is in all that concerns sexual life? Or are you ignorant of the fact that all the excesses and aberrations of which we dream at night are crimes actually committed every day by men who are wide awake?" Leaping from the behavior of individuals to that of whole groups, Freud directed his students to the example of "the great war still devastating Europe: think of the colossal brutality, cruelty and mendacity which is now allowed to spread itself over the civilized world. Do you really believe that a handful of unprincipled place-hunters and corrupters of men would have succeeded in letting loose all this latent evil, if the millions of their followers were not also guilty?"[18]

As the *Times*'s reviewer of the volume pointed out, psychoanalysis had become in England a "rage," "feverishly discussed by people who had but a slight knowledge of its meaning." Clearly, Freud's ideas resonated in the minds and souls of the British, who had before the war not paid much, if any, attention to them. His theories about aggression most likely enabled many to understand and give expression to the experiences of the war years. What Elias Canetti remarked about Freud's reception in Vienna in the 1920s must hold true for London as well: "What one had witnessed of murderous cruelty was unforgotten. Many who had participated actively had now returned. They knew well of what—on orders—they had been capable, and greedily caught hold of all the explanations for the predisposition to murder that psychoanalysis offered them." By the time of Freud's popularization in Britain, the English could readily accept the notion that impulses toward sex and aggression were intertwined; indeed, many Britons held as "a deeply rooted cultural assumption" the view of war as a release from long-suppressed libidinal energies. Caroline Playne wrote in 1931, in a book investigating "the psychological states which, all must agree, were at the back of the great upheaval" of 1914–1918, that "the madness of the war years must be conceived as the madness of men" driven by "the primitive lust of getting the best of those you hate." She spoke of "a bout of overflowing national lust," a phenomenon that was clearly sexual in nature, as indicated by her allusions to "the tidal floods of life [that] were inundating, fertilizing the dry lands of human civilization," to "the engines of life" and "the flood of passion."[19]

Magnus Hirschfeld, a sexologist and sex reformer, articulated these attitudes in *The Sexual History of the World War*. The war, he wrote, "was . . . a sudden unchaining of atavistic impulses which for five years stormed through the world unimpeded and constituted the terrible forms in which the historical necessity of a moral transformation came to expression." While repressed eroticism did not bring about the war, he noted, "war is an opportunity for throwing off, for a while, all the irksome repressions which culture imposes and for satisfying temporarily all the repressed desires." British sexologists H. C. Fischer and E. X. Dubois, authors of *Sexual Life during the World War*, concurred. "The subconscious motives of war," they argued, "include the sexual factor. There is a close connection between war and all that is comprised in the concept of eroticism, though it is not claimed that eroticism has a direct, deliberative causative effect. . . . war, no matter with what ostensible object it is waged, is to some extent similar to the contest normally fought during the mating season by the males of certain species of animals for the possession of the female." "The lust for killing goes parallel with sexual lust," they wrote, "for love and death—creation and destruction—are psychologically inseparable allies."

> According to many modern psychologists, a subconscious desire to bring about just such a change from the normal sexual life [of repressed sexual urges], is a contributory factor in causing war. . . . this theory . . . provides the only acceptable explanation of war. Sexual lust and blood lust are compelling primeval instincts—the animal in man—and it is hardly possible to conceive that whole nations throw themselves into an orgy of murder and indescribable horror without some such psychological urge. Economic interest, greed, even so-called idealism, are inadequate, in themselves, as an explanation of such a cataclysm as the Great War.[20]

Hirschfeld, extrapolating from Freud's *Beyond the Pleasure Principle* and *The Ego and the Id*, argued that "in the depths of the human soul, eroticism, cruelty and the mad desire to destroy, are all intimately connected." Sadistic impulses that had been repressed in peacetime found legitimate expression in the atrocities perpetrated in the war. "Without the sexual background," Hirschfeld asserted, "the numerous, meaningless acts of cruelty of the World War are incomprehensible." Winifred Holtby quite explicitly remarked on war's erotic effects, jotting down notes for a lecture on "The Psychology of Peace and War" in 1935. "Sixteen when the War started. The first thing it made me do was to fall in love." She attributed this in part to "the erotic attraction of death" and argued that "the erotic impulse" ranked high among the war-making instincts.[21]

The intimate cultural associations of sex and war made it possible for sexologists to theorize and present to the public the notion that sexual relations between men and women resembled war, and to exploit this reification of warlike erotic "instincts" to establish the power and legitimacy of their profession. Fischer and Dubois, calling upon the theories of Wilhelm Steckel, a Freudian analyst, declared that "woman is the enemy of man, whom she constantly combats by every means at her disposal. . . . This war between the sexes is intensified by international war. Woman then makes every effort to exploit the situation into which such an event places her to score over the opposite sex. The great upheaval involved in war is used by her as a sort of springboard. That is the explanation of the enormous progress of feminine emancipation during the last war." Hirschfeld saw it a bit differently, though he, too, relied on Stekel's formulations of a "war between the sexes" in asserting that "between men and women there rages an eternal war in which there is only an armistice but no lasting peace. The war of the sexes abated during the World War apparently only because a common foe forced both sexes to combine against him." This development would have a significant impact upon theorists of male-female relations, particularly physicians, psychiatrists and sexologists, and feminists; these last embraced the conservative images of femininity and masculinity that arose as British society sought to resolve the anxieties and political turmoil caused by the Great War by establishing harmonious marital relationships.[22] Britons, including feminists, looked to create peace and order in the public sphere of social, economic, and political relations by imposing peace and order on the private sphere of sexual relations.

The inscription of large societal anxieties and conflicts onto marital relationships operated on at least two levels. On the one hand, gender, sexuality, and the relationship between the sexes served as metaphors through which issues of power might be resolved by referring to notions of sexual difference. On the other hand, sexuality and war were understood by the culture—consciously or unconsciously—to be inextricably intertwined. Thus, the resolution of conflict through mutual, pleasurable sexual experiences within marriage was regarded by many sexologists and sex reformers as a means of reducing the threat of war by removing the sexual repressions and tensions that, they sometimes implied, helped to bring it about. "There are certain inter-relationships between the negative forces of destruction and the positive might of Eros," Hirschfeld asserted.

> For every repression and violation of Eros can, under certain conditions, produce an emergence of the destructive sadistic powers. The sexual misery of peace time, the hypocritical morality of the ruling social classes, pervert the natural impulses and finally bursts [sic] out in aberrant reactions. The liberation of violated impulses through the war, the tremendous expression which they had never been able to achieve in peace time, produced a tremendous intoxication which carried men with it beyond all reason. The primeval combat of the powers of life and death, which is forever being fought anew, came to an armistice.

"How will the primeval enmity of both these powers end up?" Hirschfeld asked. Professing his faith in the perseverance of the positive might of Eros, he replied by paraphrasing Freud in *Civilization and Its Discontents*: "We must hope that the second of the two divine forces, namely, the eternal Eros will make a great effort to maintain itself in the struggle with its equally immortal enemy."[23]

Also drawing upon Freud, Fischer and Dubois came to the same conclusion. War, they claimed, "constituted a respite from rigid moral laws that were contrary to fundamental human nature." It provided "an outlet for latent erotic needs" driven underground by society's imposition of "many sexual constraints," against which "the caveman within" civilized men revolted. "The primitive combative and sexual instincts are undoubtedly there, and have led the world into many irreparable disasters," Fischer and Dubois argued. "These instincts can neither be completely repressed, nor eliminated. But they must be given another outlet than war. Judicious and progressive sexual reform, tending to liberate the world from the false morality that ultimately leads to the degradation of war, would be an obvious first step in this direction."[24]

The discourses on sexuality that predominated in the postwar years appropriated the language and imagery of war as psychoanalysts, sexologists and sex reformers sought in the study of sexuality the means for the maintenance and salvation of civilization itself. As Havelock Ellis, the most influential sexologist in interwar Britain, wrote in *The Psychology of Sex*, his popular textbook, sex "is not merely the channel along which the race is maintained and built up, it is the foundation on which all dreams of the future world must be erected." For Ellis, as for all "scientists of sex" in the 1920s and 1930s, sexual activity was firmly located within marriage, and its chief and central aim, after the carnage wrought by the Great War, was procreation. (G. K. Chesterton, as quoted by Dora Russell, wrote that "sex without gestation and parturition is like blowing the trumpets and waving the flags without doing any of the fighting.") A more insistent ideology of motherhood[25] demanded that women leave their wartime jobs, give up their independence, and return to home and family, where their primary occupation—their obligation, in fact—would be the bearing and rearing of children.

If the sexual disorder of war was to be followed by peace, the metaphor required sexual peace, a model of marital accord achieved through mutual sexual enjoyment. Discourses about female sexuality, which before the war had emphasized women's lack of sexual impulse, and even distaste for sexual intercourse, underwent modification to accommodate the political, social, and economic requirements of the postwar period. The new accent on motherhood was accompanied by a growing emphasis on the importance of sexual activity, sexual pleasure, sexual compatibility between husband and wife. Utilizing the theories of Steckel, sexologists such as Theodore Van de Velde, Hirschfeld, and Fischer and Dubois emphasized what they believed to be the "primary, genuine sexual hostility" between men and women. While these feelings of hostility were normal, and in fact constituted the basis upon which sexual attraction could be built, they nevertheless posed danger to the success of marriages and society as a whole, and were caused by the "repression of the sexual impulse," Van de Velde claimed. "The weaker the sexual impulse, the stronger the undeniably antagonistic effect of the opposite sex."

"As long as [the sex glands] function to a negligible extent, or not at all, the instinctive sexual antagonism predominates, but, if their effect has become strong enough, then sexual attraction is predominant, to such a degree, indeed, that the previous all-powerful feelings of antagonism recede and seem to disappear entirely from the scene." Women denied sexual pleasure in marriage might easily transform their hunt for love into a hatred for the entire male sex, Van de Velde warned. Men, because they could masturbate to relieve sexual tension, ran far less risk of "thus turning against the whole female sex." Sexologists acknowledged that sexual pleasure in marriage might not be attainable for many women, a possibility that threatened the marital and social order. In cases such as these, wrote Van de Velde, "it is best, for the comparative success of the marriage, that the sexually unsatisfied woman should have children, and succeed in converting her sexual feelings into a stronger mother love (hence to sublimate them)."[26]

As marriage and marital sex bore the brunt of restoring social harmony in postwar Britain, sex manuals—how-to guides to conjugal fulfillment—became best-sellers. Marie Stopes's *Married Love*, published in 1918, sold more than 2,000 copies in the first two weeks, and 400,000 by 1923. Van de Velde's *Ideal Marriage: Its Physiology and Technique* (1926) went through forty-three printings. Such books as Isabel Emslie Hutton's *The Sex Technique in Marriage* (1932), Helena Wright's *The Sex Factor in Marriage*, and Van de Velde's *Sex Hostility in Marriage* (1931) attest to the broadly perceived need to establish sexual peace through sexual pleasure. Of Stopes's *Married Love*, Mary Stocks wrote that "this book with its spectacular sales brought more happiness to more people than any other publication of our time." As Richard Soloway has observed, Stopes's vision of enlightened matrimony, in which "the new woman could achieve all of her goals and fulfil her biological obligations . . . appealed to a new generation of women after the war and offered a compromise to sensitive, intelligent men worried about the reconciliation of feminist independence with the traditional maintenance of the family and the race." Van de Velde's *Sex Hostility in Marriage* sought to "help those numerous people, whose happiness is menaced by the spectre of hostility in marriage to combat this danger. . . . Few married couples are aware of the evil and dangerous enemy that stands so near to them." The imagery of war—"combat," Van de Velde's "attacks" on the "enemy"—testifies to the heavy load sex was being asked to carry. Domestic harmony, and thus social peace, appeared to Britons to depend upon the establishment of a managed and controlled sexuality whereby warriors could be rendered peaceable and wherein women could find, acknowledge, and express their sexuality within a framework of "scientific" approbation.[27]

With the popularization of Freudian theory in the 1920s, separate sphere ideology was further psychologized. In his earliest writings on sexuality, and in his thinking right up through the war, Freud viewed sexual development in boys and girls as parallel processes; he believed that men and women were quite similar to one another in their sexual beings. In the 1920s, however, his thinking about female sexuality changed. In "The Dissolution of the Oedipus Complex" (1924), "Some Psychical Consequences of the Anatomical Distinction between the Sexes" (1925), and "Female Sexuality" (1931), Freud formulated his ideas about the natural psychological, ethical, and mental differences between men and women produced by their fundamentally different sexual organizations.

Psychoanalysis filtered into Britain through the lens of biology. Whereas Freud had initially posited a psychological bisexuality in males and females, and asserted that masculinity, femininity, and sexuality were cultural phenomena that required explanation, British psychiatrists and sexologists put forward theories of sexuality and sexual difference that stemmed from biology. Femininity, argued Ernest Jones, "develops progressively from the promptings of an instinctual constitution." While undermining belief in the passionlessness of the female—a development that had considerable appeal for many feminists and contributed to the conceptual dilemma within which they trapped themselves—Freud's British followers thus gave credence to the belief that biological factors determined the differences between masculinity and femininity, and between male and female sexuality. "Anatomy is destiny," Freud declared in 1924 in "The Dissolution of the Oedipus Complex," in contradiction to his earlier beliefs; and while Peter Gay argues that Freud's abrupt transformation in thought derived not from any external factor but from the logic of internal theoretical difficulties, it is hard to discount the blurring of sex and gender identities occasioned by the experience of the war, and the need to reassert sexual difference as a means of reestablishing order in society. In "Some Psychical Consequences of the Anatomical Distinction between the Sexes" Freud argued that female personality development centered upon her discovery in early childhood that she lacked a penis; penis envy created in the female child a lifelong dissatisfaction with her identity as a woman. Her discomfiture could only be overcome through the substitution of a child for the penis. Moreover, the absence of a penis meant that the threat of castration had no impact on girls, resulting in their failure to fully develop a superego. Consequently, argued Freud, women demonstrated little sense of justice; they were less capable of appreciating "the great necessities of life" and were likely, more often than men, to be influenced by their emotions in making judgments. Such proofs of inferiority, Freud concluded, cannot be overlooked, despite "the denials of feminists, who are anxious to force us to regard the two sexes as completely equal in position and worth."[28]

Happiness and health for women, in other words, depended upon motherhood. *The Encyclopaedia of Sexual Knowledge*, under the general editorship of Norman Haire, a prominent British sex reformer, declared that "the physiological need of childbirth" in a woman stemmed from "the obvious fact" that "her organism is essentially fitted for maternity." "The organic need of children, which is latent in every woman, is so imperious that prolonged enforced sterility drives her body to revolt, and this revolt may manifest itself in a number of disorders and growths." This physiological need for children, argued the physicians and sexologists who contributed to the huge tome, was matched by a psychological one to fill the "void in a woman's life." Lacking the activities and opportunities of her husband, and "the care of children being the occupation most suited to her temperament, she will seek an outlet for her energy in that direction. Thus, in order to preserve her physiological and psychological equilibrium, a woman, to whatever social stratum she may belong, needs children."[29]

Those women who refused motherhood, who continued in their work or study, or who sought equality between men and women, brought down upon their heads the wrath of many psychiatrists and sexologists, who found in their presumptions a sexual pathology. "After all is said and done," declared Van de Velde, "the biological difference between masculine and feminine cannot be explained away; neither can the physical and mental contrasts between man and woman proceeding from this." Characterized by its capacity for emotion, the feminine psyche, he declared, rendered women incapable of objectivity, of weighing the sides of an argument or of distinguishing the right and wrong of things. "Just as her body is fashioned for maternity, so the mental quality dominating all others in the woman is motherhood." Permanent equality in marriage, Van de Velde asserted, was abnormal because "sexuality is always present in man and woman, and upper and lower place is inseparably allied with it." Hostility in marriage, which was now construed as partially responsible for the disorders of contemporary life, was caused by women who sought to dominate their husbands or who struggled with them for power, he cautioned. Karl Abraham, a close colleague of Freud, described feminists as women who "are unable to carry out a full psychical adaptation to the female sexual role," women who, quite mistakenly, "consider that the sex of a person has nothing to do with his or her capacities, especially in the mental field." Even Havelock Ellis, friend to Olive Schreiner and advocate of women's rights in the prewar period, had come around to this view: the idea that women might have "the same education as men, the same occupations as men, even the same sports" constituted "the source of all that was unbalanced . . . in the old women's movement."[30]

Diagnoses of a "female castration complex" or of frigidity were applied to women who ventured out of their assigned domestic, sexual sphere. Using terminology and imagery evocative of war, sexologist Walter Gallichan wrote in *The Poison of Prudery*, "These degenerate women are a menace to civilisation. They provoke sex misunderstanding and antagonism; they wreck conjugal happiness." Wilhelm Stekel agreed, insisting that "we shall never understand the problem of the frigid woman unless we take into consideration the fact that the two sexes are engaged in a lasting conflict. . . . dyspareunia [frigidity] is a social problem; it is one of woman's weapons in the universal struggle of the sexes." K. A. Weith Knudsen, a Norwegian professor of jurisprudence and economics who had a large British audience, argued that this "sexual anesthesia" "so prevalent among civilised women" "actually reinforces the threats to our civilisation, which in a higher degree than in any former culture is based on the assumption of mutual understanding and co-operation between the sexes." Gallichan blamed frigid women for producing spinsters, attributing to female agency what was, in fact, a consequence of battlefield mortality. "Many daughters of cold mothers die spinsters. They imbibe the maternal prejudices and ideas at the school age or earlier, and they grow up with a smouldering antipathy towards men." Janet Chance, a prominent sex reformer, stated that "non-orgasmic" women should be kept out of politics. "The effect of your spinster politicians, whether married or single," she wrote—conflating, significantly, frigidity and spinsterhood—"has yet to be analysed and made plain to the women they represent. I consider the lack of orgasm by women a fundamental question which deserves serious consideration."[31]

The description of feminists as abnormal, sexually maladjusted women who hated men and the equating of feminism with sex war were not, of course, new, but the context in which such charges were leveled was entirely different now. The existence of large numbers of unmarried women produced considerable anxiety. The diatribes directed at them reflected society's longing to return to the familiar, "traditional" ways of life before August 1914, a nostalgic projection that distorted memories of life in Edwardian times. Denied husbands, many of them, by the Great War, single women were visible reminders of the combat that had only recently ended. Feminism soon became linked in the public mind not merely with sex war, a somewhat familiar concept, but with armed conflict, death, and destruction. Van de Velde argued that

> the dependence of the woman on the man, and, in consequence, his supremacy in marriage and in Society, is based on biological and natural facts. . . . it is ridiculous to try . . . to reverse the parts played in life by man and woman. Society is bound to suffer from this, both men and women, and, in the end, women most of all. . . . If the primary processes of life, which are based on biological facts, are ignored, time will have its revenge. One cannot assault Nature with impunity.

Weith Knudsen warned that the feminist movement—and those who failed to take seriously the threat it posed to civilization—sought "the destruction of the white man's world." Arabella Kenealy, a lecturer at the Royal College of Physicians in Dublin, argued in a 1920 volume pointedly titled *Feminism and Sex-Extinction* that "men and women are naturally dependent upon one another in every human relation; a dispensation which engenders reciprocal trust, affection and comradeship. Feminist doctrine and practice menace these most excellent previsions and provisions of Nature by thrusting personal rivalries, economic competition and general conflict of interests between the sexes." She urged women to recognize the inevitability of sex differences and to give up their wartime jobs to men, explaining that men would use violence against women who refused to vacate their positions. Anthony M. Ludovici, in *Lysistrata, or Woman's Future and Future Woman* (1925), maintained that the "body-despising values" of feminists would lead ultimately to an "evanescence of sexual love," and thus to the disappearance of the one thing that offered "our most effective protection against the instinctive hostility of the sexes." That hostility, in the context of a civilization that promoted degeneration in men and in which women competed economically with them, threatened to "lead to riots and savage street-fighting." He envisaged a world organized according to feminist ideals and principles as one that would reproduce itself through parthenogenesis and would finally "proceed to a systematic slaughter of males."[32]

Only now, after the horrific events of the Great War, the specter of conflict between men and women could hardly be tolerated; postwar society sought above all to reestablish a sense of peace and security in an unfamiliar and insecure world. The most fundamental step in that direction appears to have been an insistence upon gender peace: a relationship of male-female complementarity in which women did not compete with men in the public sphere, did not thereby provoke men to anger—the world as envisaged by antifeminists. Prewar egalitarian feminism, with its suggestion of sex war, seems to have become associated in the public mind with a renewal of the massive conflict so recently ended.

Chapter 6

POSTWAR FEMINISM:
ESTABLISHING THE PEACE

THE DEFENSIVE POSTURE of the feminist movement during and after the Great War contrasted sharply with the confidence and assertiveness displayed in the prewar period. This defensiveness was not immediately evident, however; even as the members of the Executive Committee of the NUWSS (renamed, after suffrage had been attained, the National Union of Societies for Equal Citizenship, or NUSEC) struggled with one another to produce a program for the future, their parliamentary efforts succeeded in garnering impressive gains in women's rights. In November 1918, the Eligibility of Women Act passed unopposed, enabling women to stand for Parliament; the Bastardy Laws of 1872 were amended, increasing from five to ten shillings a week the amount a father could be made to pay to support his illegitimate child. The following year, the Sex Disqualification Removal Act opened all branches of the legal profession to women. The Matrimonial Causes Act of 1923 eliminated the double standard of divorce; in 1925, the Civil Service was forced to admit women to its competitive examinations, though provisions to pay women the salaries paid to men in the same position failed. Feminists had good reason to bask in the glow of their victories.

But these gains were offset by losses in other areas of concern to feminists, especially employment, as we have seen in chapter 5. More intangible, but no less palpable and consequential, were the losses of confidence and faith in the feminist program in the war's aftermath, when the slaughter of hundreds of thousands of men gave such pointed relief to society's emphasis on maternity, and when the enormous sacrifice of the soldiers made insistence upon a sex-based demand seem petty and uncharitable. "Feminism found itself in disgrace," declares Riley.

> There was a consensus in the inter-war years that the older generation of feminists bored and irritated younger women. For it could not, it seemed, acknowledge the depths of men's sufferings, have the grace to fall silent on "women," and instead espouse humanism. The First World War, that Calvary of men, was a sacrifice so vast that to press a nagging "sex-consciousness" was shaming. . . . The spectacle of "women" still demanding rights could be seen as cheaply partisan failures of generosity.

Ray Strachey lamented that "modern young women know amazingly little of what life was like before the war, and show a strong hostility to the word 'feminism' and all which they imagine it to connote." "Why," despaired Winifred Holtby, "in 1934, are women themselves often the first to repudiate the movements of the past hundred and fifty years, which have gained for them at least the foundations of political, economic, educational and moral equality?"[1]

The answer to her query is a complicated one. Organized feminism found itself splintered and constrained in its ability to advocate equality for women by the gendered, highly sexualized languages used to represent the Great War. By the time war ended in 1918 masculinity and femininity had been construed in multiple and contradictory ways. In the first six months of the war, the idea of women as mothers, as givers of life, emerged from rhetoric that focused on women's roles in wartime and from arguments about the relationship between feminism and pacifism. It was accompanied, indeed, it depended upon, the notion of men as warriors, life-destroyers, and—in the context of the Belgian atrocity stories—as bloodthirsty and rapacious. After 1915, as women flocked to munitions factories and auxiliary organizations, the predominant image of women as mothers gave way to that of women as warriors; in some representations, women could be seen as destroyers of men. Such a construction gained reinforcement from men who felt themselves emasculated by those at home who were responsible for prolonging the war, nearly always depicted as feminine, and, paradoxically, from women at the front who saw the broken bodies and heard the pitiable cries of men as they emerged from battle. The disparate, multiple experiences of the war boded ill for a common postwar feminist vision of, and rhetoric about, the relationship between the sexes and the reforms that would be derived therefrom.[2]

The postwar backlash against women extended beyond the question of women's employment; a *Kinder, Küche, Kirche* ideology stressing traditional femininity and motherhood permeated British culture. Holtby decried "this powerful movement to reclothe the female form in swathing trails and frills and flounces, to emphasise the difference between men and women—to recall Woman, in short, to Her True Duty—of . . . bearing of sons and recreation of the tired warrior." Cicely Hamilton observed that

> to-day, in a good many quarters of the field, the battle we thought won is going badly against us—we are retreating where once we advanced; in the eyes of certain modern statesmen women are not personalities—they are reproductive faculty personified. Which means that they are back at secondary existence, counting only as "normal" women, as wives and mothers of sons. An inevitable result of this return to the "normal" will be a revival of the old contempt for the spinster—the woman who has failed to attract a husband, and who has therefore failed in life; and an increase in the number of women who live, or endeavour to live, by their sexual attraction.[3]

Holtby's and Hamilton's critiques were not, however, typical. Feminists responded ambiguously and ambivalently to society's attempts to reestablish separate spheres. The NUSEC—the successor organization, after 1918, to the NUWSS—continued to campaign for equal suffrage and expanded its efforts to include "all such other reforms, economic, legislative, and social, as are necessary to secure a real equality of liberties, status, and opportunities between men and women."[4] The practical extension of the NUSEC's scope of activity proved difficult to determine, however, as feminists disagreed about just what reforms constituted feminist demands. Under the leadership of Eleanor Rathbone, a longtime Executive Committee member of the NUWSS, the NUSEC veered off on a "new" feminist course, seeking to appeal to a much larger and broader group of women, particularly those in the trade unions. Many "old" feminists, a good number of whom, like Vera Brittain and Winifred Holtby, had actually been too young to participate in the prewar campaign for suffrage, objected to this new direction, which reflected altered understandings of masculinity, femininity, and the relationship between the sexes.

As Maude Royden explained it in 1917, until quite recently, feminists had "emphasised above all the common humanity of women and men, and in doing so laid the foundations of all future building well and truly. But since men have always assumed that they were the norm, and alone really and wholly human, women have been obliged to seek to prove that they were not only equal to men, but so exactly like them as to be able to do their best work and develop their best capacities under like conditions." It had been unnecessary, she said, "to prove the obvious, that women were different from men; every progressive desired and *needed* to show that they were very like them." The war had demonstrated to British society that women were competent and equal to men in carrying out the functions of the state, that "women are human beings, having a human value outside sex," and in so doing had "transformed" the women's movement. "It has become necessary," Royden argued, "now to consider the points at which women differ from men, and differ not through artificial circumstances, which may be altered, but in fundamentals, and to demand the conditions which shall enable them to do their best work. . . . It is necessary to find out what is the work they can do *best*, and which are the best conditions for doing it."[5]

"New" feminism, as Eleanor Rathbone explained it, embodied the belief that women had achieved equality with men. "Women are virtually free," she announced to her NUSEC colleagues in her presidential address of 1925. Having gotten that "boring business" out of the way, feminists could now turn to the needs of women as women, not as imitators of men. "At last we can stop looking at all our problems through men's eyes and discussing them in men's phraseology. We can demand what we want for women, not because it is what men have got, but because it is what women need to fulfil the potentialities of their own natures and to adjust themselves to the circumstances of their own lives." Family endowment, also referred to as the endowment of motherhood; birth control; and, by 1927, protective legislation appeared to Rathbone and her "new" feminist supporters—many of them, like Mary Stocks, Maude Royden, Margery Corbett Ashby, Eva Hubback, and Kathleen Courtney, veterans of prewar feminist struggles—to be the best way to safeguard women's interests. Those interests, it became clear, and the justification for "new" feminist demands, centered upon the role of women in the home and "the occupation of motherhood—in which most women are at some time or another engaged, and which no man . . . is capable of performing."[6]

"New" feminist demands arose from the conviction that sexual difference rather than a common humanity characterized the "natural" relationship between men and women. Royden believed that the "best" and most absorbing work women could do was the bearing and rearing of children; she claimed that "the average woman will generally be in other walks of life not an expert but an amateur. She will be an amateur in arts and professions, an expert in human life. This . . . is . . . a permanent difference between the average woman and the average man, due to their natural qualities and vocations." As Rathbone insisted, "whatever may be the truth about the innate differences between the sexes, it is unquestionable that their differences in functions, especially the difference between the paternal and the maternal function and all its results upon social life and occupational groupings, do bring it about that each sex tends to acquire a special kind of experience and to develop its own forms of *expertise*." She believed that "this traditional difference of outlook" between men and women "corresponds to real facts of human nature and human experience."

> For example, most men are or expect to be sometime husbands and fathers, never wives and mothers. The consequences of marriage are usually, and of parenthood invariably, different for men and women. . . . It follows inevitably that questions such as birth control, family allowances, housing, smoke abatement, though they affect both sexes, do not affect both sexes equally. . . . There is probably scarcely a department of human activity in which the physiological differences between men and women and the ensuing differences in their activities have not some effect, though in many departments it may be only slight, upon the outlook of the two sexes.[7]

To "old" feminists, espousing a strictly egalitarian position, "new" feminist arguments reminded them of nothing so much as the antifeminist arguments marshaled in the nineteenth and early twentieth centuries to deny women equality with men. In 1927, the women's movement split, with "new" feminists in the NUSEC facing strong opposition from such "equalitarians" as Elizabeth Abbott, Lady Rhondda, Emmeline Pethick Lawrence, Cicely

Hamilton, Rebecca West, Winifred Holtby, and Vera Brittain, who removed themselves to newly founded organizations like the Open Door Council and the Six Point Group to continue to lobby for sex equality.

I do not mean to suggest that the "new" feminist agenda was inherently antifeminist; obviously, such demands can be quite radical. As Rathbone observed, women's needs are often very different from those of men, and a strictly egalitarian line frequently failed to address those needs. When Rose Macaulay, in a debate with Lord Ampthill, defined feminism as "attempts of women to possess privileges (political, professional, economic, or other) which have previously been denied to them on account of their sex," the *Woman's Leader* agreed that to deny women these things "is anti-feminist." But Macaulay had not gone far enough, it argued. "The mere throwing open to women of all privileges, political, professional, industrial, social, religious, in a social system designed by men for men is not going to carry us all the way to our feminist ideal. And what that ideal is, becomes clear when we define feminism as '*the demand of women that the whole structure and movement of society shall reflect in a proportionate degree their experiences, their needs, and their aspirations.'*"[8]

Moreover, by focusing on reforms that went beyond creating a level playing field for women, "new" feminism offered an essentially bourgeois organization the opportunity to expand its constituency to include the working classes, which in effect it had been ignoring since 1915, when the National Union's agreement with the Labour party to form an Election Fighting Fund was permitted to lapse after women dedicated to a cross-class movement resigned from the Executive Committee. As Margaret Ashton had written to Catherine Marshall at the time, "the middle-class woman attitude of the National Union Executive is bound to prevail." If organized feminism was to regain any semblance of a mass base, it would have to pay serious attention to the concerns of working-class women. Prominent among these concerns, as Pat Thane has demonstrated, was the "need to enhance society's valuation of woman's maternal and domestic role." Women in the Labour party, even at the height of the Depression, believed overwhelmingly in the right of married women to work; but they also sought reforms that would improve the position and status of women in the home.[9]

"New" feminism, then, had the potential to move in a profoundly transgressive direction, and to create a vastly enlarged constituency. This potential was undermined, however, by the arguments "new" feminists advanced to legitimate their demands. Not the *rights* of women, but the *needs* of women *as mothers* backed feminist appeals now. When "new" feminists made demands based upon women's traditional special needs and special functions, when they ceased to challenge the dominant discourses on sexuality, their ideology often became confused with that of antifeminists.

Family endowment is a case in point. The endowment of motherhood would provide women with economic independence, wrote Kathleen Courtney; without economic independence, which demands for equal pay could not achieve, there could be no real independence. "Few of us realise how constantly and subtly this half-conscious, but ever present sense of economic dependence of the woman upon the man corrodes her personality, checks her development, and stunts her mind, even when she is still a girl, with marriage only as yet in prospect." Mary Stocks, editor of the *Woman's Leader*, pointed out that feminists saw in the endowment of motherhood "a measure of economic advancement without which the franchise might prove an empty dignity. Only by the practical financial recognition of woman's work in the home . . . can the position of women be stabilised in the complex modern society of to-day." Eleanor Rathbone felt that endowment would alleviate married working-class women's dissatisfaction with "the conditions of their maternity; . . . their economic conditions generally; lastly . . . the subtler question of their status." While some feminists might look to equal pay as a means to eliminate women's economic dependence on men, Rathbone and her supporters believed that equal pay could not be implemented unless family allowances were first in place: men would not permit it because it would serve to undercut their pay and their ability to provide for their families. Endow the family, and men would accept equal pay for women because they would no longer be called upon to support their wives and children. Linked from the beginning with women's demands for equal pay, Alberti has argued, "Rathbone's argument for family allowances is thus staunchly feminist and based on economic arguments."[10]

Moreover, the *Woman's Leader* pointed out, the call for the endowment of motherhood "means that women, having successfully challenged the social arrangements which deny them political citizenship, are about to challenge the social arrangements which deny them economic individuality." Rathbone recognized that the existence of separate spheres, public and private, served to impoverish women and rendered them vulnerable to men's arbitrary control; providing women with economic power in the home could transform their relationship with men. As Susan Pedersen has pointed out, advocates of family endowment sought to eliminate the distinctions of public and private by making the state, rather than the male breadwinner, responsible for the maintenance of women and children within the family, and thereby "to safeguard women's sphere, while breaking its links to economic dependence and political marginality."[11] Such a policy held out truly revolutionary possibilities for women.

But in reifying the notion of women's sphere, it also had the potential to inscribe motherhood as the only possible identity for women and to render women unequal to men because "different," despite protestations to the contrary. Rathbone, for instance, betrayed her ambivalence about women's equality with men in her justifications for family endowment. Wholly ignoring the evidence of women's wartime work experience, she argued that "certain standing disadvantages" such as "her [greater] liability to sickness," her lesser physical strength, and "the overwhelming disadvantage" that she might get married and leave work meant that the woman worker, compared with the man, was not necessarily an "equally valuable or . . . equally acceptable employee." Consequently, demands for equal wages for equal work had to take into consideration "that any permanent recognised disadvantage that adheres to women workers as such should be allowed for by a *pro rata* rate reduction in their standard rates."[12] Her lack of conviction in women's abilities and their value as workers attenuated the radical possibilities of family endowment; as Banks has observed, "Rathbone herself saw family endowment primarily as a means to strengthen both the family and women's traditional place in it." Royden did too, noting, with approval, that state endowment of motherhood "would withdraw a large number of women from the labour market."[13]

As Alberti has noted, Rathbone did not claim that maternity was "a morally uplifting occupation: she described it as a craft with children as the mother's product." There can be no doubt, however, that Rathbone believed women and men to be different in their "fundamentals." Her rhetoric drew upon and furthered those discourses which insisted upon motherhood as women's primary and even exclusive function in life. Stocks defended family allowances, or the endowment of motherhood, as a feminist issue because it involved "the conscious allocation to the mothers *qua* mothers of resources adequate for the proper performance of their function." She shared Rathbone's conviction that the endowment of motherhood was a far more important demand than equal pay and equal opportunities for women, the latter arguing that "the majority of women workers are only birds of passage in their trades. Marriage and the bearing and rearing of children are their permanent occupations." When the *Woman's Leader* hailed Rathbone's book advocating the endowment of motherhood, *The Disinherited Family*, as "perhaps the most important contribution to the literature of Feminism since the publication, in 1869, of J. S. Mills' [*sic*] *Subjection of Women*," and referred to women's "peculiar and primary function of motherhood," the distance between feminism and antifeminism had been effectively traversed. As Banks has pointed out, interwar feminism "trapped women in the cult of domesticity from which earlier feminists had tried to free themselves."[14]

Women in NUSEC who identified themselves as "old" feminists, or equalitarians, rejected "new" feminism. In Elizabeth Abbott's view Rathbone and her colleagues embraced a doctrine that was not, in fact, feminist at all, that "does not accept and does not believe in many of the equality reforms defined by plain resolutions. . . . The issue is not between 'old' and 'new' feminism," she argued. "The issue is between feminism—equalitarianism—and that which is *not* feminism." Especially galling for equalitarians was the "new" feminist accusation that they were pursuing no more than a "me, too" agenda. Rather, Abbott replied,

> the demand for equality has been a demand that such rights, liberties, and opportunities as the State allows to its citizens shall not be withheld from women; a demand that wherever and whenever the State sets a value upon its citizens, it shall not set an inferior value upon women; a demand for the removal of every *arbitrary* impediment that hinders the progress, in any realm of life and work, of women. That is equality. "New Feminism" . . . calculates "withholding" and "impediment" as "protection," "inferior value" as "unavoidable difference." Feminism bluntly names them injustice.

Twice, Abbott pointed out,

> NUSEC's governing body demanded that propaganda for Equal Pay shall be carried on throughout the country. "New Feminism" rejects both definition and command, and states, and has acted upon that statement, that to demand Equal Pay for women, as defined by the Union, is not, according to its measuring line, equality. The value of the woman worker must be measured; the value of her work must be measured; above all the superior rights of a man to get better wages than a woman must be measured, and measured high. . . . The equalitarian knows that . . . it is impossible to single out any class of women and treat them as a class apart—treat them mercifully, benevolently, and *unjustly*—without in the long run lowering not only their status, but lowering the status and limiting the opportunities of all women.

"'New Feminism,'" Abbott raged, "sees in maternity an eternal disability—just as anti-suffragism saw eternal disability in other generalizations such as 'sex,' 'motherhood,' 'the home.' The equalitarian knows that it is not maternity in itself which is the disability; it is the horribly low and unequal status of woman, the everlasting conception of her as a means to an end instead of as an end in herself, that makes not only maternity but sometimes every hour of a woman's day a disability."[15]

Others, while sympathetic to the reforms themselves, objected to the implications of the "new" feminist demands. Helena Swanwick, for instance, in Alberti's words, "accepted the theoretical arguments for family endowment, but she remained wary of the idea precisely because of its association with the ideology of motherhood." She believed that "every child should be endowed, by means of allowances or free services, for all the cost of its maintenance, nurture, and training, until it can earn its own living," and conceded that many mothers would choose to be the individual charged with "personal attendance on the child," for which work she should be paid. But she objected to the notion that motherhood was a permanent occupation of even married women. Ray Strachey, while accepting the notion that "the accomplishment of motherhood gives satisfaction to a deep instinct in women, and is not only an essential achievement for the survival of the race, but also a personal and emotional satisfaction of great importance in the lives of women themselves," did not advocate for the family allowance on the grounds that it would limit women's opportunities for self-fulfillment and contribution to the state through work. Rather she asked that men "take on a greater share of the tasks of home-making" and insisted that "the intensity of the hours and competitive conditions of labour must be reduced." Such changes in social and work life would enable women to

> achieve both their kinds of usefulness, and derive both their *natural forms of satisfaction* without conflict. Then—and probably not until then—we can really discover what kinds of endeavour are naturally adapted to female minds and temperaments. Feminists have generally tended to believe that under free conditions women would prove to differ widely from each other, and to be without any special aptitudes or limitations as a sex. Whether that be true or not we do not yet know.[16]

Helen Ward advocated a third position somewhere between those of Rathbone and Abbott, urging NUSEC to maintain its adherence to "the well-tried and amazingly fruitful 'equality' principle," but recognizing that "it does well to have a varied and elastic programme, and to include in that programme various complex problems, some of them of modern development, in regard to which a straight parallelism of circumstances between men and women is not, in the nature of things, practicable." Nevertheless, Ward agreed wholeheartedly with the strict equalitarians that "certain aspects of the 'new feminism' make us uncomfortably reminiscent of the Anti-Suffrage Society in all its glory." Lady Dorothy Balfour of Burleigh urged that a hard-and-fast reliance upon the "new" feminist agenda, ignoring the equalitarian demands of the past sixty years, could produce a situation wherein "we may find ourselves building up new barriers more difficult of destruction than even those existing to-day."[17] She, like Ward, feared that the National Union might founder on the rock of "new" feminism.

They were right. The issue over which the NUSEC split in March 1927 was that of protective legislation, which prewar feminists had adamantly and consistently opposed as being discriminatory against women. At the annual council meeting, the Executive Committee of the National Union reaffirmed its commitment to the principle that "legislation for the protection of workers should be based, not upon sex, but upon the nature of the occupation." Rathbone then introduced an amendment that charged the Executive Committee with considering a number of other factors before deciding the stance it would take on the issue, including "whether the workers affected desire the regulation and are promoting it through their own organizations," and "whether the policy of securing equality through extension [of the regulation to men] or through opposition [to the regulation] is the more likely to meet with a rapid and permanent success." After intense debate, the amendment carried by a vote of 81 to 80. The council also voted by a large majority to reclassify as primary, rather than secondary, organizational objectives support for family allowances, for freedom to obtain birth control information from Welfare Centres, and for the League of Nations. In response, eleven members of the Executive Committee, including the honorary secretary and honorary treasurer, and Helen Fraser and Chrystal Macmillan, resigned, explaining that the amendment weakened and compromised the demand for equal opportunity for men and women. "To acquiesce in this change of fundamental principles would have been a betrayal of the women's movement," argued the eleven, "for which we have been working, some of us for more than thirty years."[18]

Rathbone and her followers justified protective legislation on a number of grounds. Solidarity with the labor organizations in support of protective legislation held out the promise of enlarging and consolidating NUSEC's base of support by attracting working-class women to it. Feminists could not afford, Rathbone argued, "to brush aside the views of the women concerned" and simply refuse to entertain legislation that differentiated the worker on the basis of sex "if the facts show that this might mean withholding legislation needed to protect life or health which is not yet possible to obtain for both sexes." Trade union women and their leadership might be wrong in seeking such protection for women, but "the usual principle of collective representation of interests must be respected." Moreover, "new" feminism, Rathbone explained, "refuses to ignore the possibility of real differences of need, as for example those which turn on the function of maternity. They refuse to go so far as those who, because men have no babies in the sense that women have them, would reject every provision which applies exclusively to the pre- or post-confinement period."[19]

"Old" feminists within the NUSEC and the WFL, and such equal rights organizations as the Open Door Council and the Six Point Group protested vociferously against protective legislation. The *Vote* countered the argument that protective legislation would provide better working conditions for both women and men, claiming that "we yield to no one in our demand for the best possible conditions in industry for both men and women; but we believe that the best way to secure an improvement is for men and women to work together for it, on equal terms." *Time and Tide* maintained that the only possibility of safeguarding the health and well-being of all workers lay in "getting rid of this old and out-of-date classification of men on one side, and women and children on the other, and . . . substituting a classification of men and women on one side, children and young persons on the other, and then seeking equality of opportunity and service." Lady Rhondda insisted that "it will never be possible to persuade public opinion that women are independent, fully responsible human beings and complete citizens, so long as the law protects them specially in ways in which it does not protect men. . . . these laws, though they apply to wage-earning women only[,] affect public opinion in respect to all women." Cicely Hamilton argued that protective legislation treated women "from youth to age as if they were permanently pregnant." Winifred Holtby observed that it "perpetuates the notion that [women] are not quite persons; that they are not able to look after themselves; to secure their own interests, to judge whether they are fit or unfit to continue employment after marriage, to enter certain trades, or to assume equal responsibility with men in the state. It fosters the popular fallacy that women are the weaker sex, physically and mentally." Both Holtby and Vera Brittain, along with most members of the Six Point Group and the Open Door Council, accepted family allowances and birth control as vital demands. They parted company with "new" feminists, however, over the underlying insistence that the chief occupation of all women was motherhood. Recognizing that "respect for maternity is naturally not in itself a bad thing for women," and that "English society to-day suffers from lack of respect for maternity," they were nevertheless leery, in Brittain's words, of "the tendency of fertility-worship to degenerate into the belief that women have no social value apart from their reproductive functions—a belief which immediately removes them from the category of human being." Holtby condemned "the emphasis laid on the exclusively feminine functions of wifehood and motherhood. Throughout history, whenever society has tried to curtail the opportunities, interests and powers of women, it has done so in the sacred names of marriage and maternity. . . . In the importance of sex too often has lain the unimportance of the citizen, the worker and the human being." "We need to plan our civilization so that our institutions leave room for individual difference," she argued.

> The real object behind our demand is not to reduce all men and women to the same dull pattern. It is rather to release their richness of variety. We still are greatly ignorant of our own natures. . . . We are content to make vast generalisations which quite often fit the facts well enough to be tolerable, but which—also quite often—inflict indescribable because indefinable suffering on those individuals who cannot without pain conform to our rough-and-ready attempt to make all men good and happy.[20]

Old feminists rejected an emphasis on sex—what we would call gender—in favor of one on humanity. Lady Rhondda founded *Time and Tide* in 1920 because she felt "the lack of a paper which shall treat men and women as equally part of the great human family, working side by side ultimately for the same great objects by ways equally valuable, equally interesting; a paper which is in fact concerned neither specially with men nor specially with women, but with human beings." "The New Feminism emphasises the importance of the 'women's point of view,'" objected Holtby in 1926, "the Old Feminism believes in the primary importance of the human being." The vision of society offered by "old" feminism, she declared, was one "in which men and women work together for the good of all mankind; a society in which there is no respect of persons, either male or female, but a supreme regard for the importance of the human being."[21] "Feminism still lives in England today because . . . of the incomplete recognition of women as human beings. . . . women . . . are frequently regarded as a class apart, vaguely sub-human and not quite entitled to the same opportunities as men in education and in the professions," explained a Six Point Group pamphlet in 1927. According to Vera Brittain, the feminist plea was "Recognize our full humanity, and we will trouble you no more." *Time and Tide* condemned the policy decided upon at the Headmasters' Conference in 1927 that it was neither necessary nor desirable for boys and girls to be examined by the same instrument, declaring that "there can be nothing more dangerous to the whole structure of society than this attempt of the reactionaries to train women from their earliest years for a subordinate position and to divide the community into two groups: human beings—and females."[22]

As Riley has pointed out, this emphasis on humanity tended to submerge the categorical "women" on whose behalf feminist reforms were sought in a larger humanity, with the effect of giving short shrift to the needs of significant numbers of women. Holtby admitted that "I am a feminist, and an Old Feminist, because I dislike everything that feminism implies. I desire an end to the whole business, the demands for equality, the suggestions of sex warfare, the very name of feminist." Indeed, *Time and Tide* by the 1930s had so lost its feminist perspective that it could run a regular weekly feature under the heading "Men and Books," to which such writers as Cicely Hamilton and Elizabeth Robins contributed.[23]

The insistence upon maternity as virtually the only conceivable occupation for the overwhelming majority of women drew upon the current psychoanalytic and sexological literature on sexual difference.[24] As Rathbone put it, "there is scarcely a department of human activity in which the physiological differences between men and women and the ensuing differences in their activities have not some effect, though in many departments it may be only slight, upon the outlook of the two sexes." This position was a new development, a departure from feminist thinking prior to the war. In February 1914, for instance, Maude Royden, editor of the NUWSS newspaper *Common Cause*, stated in an editorial entitled "Our Common Humanity," "The 'difference of function' which Anti-Suffragists urge as a reason for denying women the vote without insisting on their inferiority, has no reality in the facts of life. The 'functions' of men and women are not divided into political and domestic." By 1917, Royden had markedly altered her stance. Believing "that most women desire to have children, and that motherhood is to them an absorbing duty and not merely an episode," she concluded that "the average woman will generally be in other walks of life but an amateur." While men might be expert in the arts and the professions, women could only be dilettantes; their expertise lay in "human life." This "new" feminist version of separate spheres for men and women derived from what Royden described as "a permanent difference between the average woman and the average man, due to their natural qualities and vocations."[25]

Royden's ideological shift, one that took place gradually and ambivalently over the course of some ten years between 1914 and 1923, stemmed from the wartime and postwar discourses that represented war and peace in sexual terms. In 1915, for example, she observed that with regard to militaristic or pacifist thinking, "there appears to be no cleavage of opinion along sex lines." By 1920, Royden tried without success to reconcile this conviction with her growing belief that sex differences were innate, and that the fate of world peace might well rest with the recognition of these differences. "I am not fond of sweeping generalisations about the sexes, and am not less suspicious of them when they are made by scientists than when they are made by politicians or divines," Royden declared. "Yet it may be true that the male represents the 'katabolic' and the female the 'anabolic' elements in the race; the male, the destructive; and the female, the constructive or conservative. If it be true, then this coming age must be the 'woman's age' in some more real sense than the rather sentimental idea of old-fashioned 'womanliness,' or we are indeed confronted with the suicide, not perhaps of humanity, but certainly of Western civilisation." In 1923, fully converted, she lamented "that the world is too great for us, that the passions created by the war are uncontrollable, that you cannot master your own civilisation." Respite from "the wounds of war [that] are so terrible and so recent" would come once those "differences of function" Royden had repudiated in 1914 were acknowledged. The values, outlook, and behavior inherent in women's "actual experience," "the fact that to be a woman gives one a rather different angle of vision to certain things in life," offered the best prospects for peace, the greatest chance of convincing men "to cease thinking of the world as a battlefield and to begin thinking of it as a home."[26]

Feminists participated in the cultural linking of sexual disharmony and the threat of war. F. W. Stella Browne, writing in 1915, utilized the rhetoric of war in her argument for recognizing "Sexual Variety and Variability among Women, and Their Bearing upon Social Reconstruction" after the war, claiming that "much of the unhealthiness of sexual conditions at present, is due to the habit of segregating the sexes in childhood and partly in latter life, and making them into 'alien enemies' to one another." Elizabeth Robins believed that sex antagonism "is the seed of all the other Antagonisms that ravage the earth. You shall not deal faithfully with any other till you have dealt faithfully with that."[27] Many, echoing the sexologists,[28] saw in sex the salvation of civilization. Marie Stopes hinted at this in recounting the evolution of her work. "I had written 'Married Love,'" she said, "some years before it was published, but early in 1918, while the war was still raging, I felt that psychologically the time was ripe to give the public what appeared to me a sounder, more wholesome, and more complete knowledge of the intimate sex requirements of *normal* and healthy people than was anywhere available." Stella Browne, in very much the same imagery that Hirschfeld and Fischer and Dubois would conjure up after the war, warned of "very dangerous and degrading perversions which may develop under repression. I know of a case in which a sudden, inexplicable, but apparently irresistible, lust of cruelty developed in a woman of the most actively kind and tender heart, but . . . sexually unsatisfied." Rebecca West warned of the ongoing nature of sex antagonism, stating that "in this war there is no discharge" for "such of the sexes as are not intimately in harmony." Dora Russell's *Hypatia* (1925), a response to Ludovici's *Lysistrata*, opened with a statement that equated marital discord with war. "Matrimonial quarrels, like modern war," she asserted, "are carried on on a large scale, involving not individuals, nor even small groups of individuals, but both sexes and whole classes of society." Russell was one of the few feminists in the postwar period willing to speak about hostility between women and men; she saw in sexual reform the "way out of the intolerable tangle in which their quarreling has landed us." "To understand sex," she promised, "to bring to it dignity and beauty and knowledge born of science, in place of brute instinct and squalor—that is the bridge that will span the breach" between the sexes.[29]

And not just the sexes. In many of her writings Russell articulated some of the misgivings about equal-rights feminism that haunted the proponents of "new" feminism: by insisting upon equality with men, by competing with men in the marketplace, equal-rights feminists threatened to undo the international peace. In chapter 1 of *Hypatia*, which is subtitled, "Is there a Sex War?" Russell conceded that, owing to women's rebellion against "a system of masculine repression," there had indeed been one. "It was a disgraceful exhibition," she observed, slipping into a barely qualified equation of feminism and the Great War, "and would not have come to a truce so soon, but that it was eclipsed by the still more disgraceful exhibition of the European war." Completing the metonymy, she concluded, "In 1918 they bestowed the vote . . . as a reward for our services in helping the destruction of our offspring." Wholly sympathetic to the cause, Russell nevertheless gave voice to a widespread understanding of feminism as war: "Feminism led women away from the home that they might return armed and unsubdued to make marriage tolerable," she declared. Mutual sexual pleasure, she believed, offered a solution not only to antagonism between men and women, but to conflict between nations as well. "I think that through sex and through parenthood we might get people away from admiration of a social system built on war," she told a Guildhouse audience. More explicitly, she argued in *The Right to Be Happy* that "in sex-love, through physical sympathy and intimate union, we draw into ourselves as in no other way the understanding of another human personality, and the knowledge that two very different creatures can live together in exquisite harmony. Such an experience alone, widespread, would be worth ten million platforms blaring pacifism."[30]

Russell and Browne were among the few people willing to call for sexual activity and pleasure outside of marriage; they had no problem extending their formulas for happiness to the two million women who would never marry because of the disproportionate ratio of men to women after the Great War. Most feminists, however, while joining in the cries for recognizing women's sexual nature, and in fact agreeing with the prescriptions against repression of sexual impulses, could not make those claims for women outside of marriage, and struggled with the problem of what chaste and celibate women were to do about their sexual urges.[31] Helena Swanwick expressed concern about the demographic implications of the war as early as 1916, as she articulated some of problems Britons would face in the postwar period. "We know that men have sexual needs," she stated,

> we know just as well that women have also; it is stupid to pretend that they have not, or that the matter is of no importance. There are three ways of treating natural instincts: you may (1) satisfy them, (2) repress them, (3) divert them. Only extreme ascetics would deny that healthy satisfaction of natural instincts is the happiest and best way of dealing with them. But if circumstances make healthy satisfaction impossible, what then? In the past we have always pretended that the problem did not exist. It is going to be greater than ever when this devastating war is over. . . . there will be more young women than young men to mate with them. Are the older people who made the war and sent the young men to give their lives in it going to wash their hands of the consequences to the mateless maidens, to talk outrageously of them as "waste products of civilisation" (instead of admitting that, in fact, they are the victims of barbarism), and to offer nothing but lifelong repression?

She urged that sublimation, or diversion of the sex instinct in "freedom, joy, the exhilaration of creating something, comradeship and passionate living" could "transmute the life-force and make it beneficient." Repression, on the other hand, promised only "vice, or pinched and sour egotism."[32]

Maude Royden, speaking from personal experience, testified to the "tremendous sacrifice on the part of so large a number of women as is involved in their acceptance of life-long celibacy" necessitated by war deaths. "I want to emphasize with all my power," she wrote, "that the hardness of enforced celibacy presses as cruelly on women as on men. . . . The idea that existence is enough for them—that they need not work, and do not suffer if their sex instincts are repressed or starved—is a convenient but most cruel illusion." Modern psychology, Royden argued, demonstrated that the repression of sexual instincts and impulses contributed to the development of a "cramped and twisted" nature. Eschewing promiscuity or "the right to motherhood" on the part of unmarried women, Royden advised them to sublimate, to transform the "sex side of our nature," to "transmute the power of sex and 'create' in other ways," to use the impulse in the service of humanity. "You can begin now and here," she urged, "to work for a world in which that cruelty which we call war, which has cursed and blighted your lives shall never again blight the lives of other young men and women."[33] Despite their protestations against those who blamed spinsters for their fate, both Swanwick and Royden shared with sexologists the conviction that in sex—in their cases the sublimation of sex—lay the potential for civilization's salvation; by directing all that sexual energy into programs addressed to the settlement of postwar difficulties, single women could play an instrumental role in preserving both domestic and international peace.

Virtually no one dared to support the suggestion of "Cripicus" in the letters column of the *Woman's Leader* that intimate relationships with other women offered a legitimate source of happiness and satisfaction.

There are thousands of women, independent, vigorous, capable, temperamentally rich and mentally alert, who are restless, hampered, frustrated, warped, according to their various degrees, because they are denied a proper emotional life. . . . Marriage, for a variety of reasons, has been denied to them. But they are not physical or physiological or pathological abnormalities. They ask . . . the emotional satisfaction of an intimate affection and the assured spiritual and social companionship of a home. The physical side of it in many women's cases plays a very insignificant part; it would be developed, no doubt, in marriage, it is sublimated out of it—in any case it is relatively unimportant. Their yearning is the multiple and complicated need of a complex human being. They could find it, most of them, with equal success through man or woman. . . . Thousands of women are conscious of this need. Equally, thousands of women have satisfied it with an intimate relationship with another woman. . . . But just as there is a physical sympathy which has no connection whatever with sexual excitement, so there is innate in human beings a need of intimacy and an instinct of approbation—shown in the most legitimate relationships—which is wholly psychological. . . . I do hope that no woman will allow the magisterial condemnation of *The Well of Loneliness* to shorten her courage—and she will need much—in pursuing for herself honestly, wisely, and generously that life which will bring her real contentment.[34]

Peace "through sex and through parenthood" depended upon the availability of reliable contraceptives. In 1918, Francis Gurdon, the bishop of

Hull, had warned the Lower House of Convocation of the Church of England that "if we are to have a League of Nations, the Church must reconsider her attitude of blessing large families and saying 'Be fruitful and multiply.'" He advocated "moral restraint in the size of families" rather than the use of contraceptives, but his nostrums for preventing war through birth control resonated with those of sexologists and feminists. In a formulation that counterposed birth control and war, Stella Browne maintained that "it ought not to be beyond the powers of medical and chemical science to invent an absolutely reliable contraceptive. Think of the marvels of destruction in the shape of asphyxiating and corrosive gases all ready for the next great war for liberty and civilisation." Russell regarded birth control as the "keystone" of motherhood. In demanding that birth control information and contraceptive devices be made available to working-class women through Maternity Centres, she enlisted the language and imagery of war. She charged that the government, by refusing to provide birth control information, forced working-class women to produce a yearly baby in intolerable circumstances. "The crime of war is bad enough," she lamented, but "this butchery of hope and promise and human lives is one so black that the heart and mind of every woman who has borne a child should revolt against it until it is tolerated no more." Working-class women, she claimed, "know . . . contraceptives are better than infanticide and war."[35]

Moreover, women could not participate unreservedly in the joys of sexual activity if they had to worry about conception and pregnancy. Russell saw birth control as the means by which sexual freedom could be realized. Few feminists, however, shared her view. Russell, Cicely Hamilton, Vera Brittain, and Winifred Holtby were among the very few who insisted, with Stella Browne, that "the fundamental importance and value of birth control lies in its widening of the scope of human freedom and choice, its *self-determining* significance for women"; they recognized that they represented "a very small minority in the [birth control] movement in this country." Mrs. M. C. Crook wrote in to the *Woman's Leader* to proclaim that birth control "is the very foundation of all liberty and equality for women." Holtby applauded the advent of scientific birth control, as she called it, for making it possible for women to enjoy "the right to choose her own time for her achievement of maternity, the ability to plan her life and work, the freedom from that accidental element which previously rendered her an uncertain unit in social organisation." Without these new freedoms for women made possible by contraceptives, she argued, pursuant to her equalitarian stance, "it is impossible that as workers and citizens they should be as reliable, as efficient, as regular as men."[36]

Most women affiliated with feminist organizations such as the NUSEC, the WFL, and even the Six Point Group held ambiguous and ambivalent opinions about contraceptives. Even Stopes, who regarded contraceptives as vital ingredients of women's marital happiness because they removed the fear of pregnancy, often diluted her feminist message with eugenic arguments and paeans to motherhood.[37]

Prewar feminists, by and large, had avoided any mention of birth control, seeing in contraceptives the means by which women could be forced to engage in sexual intercourse against their will. Reproductive freedom meant for them the right to limit their families by demanding abstinence, not "those horrid preventive methods," as Charlotte Despard put it in 1916. As late as 1924, the WFL announced that it "has nothing whatever to do with birth control, and no connection at all with it. The whole question lies entirely outside our interests as an association of women and men banded together for definite objects"; while a 1926 article in *Time and Tide* stated that "information as to artificial methods of birth control has nothing whatever to do with feminism." But as women like Dora Russell and Stella Browne began to demand for women the right to control their bodies and their fertility, feminists within the organized bodies began to pay attention.[38]

In 1923, the *Woman's Leader*, the organ of NUSEC, opened its letters column to a discussion of the pros and cons of birth control, observing that while it was not "part of our policy to express any opinion as to the rights and wrongs of birth control," it was "plain that the conditions under which the greatest of all occupations open to women—motherhood and the rearing of children—is carried on is a question of first-class importance, not only to all who care for woman's status, but for the race." "The proper performance of their function"—maternity—justified for "new" feminists the demand that "expert and disinterested birth control advice" be made available to married women so that they might "improve the standard of [their] 'product.'" The *Woman's Leader* did not intend to make a case for birth control per se, but only a case for birth control as a feminist issue "once its justifiability is established. . . . we are not advocating birth control as good in itself," the editors wrote. Their first object of concern was not the right of women to control their own bodies, but the children those bodies produced. "Our attitude in this matter is inspired by a reverence for human personality. . . . It is a reverence which revolts at the thought that the seeds of life may be sown thoughtlessly and on unprepared ground; at the thought that its fruit may be unwanted and inadequately tended; at the thought that its increase may destroy instead of fulfilling the life from which it comes." In March 1925, NUSEC overwhelmingly passed a resolution calling on the minister of health to allow Maternity and Infant Welfare Centres to give birth control information to married women who asked for it or whose health warranted such an action. As the *Woman's Leader* put it, NUSEC was "not calling for general indiscriminate propaganda in favour of birth control." Its demand had "the strength of extreme moderation" and could be defended on the grounds that it would eliminate other sources of birth control information which did not "discriminate in terms of clientele" and was sold "to unmarried people." Furthermore, contraceptive advice in the hands of the right people would help put abortionists out of business. Only belatedly did the paper refer to "the intolerable burden of undesired parenthood." As Stocks put it, NUSEC demanded that "the question of family limitation shall be viewed in its right perspective, as part and parcel of the greater question of maternity and child welfare."[39]

This position on contraceptives derived from the "new" feminist direction in which NUSEC was heading under Eleanor Rathbone's leadership. "New" feminism, as we have seen, started from the premise that women's needs and interests were not identical to those of men, and that demands for equality with men, or "old" feminism, failed to address those areas specific to women. As Alberti has argued, "for many birth-control campaigners the issue was not individual liberty, but increased economic freedom and improved health for women," an intrinsic part of the "legitimate economic aim" of "liberating the mothers." The rhetoric marshaled to support "new" feminist claims, however, justified them on the basis of women's special needs and special functions. The *needs* of women *as mothers* rather than the *rights* of women backed "new" feminist appeals. Sexual difference rather than equality characterized the relationship between men and women as "new" feminists understood it. Thus birth control could be advocated not as a means of enlarging a woman's freedom in general, but as a reform that would provide "maximum freedom to determine under what conditions she will or will not *perform her function*, and how far by reasonable 'limitation of output' she may improve the standard of her 'product.' " As Olive Banks has argued,

> the changing attitude of the feminists towards birth control is . . . less revolutionary than it sounds. Their conversion parallels and reflects conventional behaviour and conventional attitudes, when birth control ceased to be radical in itself, and when it was beginning to be linked to population policies and welfare reform rather than feminism as such. Only for a brief period in 1920, when, under the leadership of radical feminists like Stella Browne and Dora Russell, women in the movement tried to change the policies of the Labour and Communist parties, do we meet with a specifically feminist approach.[40]

The insistence on sexual difference received its impetus from two contradictory and paradoxical developments of the war. On the one hand, the vastly different experiences of the front and of the home created an almost insurmountable barrier between the individuals—men and women—who inhabited those realms, especially as the home came to be represented in the gendered language of sexual difference by feminists who turned their considerable resources to activities that highlighted mothers and babies. The dichotomy of women as mothers at home and men as soldiers at war per-

vaded wartime and postwar culture. We see this dichotomy expressed in
Royden's demand for the endowment of motherhood. "No one says a man
must depend on his wife for maintenance because he is a soldier," she argued. "No man, though he be a millionaire, refuses his soldier's pay. So
should it be with women. . . . You cannot, indeed, pay for all that motherhood means, but neither can you pay for a man to die. Yet soldiers are 'endowed' by the State."[41] Men are by nature soldiers, whose business is war,
women by nature mothers, whose business is peace.

On the other hand, the apparent blurring of gender lines brought about by
the requirements of total war led many in society to embrace dichotomies
based on sexual difference as a way to re-create a semblance of order and
peace. Egalitarian feminism threatened to renew the conflict so recently
ended; "new" feminists often represented demands for equality in imagery
that recalled antagonism, fighting, war. Eleanor Rathbone, in a 1917 article
challenging the efficacy of the equal pay demand, claimed that it "opens up
unpleasant possibilities of class antagonism and sex antagonism." In 1918, in
a pamphlet entitled *Equal Pay and the Family*, Kathleen Courtney warned
that the successful strike of women bus conductors for equal pay with their
male counterparts threatened to spread to every branch of transport and
industry. "Principles are a dangerous form of social dynamite," she noted in
the idiom of munitions and war, "and this particular explosive will shatter
many things before its force is exhausted."[42] In 1925, Rose Macaulay, explaining that "attempts of women to obtain privileges (political, professional,
economic, or other) which have previously been denied to them on account
of their sex" did not encompass the whole of feminism, cited boxing as an
example. "The feminist is not profoundly concerned with securing such
modifications of the National Sporting Club's rules as shall enable her to put
a woman into the ring against Kid Lewis," she wrote. The following year, in
response to *Time and Tide*'s criticism of "new" feminism, the *Woman's
Leader* carried an article in which the concerns of "new" feminists with
"improving the social, legal, and economic status of many thousands of
mothers" was set against that of "an undeniably equalitarian proposal for, let
us say, securing the participation of women in the activities of the boxing
ring." As Royden intimated in a letter to the NUSEC when equalitarians
resigned over protective legislation, "new" feminism meant sexual difference, and thus peace; "old" feminism threatened to renew hostility between
the sexes and thus international war. "When I reflect that the legalistic interpretation of equality must lead us to abandon our work for the League of
Nations . . . and concentrate on agitation in favour of women being admitted
on equal terms to all ranks of the Army, Navy, and Air Force," she wrote,
unwittingly caricaturing the positions of "new" and "old" feminism respectively as representing peace and war, "it seems to me that it was time that
the Union should clear its mind on what it meant by 'equality.'" Rathbone

put it more directly, arguing that sexual difference, the "traditional differ-ence of outlook" on the part of men and women, which "corresponds to real facts of human nature and human experience," promised to bring happiness to society, and "a more sustained and determined fight against cruelty in all its forms, and especially against the cruelty of war."[43]

The "new" feminist emphases upon women as mothers and upon sexual difference caused a great deal of concern among many "old" feminists, who argued a more strictly egalitarian agenda. Equalitarian feminists such as Holtby, Brittain, Swanwick, and Ray Strachey contested the sexological and psychoanalytic literature that underpinned the stress on sexual differ-ence and threatened to reinscribe separate spheres for men and women. In a review in the *Woman's Leader* in 1925 entitled, "Woman's Sphere Once More," Strachey observed that "there are a great many books about women with a capital W, and most of them are absurd. The latest craze, apparently, is to discuss the 'essential' differences of men and women, and to call in all the new psycho-analytical vocabulary for the purpose of saying the same old things in a new form." *Time and Tide* referred to the Report on the Differentiation of the Curriculum for Boys and Girls in Secondary Schools, issued in 1923, in support of its claim that "the educable capacity of the sexes differs so slightly, and the evidence for difference is so conflicting as to justify a verdict of equality if not 'sameness.' . . . The mysterious quality of 'femaleness' peculiar to the female sex is as illusive as ever," it crowed. It attributed those "psychological differences of sex" that do exist, quoting Helen Thompson, "not to difference of capacity, but to differences in the social influences brought to bear on the developing individual from infancy to adult years." *Time and Tide*'s reviewer of Norman Haire's *Encyclopaedia of Sexual Knowledge* challenged the claim, cited in chapter 5, that "in order to preserve her physiological and psychological equilibrium, a woman . . . needs children," calling it "a sentimental and typically Victorian lie."[44]

Winifred Holtby insisted, against the current sexological literature, that "we still are greatly ignorant of our own natures. We do not know how much of what we usually describe as 'feminine characteristics' are really 'mascu-line,' and how much 'masculinity' is common to both sexes. . . . We do not even know—though we theorise and penalise with ferocious confidence—whether the 'normal' sexual relationship is homo- or bi- or hetero-sexual." She condemned "that emphasis on sex difference characteristic of a creed which places instinct above reason," blaming Freud and authors such as D. H. Lawrence for the twentieth-century "dethrone[ment]" of human rea-son by "nerves and memory." "Freudian psychology has sanctioned the ex-treme veneration of sex. The followers of D. H. Lawrence have taught us to venerate instinct, emotion, and the intuitive vitality of the senses," she wrote. Society drew upon these thinkers to justify its insistence on marriage and maternity for women, "hounding them into marriage, into maternity, with the best intentions—and usually with the full co-operation of the women." Women in Britain "have been cast . . . for the role of wives, mothers, expectant and desirous mistresses. The whole force of Freudian revelation, the 'modern' morality and the fashionable insistence upon nerves rather than reasons, lies behind that choice. They have been told that without complete physical satisfaction they will remain dwarfed and crippled."[45]

Whereas Vera Brittain optimistically claimed that "one of the most valuable achievements of the feminist movement has been to uproot, gradually but persistently, the popular notion that some infallible guiding quality . . . known as 'instinct,' is inherent in every woman," Swanwick held that "the women's movement and the war and the permeation of Freud's ideas (though grotesquely deformed)" had brought about the displacement of reason by "the force of instincts, especially those of herd and sex." She lamented this development, noting, "I don't like to see man, when he notes more exactly what he is, confusing that with *what he ought to be*. I believe intensely in the sovereignty . . . of reason [Swanwick's emphasis]." She placed her hopes in "signs . . . that the recognition of the force and even the value of some instincts need not involve the total abdication of reason." Holtby, writing four years later, after Hitler had come to power, was not so confident in the outcome. "A sense of bitterness infects many public utterances, speeches and articles, made on the subject of women's position in the state," she warned. "The problems which feminists of the nineteenth century thought to solve along the lines of rationalism, individualism and democracy, present new difficulties in an age of mysticism, community and authority."[46]

"Old" feminists were able to hold on to understandings about masculinity and femininity and about male and female sexuality that recalled the prewar period. Their ability to contest the meanings about gender that were accepted not simply by the culture around them but by other feminists as well stems in part from the imagery they employed to articulate their experiences of the war. So neat a schema equating women who remained at home with those who embraced "new" feminism, or those who went to the front with those holding equalitarian or "old" feminist views, clearly will not stand up to scrutiny; many women, like Ray Strachey, Helen Fraser, Elizabeth Robins, and Rebecca West, who strongly advocated equality with men, got nowhere near the front. But it is striking that some of the most vocal supporters of "old" feminism—Hamilton, Brittain, Holtby, Lady Rhondda—all saw action in some fashion. In any event, the value "old" feminists placed on reason—invoking themes of knowledge and enlightenment—contrasted sharply with the notion of instinct and its companions (mystery, intuition, darkness) that underlay the sexological literature upon which "new" feminism was based, a contrast that also characterizes feminists' differing representations of the war as experienced from front and home.

Above all, postwar feminism, both "old" and "new," eschewed even the slightest hint of sex war. Rebecca West noticed in 1923 the "modern timidity about mentioning that there is such a thing as sex-antagonism." Christabel Pankhurst, one of the chief prewar ideologists of feminism as a response to war waged by men upon women, sought in 1921 to soften her stance, writing that "one sex should honour and reverence the other." Cicely Hamilton, another veteran of suffrage militancy, charged in a 1921 article entitled "Women Who Repel Men," that a recent attack on Newnham College was the fault, as Sheila Jeffreys has reported it, of "the women's reluctance to compromise and be amenable to men. She advised the women to play down their independence." Holtby and Brittain, despite their strong support for "old" feminism, never spoke of the relationship between the sexes as one of antagonism. As Riley has pointed out, "'sex-consciousness' and 'sex-antagonism' were deeply pejorative terms in 1918. . . . To look for comradeship between the sexes at the end of [the war] seemed to be more honourable, and lively, than to nurse the corpse of old sexual battles."[47] Only the intrepid Elizabeth Robins and Rebecca West attributed the backlash against women to sex antagonism, and urged feminists to name and fight against it. "The renewed vitality in that influence from which women have been compelled to suffer, but never under peril to dare name: Sex-Antagonism," insisted Robins, was responsible for "the highly critical condition" of women's status in 1924. But it could only hurt women's cause further to avoid drawing attention to sex antagonism because it "seems even to certain good suffragists doubly ingracious in view of what are looked on as generous concessions," or because, indeed, such plain naming appeared "dangerous, to those women still wholly 'dependent' on masculine good-will: dangerous, above all, to those women at the beginning of independence," she argued. "There is no 'right' way but uprightness of body and mind; no way but courage to face and even to call out Antagonism, that it may stand naked to the world. Then it can be dealt with—only then." Moreover, Robins declared, assertions of the complementarity of the sexes would be to no avail; women must realize that their efforts to work cooperatively with men to achieve a civilized society have failed. "Briefly," she stated baldly, "the thesis here is this: that the short cut to real union [between the sexes] lies through temporary abandonment of insistence on union."[48]

West, writing in 1925, dared to announce,

> I am an old-fashioned feminist. I believe in the sex-war. . . . When those of our army whose voices are inclined to coo tell us that the day of sex-antagonism is over and that henceforth we have only to advance hand in hand with the male I do not believe it. . . . when [a postwar feminist] says in a speech that "women must learn to work with men," I disagree. I believe that women know how to work with men. But I believe that it is the rarest thing in the world for a man to know how to work with women without giving way to an inclination to savage

his fellow workers of the protected sex. . . . The woman who forgets this, who does not realise that by reason of her sex she lives in a beleaguered city, is a fool who deserves to lose (as she certainly will) all the privileges that have been won for her by her more robustly-minded sister.[49]

West's prophecy soon proved to be correct. "New" feminism, espousing an ideology of sexual difference and separate spheres for women and men, could not sustain itself as a distinct political, social, and economic movement, and soon was swallowed up and disappeared, along with many of the gains women had won. How do we account for this change in feminist ideology, this abandonment of a position of equality with men, this emphasis on sexual difference and complementarity of the sexes?

Cicely Hamilton understood the defensive posture of feminism to be a response to the aggression and anger displayed by returning soldiers. "With no enemy to subjugate, in the shape of man or beast," she maintained in 1927, "an unemployed instinct may turn on women and subdue them to complete femininity. . . . The peace in our time for which we all crave will mean a reaction, more or less strong, against the independence of women." Vera Brittain concurred. She believed postwar antifeminism to be an aspect of "post-war reaction, in which war neurosis had been transformed into fear—fear especially of incalculable results following from unforeseen causes; fear of the loss of power by those in possession of it; fear, therefore, of women." Irene Rathbone's Joan explained that "men came back to homes which had been running perfectly well without them; to children whom they didn't know; to wives who had been free and well-off on separation allowances, and who resented having to submit once more to male interference, and to perpetual male presence." Mary Borden put it a bit differently but shared Brittain's and Hamilton's conviction that the war had created such stresses on men's psyches that they reacted with violence, not that men were inherently violent to begin with. One of her characters in *The Forbidden Zone* forced his wife, the narrator, to listen to his cynical and horrifying descriptions of the hospital to which he had been brought after being wounded, refusing to heed her pleas that he stop.

> He wondered why he had told her these things. He loved her. He hated her. He was afraid of her. He did not want her to be kind to him. He could never touch her again and he was tied to her. He was rotting and he was tied to her perfection. He had no power over her any more but the power of infecting her with his corruption. He could never make her happy. He could only make her suffer. His one luxury now was jealousy of her perfection, and his one delight would be to give in to the temptation to make her suffer. He could only reach her that way. It would be his revenge on the war.[50]

While Hamilton, Brittain, and Borden viewed male aggression as largely a learned response, others saw in the war a lesson about the nature of mascu-

linity, which led them to reevaluate their beliefs about femininity as well. A
number of feminists pointed to the war as the key event in effecting the
transformation in their thinking. Catherine Gasquoine Hartley, for one, attributed her switch to what was essentially a "new" feminist position to the
massive male aggression manifested by the war. Whereas once she had
dreamed of "a golden age which was to come with the self-assertion of
women," with the outbreak of war, she explained in 1917, "we women were
brought back to the primitive conception of the relative position of the two
sexes. Military organisation and battle afforded the grand opportunity for
the superior force capacity of the male. Again man was the fighter, the pro-
tector of woman and the home. And at once his power became a reality." The
aggression unleashed in the war, so unprecedented, so destructive, so horrifying in its effects, seems to have convinced Gasquoine Hartley that masculinity was inherently violent and brutal. Such an understanding necessitated
that women, if they were ever to be really free, must accept "the responsibilities and limitations of their womanhood. And by this I mean a full and glad
acceptance of those physical facts of their organic constitution which make
them unlike men, and should limit their capacity for many kinds of work. It
can never be anything but foolishness to attempt to break down the real
differences between the two sexes." Prior to the war feminists had been
seeking "to break through the barriers of sex. We have been pursuing
power," Gasquoine Hartley wrote, but the war had shown her the error of
her ways. "We saw how war spoke with a more powerful voice, and the
women who had been snatching at power felt the quickening of a quite new
spirit of humbleness."[51]

Christabel Pankhurst hinted at much the same fear when she wrote in
1924, "Some of us hoped more from woman suffrage than is ever going to be
accomplished. My own large anticipations were based upon ignorance
(which the late war dispelled) of the magnitude of the task which we women
reformers so confidently wished to undertake when the vote should be
ours." Pankhurst's prewar writings made it clear that she sought in the vote
the means by which women would end the sexual abuse and degradation of
women. Her disillusionment resulted from her observation of the Great
War's massive destruction, the manifestation, for her as for so many others,
of an innate male aggression. As she put it, "war arises from passions and
ambitions which do not yield to the influence of votes." Elizabeth Robins,
one of the few in the postwar period to articulate the notion of sex war,
hoped that women's prewar gains were solid enough to withstand "this sexual antagonism which debars women from an effectual share in public policies," but her statements carried little conviction. The war, after all, she
pointed out, carried a vital lesson "to instruct us. . . . That lesson is in sum:
the Imminence of Barbarism." By that she meant both "the readiness of
soldiers abroad to commit atrocity" and Britons' willingness to abrogate their

liberties in the prosecution of the war.[52] Britons' willingness to perpetuate the loss of their liberties in the face of atrocities committed at home was a distinct, if implied, possibility.

In these constructions, and those of feminists who saw in sex the salvation of civilization and the route to world peace, the metaphors of war have come home: the return of the soldier has placed Britain, or at least the women of Britain, under military occupation. Where once they had conceived masculinity and femininity to be the products of laws, attitudes, and institutions that encouraged an unfettered and aggressive male sexuality and a passive, even nonexistent female sexuality, "new" feminists now took up a variation of the "drive-discharge" model that relied upon the notion of biological drives to explain male behavior. The social bases of masculinity and femininity gave way to a biologically determined, innate male and female sexuality, which in turn suggested that women must act differently in order to protect themselves and society from the aggression unleashed by war. The rhetoric of separate spheres had become infected with the rhetoric of war. In classic antifeminist terms, these feminists gave voice to the cultural belief that the war had demonstrated the need for re-creating barriers between men and women, for the recognition of sexual difference, if society were to return to a condition of normalcy, defined in biological or natural terms. But because many of the legal barriers excluding women from public life were being dismantled, the institutional practices enforcing separate spheres came to be replaced by psychological ones. The power of psychologized separate spheres, the extent of the psychic and linguistic internalization of military occupation by the women of Britain, insured that all the parliamentary reforms in the world would be of little avail to those seeking equality with men.

CONCLUSION

CONSERVATIVE and reactionary images of masculinity and femininity emerged as British society sought in the establishment of harmonious marital relationships a resolution to the anxieties and political turmoil caused by the Great War. The inscription of large societal anxieties and conflict onto marital relationships operated on at least two levels. First, gender, sexuality, and the relationship between the sexes served as metaphors through which issues of power might be resolved. As Joan Scott has argued, war is "the ultimate disorder, the disruption of all previously established relationships, or the outcome of earlier instability. War is represented as a sexual disorder; peace thus implies a return to 'traditional' gender relationships, the familiar and natural order of families, men in public roles, women at home, and so on."[1] Britons sought a return to the "traditional" order of the prewar world, an order based on natural biological categories of which imagined sexual differences were a familiar and readily available expression.

Second, sexuality and war were understood by the culture—consciously or unconsciously—to be inextricably intertwined. War became, in many accounts, a metaphor for gender and sexual relations. The resolution of conflict through mutual, pleasurable sexual experiences within marriage was regarded by many sexologists and sex reformers as a means of reducing the threat of war by removing the sexual repressions and tensions that, as they often implied and sometimes asserted outright, helped to bring it about. The discourses on sexuality that predominated in the postwar years appropriated the language and imagery of war as psychoanalysts, sexologists, and sex reformers sought in the study of sexuality the solutions to the maintenance of domestic and international peace.

Just as nineteenth-century physicians and scientists had created sexual discourses that upheld a particular social and gender system by establishing individuals' political identity on the basis of their sexuality,[2] twentieth-century psychiatrists, sexologists, and sex reformers built up a vast literature about masculinity and femininity and male and female sexuality that served to restore order in the face of dramatic upheavals in the political, economic, social, and gender structures of Britain. A gender system of separate spheres for men and women based upon scientific theories of sexual difference, a new emphasis upon motherhood, and an urgent insistence upon mutual sexual pleasure within marriage provided parameters within which "normal" activity was to be carried out and a return to normalcy effected. Most feminists, no less interested in the establishment of peace and order, adopted these discourses as they articulated their demands. "New" feminism failed

to challenge, and in fact contributed to, a reconstruction of gender that cir-
cumscribed the roles, activities, and possibilities of women. In so doing, it
abandoned the radical critiques of gender and sexuality that marked its prewar ideologies, critiques that had probably become anachronistic, irrelevant
to the discourses that predominated in postwar Britain. As Riley has argued,
"women's" thorough implication in "the social"—especially as it became, in
the interwar years, obsessively focused on maternity and motherhood—limited feminism's ability to exist and operate effectively, having been constructed in such a way as to entirely dislocate the "political." "The impasse
for feminism was acute in the 1920s and 1930s. It could not just repeat the
charges issued by the 'old feminism'; nor could it simply discuss the position
of women as class members with 'special needs.' The result was a nervous
hesitation between 'equality' and 'difference,' or a search for a fragile me-
dian position which saw women as 'different but equal.'"[3]

Whereas prewar feminists could assert women's independence and
equality of the sexes in the conviction that they would ultimately ensure a
better world for both women and men, the traumas of the Great War helped
to establish in the cultural consciousness what Fussell has called the "modern *versus* habit: one thing opposed to another, not with some Hegelian
hope of synthesis involving a dissolution of both extremes . . . , but with a
sense that one of the poles embodies so wicked a deficiency, or flaw or
perversion that its total submission is called for."[4] "New" feminists seem to
have internalized this mental habit only slightly less than the rest of British
society. Violence, war, and conflict could only be avoided, it appeared to
British society after 1918, if separate spheres for men and women were re-
drawn, although these were no longer necessarily marked as public and private by laws and institutional practices that had barred women from public
life in the past. A psychologized version of separate spheres—one consequence of war's depiction in the imagery of sexual violence, and of postwar
sexological and psychoanalytic discourses that represented sexual relations
in the imagery of war—proved to be just as effective in limiting women's
scope and agency as barriers between public and private spheres had been
in the past. "New" feminism, by accepting the terms of the larger culture, by
putting forward a politics of sexual difference, found itself severely constrained in its ability to advocate equality and justice for women.

Women like Brittain, Holtby, Cicely Hamilton, and Lady Rhondda, on
the other hand, could sustain their confidence in a benevolent masculinity
and a strong and confident femininity by virtue of their experiences with
men on the front lines, and could thereby forgo the solace of a separate
sphere. Moreover, they were convinced that the "new" feminist emphases
on sexual difference would not serve to prevent domestic and international
conflict, but might actually help to bring them about, with disastrous consequences for feminism, democracy, and liberty generally. Holtby offered the

words of the British fascist Oswald Mosley as a warning to those who valorized maternity and domesticity for women. "The part of women in our future organization will be important, but different from that of men," Mosley had written. "*We want men who are men and women who are women*."[5] Cicely Hamilton spoke of fascism's antifeminism in her autobiography; in *Time and Tide* in 1934, she observed, in terms that linked Jews and femininity, Germans and masculinity, "the Jew, in German eyes, stands for luxury: what Hitler preaches is contempt of luxury, hardness of body and of mind."[6] She could not know of the holocaust to come, but her imagery indicates an unease about the fate of Jews—and women—in Germany. In a review of a book by James Drennan about Oswald Mosley, Ellen Wilkinson noted the author's approval of Mosley's emphasis on traditional masculinity as he summoned "the manhood of Britain to a disciplined and peaceful revolution" that would replace the effeminate world of politics with decisive, physical action. "With his wrestling, boxing and fencing [Mosley] has walked in the tradition of the Regency Buck in a time when people have gotten into the habit of expecting younger politicians to have horn-rimmed spectacles and soft white hands and spend their holidays at Geneva," Drennan crowed. But this kind of gendered imagery, "this fencing-master idea of politics," Wilkinson insisted, "is playing the devil with modern Europe."[7] Irene Clephane warned against "the retrograde influence at work trying to force women back to the position they occupied a century ago"; she appreciated the irony—and the danger—involved in the appearance of

> young women dressed in black shirts, standing on the pavement edges offering for sale the literature of the fascists, one of whose aims is to deprive women of the very freedom which makes it possible for them to stand unmolested as they do. . . . There is certainly something definitely inappropriate in this presence in public places of women who have attached themselves to a system of thought that has reverted to the teaching that woman's place is exclusively the home. Perhaps they think there is no danger to them, even if their party gains the ascendancy. They are mistaken: in Germany, where sex freedom and sex equality were realities under the Weimar constitution, women are being squeezed out of public life as relentlessly as the Jews. . . . [women's freedom] would vanish, along with every other freedom, should a fascist regime be introduced.[8]

By the early thirties, it was clear to many feminists that another war was coming; Rathbone expressed a belief that this development was encouraging Britons to come around to the idea of family endowment. "The plaint of the recruiting sergeant and the echoes of marching feet abroad do not tend to reassurance," she wrote in 1936, implying that the home, buttressed by the payment of a wage to mothers, offered an effective antidote to the anxiety created by the threat of war, even to the fact of war itself.[9] The psychologically brutalized, victimized, Belgianized women of Britain, symbolically oc-

cupied by an army of returning soldiers, may have found comfort and protection in the promises of "new" feminism.

The Great War shattered the category of "women" in ways that may have
made it impossible, before the 1960s, for feminists to effectively recover
their movement, its goals, and its critique of the gender system. Feminism's
revival would require the intervention of yet another world war, a war whose
brutalities, technological power, and horrifying efficiencies effaced any distinction between home and front, between civilian and soldiers, between
women and men. Only after that war had destroyed the system of gender
relations created by the First World War could a new articulation of feminism arise.

NOTES

INTRODUCTION

1. The phrase belongs to Raymond Sontag, who in turn borrowed it from Gabriel Marcel's play, *Le monde cassé*, of 1933. See Raymond J. Sontag, *A Broken World, 1919–1939* (New York, 1971), p. xv.

2. See Charles S. Maier, *Recasting Bourgeois Europe: Stabilization in France, Germany, and Italy in the Decade after World War I* (Princeton, 1975).

3. See Paul Fussell, *The Great War and Modern Memory* (New York, 1975); Victoria De Grazia, *How Fascism Ruled Women: Italy, 1922–1945* (Berkeley, 1992); Sandra Gilbert, "Soldier's Heart: Literary Men, Literary Women, and the Great War," *Signs* 8, no. 3 (1983): 422–50; Eric J. Leed, *No Man's Land: Combat and Identity in World War I* (Cambridge, 1979); Bonnie G. Smith, *Changing Lives: Women in European History since 1700* (Lexington, Mass., 1989).

4. See, for example, Arthur Marwick, *The Deluge: British Society and the First World War* (New York, 1965); Gail Braybon, *Women Workers in the First World War: The British Experience* (London, 1981). More recent work in cultural history suggests that a postwar antifeminist backlash, emphasizing sexual difference and separate spheres for men and women, contributed to the elimination of many of the gains women had made in previous years. See Margaret Randolph Higonnet et al., eds., *Behind the Lines: Gender and the Two World Wars* (New Haven, 1987).

5. Mary Louise Roberts suggested many of the lines of investigation and analysis that I have undertaken here. I am indebted to her for her generosity in sharing her ideas with me and for the stimulation of my own they generated. See Mary Louise Roberts, "Scars upon My Heart: Women's Experience in World War I" (unpublished paper, 1 May 1986). In her most recent work, Roberts analyzes the ways in which gender is used to refer to cultural crisis in postwar France, and the consequences of such usage for gender identity and gender relations. See "'This Civilization No Longer Has Sexes': *La Garçonne* and Cultural Crisis in France after World War I," *Gender and History* 4, no. 1 (1992): 49–69; and *The Reconstruction of Gender in Postwar France, 1917–1927* (Chicago, forthcoming).

6. Brian Harrison, *Prudent Revolutionaries: Portraits of British Feminists between the Wars* (Oxford, 1987), pp. 323, 322; Jane Lewis, "Feminism and Welfare," in Juliet Mitchell and Ann Oakley, eds., *What Is Feminism?* (New York, 1986), pp. 88, 94; Johanna Alberti, *Beyond Suffrage: Feminists in War and Peace, 1914–1928* (New York, 1989), pp. 219, 135; Sheila Jeffreys, *The Spinster and Her Enemies: Feminism and Sexuality, 1880–1930* (London, 1985), pp. 155–56.

7. Harrison, *Prudent Revolutionaries*, p. 8; Alberti, *Beyond Suffrage*, pp. 3, 135, 69.

8. Susan Kingsley Kent, *Sex and Suffrage in Britain, 1860–1914* (Princeton, 1987).

9. Harold L. Smith, "The Problem of Equal Pay for Equal Work in Great Britain during World War II," *Journal of Modern History* 53 (December 1981): 652–72; Harold L. Smith, "Gender and Pay: The Equal Pay for Equal Work Issue in Britain

in the 1920s" (unpublished manuscript, 1991); Martin Pugh, *Women and the Women's Movement in Britain, 1914–1959* (London, 1992), p. xii; Alberti, *Beyond Suffrage*, pp. 130–34.

10. Parveen Adams and Jeff Minson, "The 'Subject' of Feminism," *m/f* 2 (1978): 60.

11. Denise Riley, *"Am I That Name?" Feminism and the Category of "Women" in History* (London, 1988), pp. 1–2, 3, 5.

12. Ibid., p. 48, chap. 3, passim.

13. See Kent, *Sex and Suffrage*, passim.

14. Susan Pedersen has noted that "for the wives [of servicemen], . . . the state became a surrogate husband . . . and the conditions of receipt [of separation allowances] included fidelity to their absent husbands." She cites the Ministry of Pensions' declaration "that the woman by her infidelity has forfeited her right to be supported by her husband," and therefore by the state. See Susan Pedersen, "Gender, Welfare, and Citizenship in Britain during the Great War," *American Historical Review* 95, no. 4 (1990): 985, 999.

15. We can find this in Vera Brittain's *Testimony of Youth* (1933; reprint, London, 1978), in Irene Rathbone's *We That Were Young* (1932; reprint, New York, 1989), and in such novels as *Not So Quiet . . . Stepdaughters of War* (1930; reprint, New York, 1989), by Helen Zenna Smith, to name just a few.

16. See Fussell, *The Great War and Modern Memory*, p. 334; and Leed, *No Man's Land*, p. 76.

17. See Antoinette Burton, "The Feminist Quest for Identity: British Imperial Suffragism and 'Global Sisterhood,' 1900–1915," *Journal of Women's History* 3, no. 2 (1991): 46–81.

18. I am indebted to Mary Poovey, who explained this all to me in the clearest possible way.

CHAPTER 1
THE SEXUAL REPRESENTATION OF WAR, 1914–1915:
REESTABLISHING SEPARATE SPHERES

1. George Dangerfield, *The Strange Death of Liberal England, 1910–1914* (New York, 1961), passim; Samuel Hynes, *A War Imagined: The First World War and English Culture* (New York, 1991), pp. 7, 6.

2. Leed, *No Man's Land*, pp. 59, 41, 42, 47, 53, 70, 71.

3. Ian Hay, *The First Hundred Thousand: Being the Unofficial Chronicle of a Unit "K(1)"* (New York, n.d.), p. 120. This book first appeared as serialized articles in *Blackwood's Magazine* in the fall and winter of 1914–1915. It was published in book form in December 1915. Hynes, *A War Imagined*, p. 48.

4. H. G. Wells, *Mr. Britling Sees It Through* (New York, 1916), pp. 119, 182, 226.

5. Edmund Gosse, "War and Literature," *Edinburgh Review* 220 (October 1914): 313. Quoted in Hynes, *A War Imagined*, p. 12. "They were blaming England" for the war, Hynes notes. "Or if not exactly England, then the softness into which England had fallen in the pre-war years. Part of the argument was that English self-indulgence, and English tolerance of disruptive movements like Irish nationalism and Suffragism had encouraged the Germans to think that England would not and could not fight" (p. 16). House of Lords Parliamentary Debates, 17 December 1917,

col. 212. Rebecca West, "Socialism in the Searchlight," *Daily Chronicle*, 6 November 1916, in Jane Marcus, ed., *The Young Rebecca: Writings of Rebecca West, 1911–1917* (New York, 1982), p. 392. Hynes, *A War Imagined*, p. 19.

6. Leed, *No Man's Land*, p. 45. See Gail Braybon and Penny Summerfield, *Out of the Cage: Women's Experiences in Two World Wars* (London, 1987), p. 32.

7. Carolyne Playne, *Society at War, 1914–1916* (Boston, 1931), p. 94. Vera Brittain, *War Diary, 1913–1917: Chronicle of Youth*, ed. Alan Bishop with Terry Smart (London, 1981), 6 August 1914, p. 89; 7 August 1914, p. 89. M. M. Sharples, "How to Help," *Common Cause*, 19 February 1915, p. 722.

8. Quoted in the introduction to Rathbone, *We That Were Young*, p. x.

9. Rose Macaulay, *Non-Combatants and Others* (London, 1916), pp. 98, 121. On Freud, see chapter 5 below.

10. Alberti, *Beyond Suffrage*, p. 38. "What War Means," *Common Cause*, 7 August 1914, p. 377.

11. Alberti, *Beyond Suffrage*, p. 39. "Resolutions for February 1915 NUWSS Annual Council Meeting," NUWSS Executive Committee Minutes, Fawcett Library. Millicent Garrett Fawcett, *What I Remember* (1925; reprint, Westport, Conn., 1976), p. 218. "Kingsway Hall Meeting," *Common Cause*, 23 October 1914, p. 499. See *Common Cause*, 4 September 1914, p. 414; 16 October 1914, p. 487; 12 March 1915, p. 763; "At the outbreak of war, thoughtful women at once realised that now, more than ever, we must try to save the babies." Ada Nield Chew, "'Womanly' Work," *Common Cause*, 19 February 1915, p. 724; "The Empire's Babies," NUWSS "Weekly Notes," December 1915, Fawcett Library. E. Sylvia Pankhurst, *The Home Front: A Mirror to Life in England during the First World War* (1932; reprint, London, 1987), p. 173. S. Bulan, "The Untrained Nurse in National Emergency," *Englishwoman* 69 (September 1914): 267.

12. *Common Cause*, 14 August 1914, pp. 386, 391; 21 August 1914, p. 398. Pankhurst, *The Home Front*, p. 72; *Common Cause*, 9 October 1914, p. 470.

13. "Mothering Our Soldiers," *Common Cause*, 18 September 1914, p. 438. "Woman's Part in War Time. Care of the Home," *Common Cause*, 20 November 1914, p. 551. M. M. Sharples, "How to Help," *Common Cause*, 19 February 1915, pp. 722, 723.

14. Quoted in Alberti, *Beyond Suffrage*, p. 45. Catherine E. Marshall, "Women and War" (1915), in Margaret Kamester and Jo Vellacott, eds., *Militarism versus Feminism: Writings on Women and War* (London, 1987), p. 38. Quoted in Alberti, *Beyond Suffrage*, p. 38; Helena Swanwick, "Daughters," *Common Cause*, 2 October 1914, p. 463.

15. Helena Swanwick, *The War in Its Effect upon Women* (1916; reprint, New York, 1971), p. 29. Jo Vellacott has argued that "while many feminists, female and male, saw women as having distinct and complementary qualities to contribute, they seldom labelled men as inherently militaristic nor women as inevitably nurturing. . . . The feminist language of the time, with its heavy emphasis on an almost mystical quality of mothering, should not blind us to the radical nature of what was being said." Margaret Kamester and Jo Vellacott, eds., *Militarism versus Feminism: Writings on Women and War* (London, 1987), pp. 13–14. The heavy emphasis on mothering, however, was a new development, born of the war; prewar feminists did not place the same kind of weight on it. More to the point, the language of the pacifist

feminists was not clear to the women utilizing it or to contemporaries; and it would help to give rise to a general change in what the category "women" would be arrayed against in the postwar period. "What War Means," *Common Cause*, 7 August 1914, p. 377. Helena Swanwick, *Women and War* (1915; reprint, New York, 1971), pp. 1, 2. Helena Swanwick, "The Implications of the Women's Suffrage Movement—A Reply," *Englishwoman* 77 (May 1915): 176. Swanwick, *War in Its Effect upon Women*, p. 3. "Defence," *Common Cause*, 18 September 1914, p. 437. Marshall, "Women and War," p. 40.

16. Macaulay, *Non-Combatants and Others*, pp. 40, 140–41, 185, 164–65, 170.

17. Quoted in Midge MacKenzie, *Shoulder to Shoulder* (New York, 1988), p. 280. Anne Wiltsher, *Most Dangerous Women: Feminist Peace Campaigners of the Great War* (London, 1985), p. 39. Christabel Pankhurst, *The War: A Speech Delivered at the London Opera House, September 8, 1914* (London, 1914), p. 12.

18. Charlotte Despard, "To Our Readers," *Vote*, 14 August 1914, p. 278. C. Nina Boyle, "The Crimes of Statescraft [*sic*]," *Vote*, 7 August 1914, p. 268.

19. Reported in "The Women's Freedom League and the National Crisis," *Vote*, 14 August 1914, p. 278. Charlotte Despard, "Your Country Needs You," *Vote*, 18 September 1914, p. 317. *Vote*, 7 August 1914, masthead. *Vote*, 21 August 1914.

20. *Common Cause*, 9 October 1914, p. 476. See Margaret Llewelyn Davies, ed., *Maternity: Letters from Working Women* (1915; reprint, New York, 1978), passim. See Alberti, *Beyond Suffrage*, p. 58. *Common Cause*, 4 September 1914, p. 414. "Notes and News," *Common Cause*, 9 October 1914, p. 469. "Women's Interests Committee" Minutes, NUWSS, Fawcett Library.

21. In Maurice Rickards and Michael Moody, eds., *The First World War: Ephemera, Mementoes, Documents* (London, 1975), items 24, 168.

22. As Bonnie Smith has observed, "gender tensions" so evident before the war "dissolved as men went off to the battlefield. . . . War made the feelings of men and women toward one another clear again. Across the great divide that split home from battlefield—an extreme version of separate spheres—societies resurrected gender harmony"(*Changing Lives*, pp. 367–68).

23. Trevor Wilson, *The Myriad Faces of War: Britain and the Great War, 1914–1918* (Cambridge, 1986), p. 25. Peter Buitenhuis, *The Great War of Words: Literature as Propaganda, 1914–18 and After* (London, 1989), p. 12.

24. Quoted in James Morgan Read, *Atrocity Propaganda, 1914–1919* (New Haven, 1941), p. 18; pp. 36–37, 38; 37–38.

25. "The National Union and Atrocities," *Common Cause*, 25 September 1914, p. 453.

26. Hynes, *A War Imagined*, p. 52. M. L. Sanders and Philip M. Taylor, *British Propaganda during the First World War, 1914–1918* (London, 1982), pp. 144, 143.

27. Committee on Alleged German Outrages, *Evidence and Documents Laid before the Committee on Alleged German Outrages* (London, 1915), pp. 4, 9, 10, 14, 19, 21, 107, 109, 111, 112.

28. Hynes, *A War Imagined*, p. 56.

29. Wilson, *Myriad Faces of War*, pp. 732, 740.

30. Hynes, *A War Imagined*, p. 53. Cate Haste, *Keep the Home Fires Burning: Propaganda in the First World War* (London, 1977), p. 54. Rickards and Moody, *The First World War*, item 24.

31. "The Germans in England: What an Invasion Would Mean," *Suffragette*, 21 May 1915, p. 92; Flora Drummond, "Our Present Duty," *Suffragette*, 21 May 1915, p. 85.

32. David Mitchell, *Monstrous Regiment: The Story of the Women of the First World War* (New York, 1965), pp. 39–40. Philip Gibbs, *Now It Can Be Told* (New York, 1920), p. 69. Wilson, *Myriad Faces of War*, p. 158. Quoted in Gibbs, *Now It Can Be Told*, p. 68. Rickards and Moody, *The First World War*, item 73.

33. Rickards and Moody, *The First World War*, item 101. Quoted in Wilson, *Myriad Faces of War*, p. 706.

34. Magnus Hirschfeld, *The Sexual History of the World War* (New York, 1937), p. 29. Quoted in Vera Brittain, *Testament of Friendship* (London, 1940), p. 52. Lady Randolph Churchill, ed., *Women's War Work* (London, 1916), p. 157.

35. Marwick, *The Deluge*, pp. 111, 108. Irene Clephane, *Towards Sex Freedom* (London, 1935), pp. 197–98. *Common Cause*, 27 November 1914, p. 563. A. Maude Royden, "Morals and Militarism," *Common Cause*, 30 April 1915, pp. 46–47. Leed, *No Man's Land*, p. 45.

36. *The Times History of the World War* 4, no. 52, 17 August 1915, p. 509. Lucy Bland, "In the Name of Protection: The Policing of Women in the First World War," in Julia Brophy and Carol Smart, eds., *Women-in-Law: Explorations in Law, Family and Sexuality* (London, 1985), pp. 27–28, 28, 29, 30. Hynes, *A War Imagined*, p. 89.

37. "A National Shame," *Common Cause*, 28 August 1914, pp. 406–7. "Notes and News," *Common Cause*, 9 October 1914, p. 469; "A Way for Girls to Help," *Common Cause*, 23 October 1914, p. 494. See *Common Cause*, 28 August 1914, p. 406; 9 October 1914, p. 469; 23 October 1914, p. 494; 1 January 1914, p. 631. Katherine E. Harley, "Active Service Cadet Corps," *Common Cause*, 13 November 1914, p. 531. Reported in *Common Cause*, 27 November 1914, p. 560.

CHAPTER 2
THE SEXUAL REPRESENTATION OF WAR, 1915–1918:
SEX, WAR, AND SEX WAR

1. Wilson, *Myriad Faces of War*, p. 510.

2. See Mary Poovey on the "gaps" opened up by the "uneven development" of gender ideologies that enable the formulation of resistance to those ideologies. *Uneven Developments: The Ideological Work of Gender in Mid-Victorian England* (Chicago, 1988), passim.

3. "Women as Non-Combatants," *Common Cause*, 1 January 1915, p. 625. E. F. Rathbone, "In Case of Invasion," *Common Cause*, 1 January 1915, p. 631.

4. "'In Case of Invasion,'" *Common Cause*, 8 January 1915, pp. 637–38. Fanny Smart, "Open Letter: Women and Defence," *Englishwoman* 73 (January 1915): 76, 78–80, 77.

5. See *Common Cause*, 9 April 1915; 23 April 1915; 7 May 1915; 14 May 1915; 7 July 1916; 14 July 1916; 21 July 1916; August 1916.

6. Quoted in Lisa Tickner, *The Spectacle of Women: Imagery of the Suffrage Campaign, 1907–14* (Chicago, 1988), pp. 230–31. "War Service for All," *Suffragette*, 4 June 1915, p. 118. Tickner, *Spectacle of Women*, pp. 231, 230.

7. Tickner, *Spectacle of Women*, pp. 231–33. Deborah Thom, "Women and Work in Wartime Britain," in Richard Wall and Jay Winter, eds., *The Upheaval of War: Family, Work and Welfare in Europe, 1914–1918* (Cambridge, 1988), p. 303. Tickner, *Spectacle of Women*, p. 234.

8. Christabel Pankhurst, "We Will Not Be Prussianised," *Suffragette*, 16 April 1915, p. 6. Tickner, *Spectacle of Women*, pp. 232–33, 231. Mrs. Pankhurst, "A Speech Delivered at the London Pavilion, October 5, 1915," quoted in MacKenzie, *Shoulder to Shoulder*, p. 294.

9. Quoted in Braybon, *Women Workers*, p. 155. C. Nina Boyle, "We Present Our Bill," *Vote*, 19 February 1915, p. 504; "The Government's Appeal to Women for War Service," *Vote*, 26 March 1915, p. 541. Quoted in Knight, "Introduction" to Rathbone, *We That Were Young*, p. xiii. Harriot Stanton Blatch, *Mobilizing Woman-Power* (New York, 1918), p. 55.

10. Rebecca West, "Hands That War: The Cordite Makers," *Daily Chronicle*, 1916, quoted in Jane Marcus, ed., *The Young Rebecca: Writings of Rebecca West, 1911-1917* (New York, 1982), pp. 381, 382.

11. Mrs. Alec-Tweedie, *Women and Soldiers* (London, 1918), pp. 1, 2, 26. Quoted in Gilbert, "Soldier's Heart," p. 425. Winifred Holtby, *Women and a Changing Civilization* (1935; reprint, Chicago, 1978), p. 164.

12. Helen Fraser, *Women and War Work* (1917; New York, 1918), p. 267. Alec-Tweedie, *Women and Soldiers*, p. 23. Blatch, *Mobilizing Woman-Power*, p. 58. Mary Agnes Hamilton, "Changes in Social Life," in Ray Strachey, ed., *Our Freedom and Its Results* (London, 1936), pp. 250, 251.

13. Quoted in Jenny Gould, "Women's Military Services in First World War Britain," in Margaret Randolph Higonnet et al., eds., *Behind the Lines: Gender and the Two World Wars* (New Haven, 1987), p. 119. Charlotte Haldane, *Motherhood and Its Enemies* (London, 1927), p. 94. Playne, *Society at War*, p. 140.

14. Ford Madox Ford, *Parade's End* (New York, 1979), p. 293. Frederic Manning, *Her Privates We* (London, 1986), pp. 12, 220, 51.

15. Ford, *Parade's End*, pp. 303, 309. Gilbert, "Soldier's Heart," p. 448. Elaine Showalter, *The Female Malady: Women, Madness, and English Culture, 1830–1980* (New York, 1985), p. 171. Robert Graves, *Good-bye to All That* (1929; 2d ed., New York, 1957), p. 263.

16. Manning, *Her Privates We*, pp. 183–84. My sincere thanks to Bonnie Smith for suggesting this last point.

17. Alec-Tweedie, *Women and Soldiers*, p. 93. Quoted in Bland, "In the Name of Protection," p. 47. *Statutory Rules and Orders* (1918), pp. 331–32, quoted in Bland, "In the Name of Protection," p. 32. Alec-Tweedie, *Women and Soldiers*, p. 85.

18. Wilson, *Myriad Faces of War*, p. 724. Siegfried Sassoon, *Memoirs of an Infantry Officer* (New York, 1930), p. 291. Wilson, *Myriad Faces of War*, pp. 724, 725.

19. H. M. Swanwick, *I Have Been Young* (London, 1935), p. 252. Hamilton, "Changes in Social Life," p. 251.

20. Clephane, *Towards Sex Freedom*, pp. 195–96. Mrs. C. S. Peel, *How We Lived Then, 1914–1918: A Sketch of Social and Domestic Life in England during the War* (London, 1929), p. 68. Hamilton, "Changes in Social Life," p. 252. Clephane, *Towards Sex Freedom*, pp. 197–98. Quoted in Brittain, *Testament of Friendship*, p. 52.

21. D. H. Lawrence, "Tickets, Please," in *England, My England* (London, 1924), pp. 52, 62–63. Wells, *Mr. Britling Sees It Through*, pp. 276–77.

22. Wilson, *Myriad Faces of War*, pp. 411–12. Quoted in Hynes, *A War Imagined*, pp. 226–27; pp. 228, 226–27.

23. See Blatch, *Mobilizing Woman-Power*, p. 58. This theme is treated at length in Gilbert, "Soldier's Heart." Wells, *Mr. Britling Sees It Through*, pp. 263–64.

24. "Weekly Notes," 13 November 1917, p. 2, NUWSS, Fawcett Library. Blatch, *Mobilizing Woman-Power*, p. 47. Mabel Potter Daggett, *Women Wanted: The Story Written in Blood Red Letters on the Horizon of the Great World War* (London, 1918), pp. 24, 299.

25. Hirschfeld, *The Sexual History of the War*, p. 37. Hynes, *A War Imagined*, p. 92. Wilson, *Myriad Faces of War*, p. 705. In Haste, *Keep the Home Fires Burning*, p. 54.

26. Alec-Tweedie, *Women and Soldiers*, p. 6.

27. Gibbs, *Now It Can Be Told*, pp. 534, 537. Manning, *Her Privates We*, p. 153.

28. Fussell, *The Great War and Modern Memory*, p. 86. Sassoon, *Memoirs of an Infantry Officer*, p. 280. Leed, *No Man's Land*, pp. 109–110.

29. Siegfried Sassoon, "Glory of Women," in Jon Silken, ed., *The Penguin Book of First World War Poetry*, 2d ed. (Harmondsworth, 1981), p. 132. "Blighters," quoted in Gilbert, "Soldier's Heart," pp. 430–31; "Yellow-Pressmen," quoted in Fussell, *The Great War and Modern Memory*, p. 86.

30. Showalter, *The Female Malady*, p. 173. Gilbert, "Soldier's Heart," pp. 423, 424. Alec-Tweedie, *Women and Soldiers*, p. 5.

31. Leed, *No Man's Land*, p. 22. Wells, *Mr. Britling Sees It Through*, p. 373. Fussell, *The Great War and Modern Memory*, p. 124. Gibbs, *Now It Can Be Told*, p. 79. Ford, *Parade's End*, p. 310.

32. Wells, *Mr. Britling Sees It Through*, pp. 388, 386.

33. Emmeline Pankhurst, "What is Our Duty?" *Suffragette*, 23 April 1915, pp. 25, 26. Mary Lowndes, "The Recrudescence of Barbarism," *Englishwoman* 70 (October 1914): 27. *Vote*, 11 September 1914, p. 309. C. Nina Boyle, "We Present Our Bill," *Vote*, 19 February 1915, p. 504. C. Nina Boyle, "The Male Peril," *Vote*, 27 August 1915, p. 727.

34. R. H. Tawney, "Some Reflections of a Soldier," *Nation*, 21 October 1916, p. 106n. Swanwick, *Women and War*, p. 2. Hynes, *A War Imagined*, pp. 110, 114.

35. Hynes, *A War Imagined*, pp. 126, 123, 125. Elsie Bowerman diary, 26 February 1917, p. 89, Elsie Bowerman Collection, Fawcett Library.

36. Hynes, *A War Imagined*, p. 120. Wilson, *Myriad Faces of War*, pp. 395–96. Hynes, *A War Imagined*, p. 100.

37. Peel, *How We Lived Then*, p. 71. Playne, *Society at War*, p. 130.

38. Playne, *Society at War*, p. 130. Tawney, "Some Reflections of a Soldier," pp. 104–6. See Hynes, *A War Imagined*, pp. 118, 117. Herbert Read, "The Scene of War: The Happy Warrior," in Peter Vansittart, ed., *Voices from the Great War* (New York, 1981), p. 118: "His wild heart beats with painful sobs, / His strained hands clench an ice-cold rifle, / His aching jaws grip a hot parched tongue, / And his wide eyes search unconsciously. / He cannot shriek. / Bloody saliva / Dribbles down his shapeless jacket. / I saw him stab / and stab again / A well-killed Boche. / This is the happy warrior, / This is he. . . ."

39. Ford's four novels, *Some Do Not . . .* (1924), *No More Parades* (1925), *A Man Could Stand Up—* (1926), and *The Last Post* (1928), were consolidated and given the title *Parade's End*. Ford, *Parade's End*, p. 233. Graves, *Good-bye to All That*, p. 237.

CHAPTER 3
FEMINISTS AT THE FRONT: REINVENTING MASCULINITY

1. May Sinclair, *A Journal of Impressions in Belgium* (New York, 1915), p. 2. Letter from Elsie Bowerman to her mother, 5 July 1916, Elsie Bowerman Collection, Fawcett Library. Mary Dexter, *In The Soldier's Service: War Experiences of Mary Dexter, 1914–1918* (Boston, 1918), p. 3. A F.A.N.Y. in France, *Nursing Adventures* (London, 1917), p. 132.

2. A F.A.N.Y. in France, *Nursing Adventures*, p. 132. May Sinclair, *The Romantic* (New York, 1920), pp. 193–94.

3. Sinclair, *Journal of Impressions*, pp. 69, 40, 41.

4. Brittain, *War Diary*, pp. 87, 105, 115. Margery Corbett Ashby to Brian Ashby, 11 April 1918; 1 April 1918, Margery Corbett Ashby Collection, Fawcett Library. Brittain, *War Diary*, 19 March 1915, pp. 161–62, 157–58.

5. Claire Leighton, introduction to Brittain, *War Diary*, p. 11. Kate Courtney, *Extracts from a Diary during the War* (privately printed, 1927), 7 August 1917, p. 128. Brittain, *War Diary*, 7 and 9 October 1915, pp. 286, 287. Quoted in Brittain, *Testament of Youth*, p. 216.

6. Margery Corbett Ashby to Brian Ashby, 1 April 1918, Margery Corbett Ashby Collection, Fawcett Library. Brittain, *War Diary*, pp. 102, 113, 116, 108, 110, 117. Mary Stocks spoke of the "acute and unrelieved personal anxiety" she endured while her husband fought in France. Quoted in Alberti, *Beyond Suffrage*, p. 49.

7. Brittain, *Testament of Youth*, pp. 214–15, 143.

8. Brittain, *War Diary*, 17 April 1915, pp. 178–79. Lynn Knight, introduction to Rathbone, *We That Were Young*, p. xv. Brittain, *Testament of Youth*, pp. 213–14. Brittain, *War Diary*, 26 April 1915, p. 186. Brittain, *Testament of Youth*, p. 166. Rathbone, *We That Were Young*, p. 129.

9. Sinclair, *Journal of Impressions*, pp. 4, 14, 7, 7–8, 21, 33, 36.

10. Brittain, *War Diary*, 1 August 1915, p. 226. Millicent, duchess of Sutherland, *Six Weeks at the War* (Chicago, 1915), p. 27.

11. Quoted in Brittain, *Testament of Friendship*, pp. 40, 41, 42, 53.

12. Viscountess Rhondda, *This Was My World* (London, 1933), pp. 239, 243–44, 245, 246, 247–48, 248–49, 257, 259. See Manning, *Her Privates We*; Graves, *Good-bye to All That*; letter from Roland Leighton to Vera Brittain, 17 April 1915, in Brittain, *War Diary*, pp. 176–77.

13. Claire Leighton, introduction to Brittain, *War Diary*, p. 11. Brittain, *War Diary*, 3 January 1916, 26–27 January 1916, pp. 305, 311; 29 February 1916, pp. 316–17.

14. Sinclair, *Journal of Impressions*, p. 283. Viscountess Rhondda, *This Was My World*, p. 259.

15. *WAAC: The Woman's Story of the War* (London, 1930), pp. 199–200. Elsie Bowerman diary, 1 January 1917, Elsie Bowerman Collection, Fawcett Library.

16. Quoted in Mitchell, *Monstrous Regiment*, p. 179. Brittain, *Testament of Youth*, p. 220. Brittain, *War Diary*, 23 March 1916, p. 324. Brittain, *Testament of Youth*, pp. 375, 339, 279, 410.

17. Knight, introduction to Rathbone, *We That Were Young*, pp. x, xii.

18. Rathbone, *We That Were Young*, pp. 194, 195, 200, 201, 202. *A War Nurse's Diary: Sketches from a Belgian Field Hospital* (New York, 1918), pp. 20, 98–99. A F.A.N.Y. in France, *Nursing Adventures*, p. 15. *WAAC*, p. 195.

19. Dexter, *In the Soldier's Service*, pp. 193–94. Smith, *Not So Quiet . . .* , pp. 11, 12, 59.

20. Knight introduction to Rathbone, *We That Were Young*, p. ix. Mary Borden, *The Forbidden Zone* (London, 1929), pp. 142–43.

21. Brittain, *Testament of Youth*, p. 374. Borden, *The Forbidden Zone*, pp. 54–55. *WAAC*, p. 36. Vera Brittain, *Lady into Woman* (London, 1953), pp. 203–4.

22. Borden, *The Forbidden Zone*, pp. 51–52. Dexter, *In the Soldier's Service*, pp. 158, 188. May Sinclair, *The Tree of Heaven* (New York, 1917), p. 366.

23. Viscountess Rhondda, *This Was My World*, pp. 261, 262–63.

24. Brittain, *War Diary*, 12 May 1915, p. 195; 5 August 1915, p. 228; 6 March 1916, p. 320. Brittain, *Testament of Youth*, pp. 360, 217.

25. Dexter, *In The Soldier's Service*, 10 September 1917, pp. 138, 139; January 1918, p. 166; 19 May 1918, p. 203. *A War Nurse's Diary*, p. 66.

26. Rathbone, *We That Were Young*, p. 45. Cicely Hamilton, *Life Errant* (London, 1935), p. 108. Gibbs recounted that "in those long days of trench warfare and stationary lines it was boredom that was the worst malady of the mind; a large, overwhelming boredom to thousands of men who were in exile from the normal interests of life and from the activities of brain-work; an intolerable, abominable boredom, sapping the will-power, the moral code, the intellect." *Now It Can Be Told*, p. 137. Rathbone, *We That Were Young*, p. 212.

27. Smith, *Not So Quiet . . .* , pp. 17–18. Hamilton, *Life Errant*, p. 145. Brittain, *Testament of Youth*, pp. 412, 417.

28. Rathbone, *We That Were Young*, pp. 239, 269.

29. Borden, *The Forbidden Zone*, pp. 60, 155–56. Brittain, *Testament of Youth*, pp. 496–97. My thanks to Stephanie Cole for bringing this to my attention.

30. *WAAC*, pp. 98, 222.

31. A F.A.N.Y. in France, *Nursing Adventures*, pp. 121, 116. Rathbone, *We That Were Young*, pp. 217, 210, 209, 219, 236, 394. Brittain, *War Diary*, 28 May 1915, 15 June 1915, pp. 202, 208. Enid Bagnold, *A Diary without Dates* (New York, 1935), p. 101. Smith, *Not So Quiet . . .* , pp. 29–30. Borden, *The Forbidden Zone*, pp. 60, 61.

32. Hamilton, *Life Errant*, p. 117. Smith, *Not So Quiet . . .* , p. 57. Brittain, *Testament of Youth*, p. 216. A F.A.N.Y. in France, *Nursing Adventures*, p. 21. Borden, *The Forbidden Zone*, p. 60.

33. a F.A.N.Y. in France, *Nursing Adventures*, p. 4; Brittain, *Testament of Youth*, pp. 371, 372. Sinclair, *Journal of Impressions*, pp. 146–47. *WAAC*, p. 56.

34. Sinclair, *Journal of Impressions*, pp. 136, 169–70. Sinclair, *The Romantic*, passim.

35. Brittain, *War Diary*, 8 January 1913, 4 March 1913, pp. 26–27, 30–31. Brittain, *Testament of Youth*, p. 48. Rathbone, *We That Were Young*, pp. 139–40.

36. *WAAC*, p. 12.

37. Brittain, *Testament of Youth*, pp. 165–66.

38. Rathbone, *We That Were Young*, pp. 212–13. Brittain, *Testament of Youth*, pp. 165–66.

39. Brittain, *War Diary*, 22 August 1915, p. 256. Rathbone, *We That Were Young*, pp. 139–40, 141.

40. *WAAC*, pp. 21, 33, 34, 35.
41. Borden, *The Forbidden Zone*, pp. 53–54, 61–62, 63, 49.
42. Ibid., p. 147. *WAAC*, pp. 35–36.
43. Sinclair, *The Tree of Heaven*, pp. 369, 396, 397.
44. Quoted in Alberti, *Beyond Suffrage*, p. 223. A.M.L., "Women and Public Affairs," *Time and Tide*, 14 October 1921, p. 978.

CHAPTER 4
THE VOTE: SEX AND SUFFRAGE IN BRITAIN, 1916–1918

1. *Suffragette*, 7 August 1914. Quoted in Andrew Rosen, *Rise Up, Women! The Militant Campaign of the Women's Social and Political Union, 1903–1914* (London, 1974), p. 248.
2. Pankhurst, *The War*, pp. 1, 2, 3, 16, 4, 6. In *Unshackled: The Story of How We Won the Vote* (1959; reprint, London, 1987), Pankhurst concluded her tale of suffrage militancy in the summer of 1914 with the exclamation, "Then, suddenly, *the other war* broke out!" (my emphasis; p. 286). Christabel Pankhurst, *America and the Great War: A Speech Delivered at Carnegie Hall, New York, October 24, 1914.* (London, 1914), pp. 10, 15, 16. Christabel Pankhurst, *International Militancy: A Speech Delivered at Carnegie Hall, New York, January 13, 1915* (London, 1915). *Suffragette*, 7 May 1915, p. 51.
3. C. Nina Boyle, "The Crimes of Statescraft [*sic*]," *Vote*, 7 August 1914, p. 268. West, "Socialism in the Searchlight," p. 392. Beatrice Harraden, *Our Warrior Women* (London, 1916), p. 5. Fraser, *Women and War Work*, pp. 26–27. "The War and Women," *Vote*, 15 January 1915, p. 463.
4. Wiltsher, *Most Dangerous Women*, p. 22. Jo Vellacott, "Feminist Consciousness and the First World War," *History Workshop* 23 (Spring 1987): 87. Wiltsher, *Most Dangerous Women*, pp. 22, 23. Quoted in Vellacott, "Feminist Consciousness," p. 88.
5. Sandra Stanley Holton, *Feminism and Democracy: Women's Suffrage and Reform Politics in Britain, 1900–1918* (Cambridge, 1986), p. 135. Vellacott, "Feminist Consciousness," p. 82; p. 98 n. 6. Swanwick, *Women and War*, pp. 3–4, 5–6. Quoted in Wiltsher, *Most Dangerous Women*, pp. 63–64. A. Maude Royden, "War and the Woman's Movement," reprinted from Charles Roden Buxton, ed., *Towards a Lasting Settlement* (London, n.d. [1915]), n.p. Catherine Marshall believed that "in a state where the social order is based on the power to exercise force women must always go to the wall, just as in a community of nations in which force is the deciding factor in international differences the smaller nations must always go to the wall." "The Future of Women in Politics," in Margaret Kamester and Jo Vellacott, eds., *Militarism versus Feminism: Writings on Women and War* (London, 1987), p. 45.
6. Quoted in Wiltsher, *Most Dangerous Women*, pp. 64–65. Holton, *Feminism and Democracy*, p. 135. Quoted in Wiltsher, *Most Dangerous Women*, p. 68.
7. Quoted in Holton, *Feminism and Democracy*, p. 135. Resolutions for NUWSS Annual Council Meeting for February 1915, Fawcett Library.
8. Resolutions for NUWSS Annual Council Meeting, February 1915, Fawcett Library. Quoted in Holton, *Feminism and Democracy*, p. 135.
9. Resolutions for the NUWSS Annual Council Meeting, February 1915, Fawcett Library. Quoted in Wiltsher, *Most Dangerous Women*, pp. 71–72.

10. NUWSS Executive Committee Meeting Minutes, 4 March 1915, pp. 3–5. For Royden's resignation from *Common Cause*, see NUWSS Executive Committee Meeting Minutes, 18 February 1915.

11. Quoted in Wiltsher, *Most Dangerous Women*, p. 69. NUWSS Executive Committee Meeting Minutes, 18 March 1915, pp. 5, 6. Oliver Strachey, "The Implications of the Women's Suffrage Movement," *Englishwoman* 76 (April 1915): 3, 4.

12. NUWSS Executive Committee Meeting Minutes, 6 May 1915, pp. 6, 7, 5–6.

13. Ibid., 15 April 1915, p. 9.

14. George N. Barnes, "British Labour and the War," *Englishwoman* 71 (November 1914): 89. Helen Fraser, "Men, Women, and War," *Englishwoman* 75 (March 1915): 245.

15. "It was to the women's advantage in 1917 that during the first three years of war no major branch of their movement had become associated with the cause of a negotiated peace, though many individuals were. Anti-suffragists in Parliament were only too anxious to deploy the argument that women as voters would hinder Governments from waging war." Martin Pugh, "Politicians and the Woman's Vote, 1914–1918," *History* 59, no. 197 (1974): 361. Wiltsher, *Most Dangerous Women*, p. 81.

16. Fawcett, *What I Remember*, pp. 226–27. House of Commons Parliamentary Debates, 15 August 1916, cols. 1700–1701. Quoted in Fawcett, *What I Remember*, p. 228. House of Commons Parliamentary Debates, 28 March 1917, cols. 469–470.

17. Brian Harrison, *Separate Spheres: The Opposition to Women's Suffrage in Britain* (London, 1978), p. 204. Pugh, "Politicians and the Woman's Vote," p. 359; Martin Pugh, *The Tories and the People, 1880–1935* (Oxford, 1985). My thanks to Harold Smith for pointing out this last argument. Holton, *Feminism and Democracy*, pp. 130, 125.

18. The exception to this rule is the WFL, which vowed on 7 August 1914 to continue its suffrage work. "Let us," wrote Charlotte Despard, president of the organization, "by every means in our power, while helping so far as we can the innocent sufferers in all such times . . . keep our own flag flying, and emphasise our demand to have a voice in decisions as to momentous events on which hang the destinies of the nation." "Our President's Message," in *Vote*, 7 August 1914, p. 263. In an article that invoked the language and imagery of the war, C. Nina Boyle warned suffragists that "there will be no end to the demands made upon their patriotism; and one of the very first . . . that will be asked of those within the Women's Movement will be that they abandon the Movement *pro tem*, and give their money, work and energy to other activities in which their services may be entertained but all authority denied. . . . We urge most earnestly all women who have the real eventual welfare of their country and their race at heart not to let themselves be turned aside at this juncture. . . . we make a strong appeal to all Suffragists to stand to their guns and man their own forts, and not to let themselves be drawn out of their Movement for any purpose whatsoever" ("The Crimes of Statescraft [*sic*]," *Vote*, 7 August 1914, p. 268).

19. Mary Stocks, *Eleanor Rathbone: A Biography* (London, 1950), p. 81. Holton, *Feminism and Democracy*, p. 116.

20. Rosen, *Rise Up, Women!*, pp. 263–65. House of Commons Parliamentary Debates, 19 June 1917, cols. 1656, 1662; 28 March 1917, cols. 521–22.

21. Brian Harrison, "Women's Suffrage at Westminster, 1866–1928," in Michael Bentley and John Stevenson, eds., *High and Low Politics in Modern Britain* (Oxford,

1983), p. 118. See Pankhurst, *Unshackled*, pp. 292–93. Les Garner, *Stepping Stones to Women's Liberty: Feminist Ideas in the Women's Suffrage Movement, 1900–1918* (Rutherford, N.J., 1984), p. 95.

22. Harrison, "Women's Suffrage at Westminster," p. 118. Garner, *Stepping Stones*, pp. 101, 103, 102. Quoted by Asquith, House of Commons Parliamentary Debates, 28 March 1917, col. 465. House of Commons Parliamentary Debates, 22 May 1917, col. 2221.

23. House of Lords Parliamentary Debates, 17 December 1917, cols. 216–17; 17 December 1917, cols. 178, 212; 19 December 1917, col. 278.

24. Quoted in Harrison, *Separate Spheres*, pp. 217–20, 216. House of Lords Parliamentary Debates, 19 December 1917, col. 300.

25. For the earl of Selborne's remarks, see House of Lords Parliamentary Debates, 10 January 1918, col. 473. For Curzon's intention to abstain, see House of Lords Parliamentary Debates, 10 January 1918, cols. 522–23. Harrison, *Separate Spheres*, p. 220.

26. Dangerfield, *The Strange Death of Liberal England*, passim. House of Commons Parliamentary Debates, 28 March 1917, col. 493. House of Lords Parliamentary Debates, 19 December 1917, col. 277.

27. Harrison, *Separate Spheres*, p. 210. House of Commons Parliamentary Debates, 28 March 1917, cols. 496–98. House of Lords Parliamentary Debates, 10 January 1918, col. 471. Quoted in Harrison, *Separate Spheres*, p. 202.

28. House of Commons Parliamentary Debates, 16 August 1916, cols. 1917–18; 28 March 1917, col. 493. Edith Cavell, a nurse caught in Belgium when the war broke out, was executed by the Germans in October 1915 for helping British soldiers escape occupied territory. See Wilson, *Myriad Faces of War*, p. 744.

29. House of Commons Parliamentary Debates, 14 August 1916, cols. 1451–52.

30. Ibid., cols. 1460–62.

31. Ibid., 16 August 1916, col. 1960. Quoted in Rosen, *Rise Up, Women!*, p. 260. *Britannia*, the successor to the WSPU's *Suffragette*, was twice closed down by Herbert Samuel's Home Office in the spring of 1916 for impugning the loyalty of Sir Eyre Crowe, a prominent official at the Foreign Office. When these measures failed to muzzle the Pankhursts, Samuel "arranged with the Post Office for issues to be stopped in the mail." Obviously, *Britannia* continued to express the patriotic, if misguided, sentiments of the WSPU in spite of the Home Office's best efforts. See Bernard Wasserstein, *Herbert Samuel: A Political Life* (Oxford, 1992), p. 190.

32. House of Commons Parliamentary Debates, 16 August 1916, col. 1901; 28 March 1917, col. 530. House of Lords Parliamentary Debates, 9 January 1918, col. 449. NUWSS, "Weekly Notes," 3 January 1916, p. 3, Fawcett Library.

33. House of Commons Parliamentary Debates, 22 May 1917, cols. 2189–90. House of Lords Parliamentary Debates, 9 January 1918, cols. 448–49.

34. NUWSS Executive Committee Minutes, 3 August 1916, p. 3. "Interview between Mr. Bonar Law, Mrs. Fawcett & Mrs. O. Strachey, 11th February, 1917" (typescript copy inserted into the NUWSS Executive Committee Minutes, n.d.), Fawcett Library.

35. House of Commons Parliamentary Debates, 28 March 1917, col. 499; 23 May 1917, col. 2428.

36. Pugh, *Women and the Women's Movement*, pp. 41, 42.

37. M. G. Fawcett, "A Step Forward! The Report of the Speaker's Conference on Electoral Reform," *Common Cause*, 9 February 1917, p. 578. Millicent Garrett Fawcett, *The Women's Victory—and After: Personal Reminiscences, 1911–1918* (London, 1920), p. 146. Harrison, "Women's Suffrage at Westminster," p. 121. Dora Montefiore, *From a Victorian to a Modern* (London, 1927), p. 194. Pugh, "Politicians and the Woman's Vote," p. 372.

38. I am grateful to Harold Smith for suggesting this line of thought.

39. Pugh, "Politicians and the Woman's Vote," p. 358. For a complete account of the developments leading to women's suffrage, see also Martin Pugh, *Electoral Reform in War and Peace, 1906–18* (London, 1978). Riley, *"Am I That Name?"*, pp. 67, 68.

40. Maud Selborne, "The Suffrage Compromise," *Englishwoman* 103 (July 1917): 15. Pugh, *Women and the Women's Movement*, pp. 34, 41, 42.

41. See Vron Ware, *Beyond the Pale: White Women, Racism and History* (London, 1992); and Burton, "The Feminist Quest for Identity," pp. 46–81.

42. Fawcett, *What I Remember*, p. 239.

43. Pugh, *Electoral Reform in War and Peace*, pp. 75–76. Millicent Garrett Fawcett, "The War Conscience in Time of Peace," *Englishwoman* 96 (December 1916): 196, 202. Millicent Garrett Fawcett, "Lift Up Your Hearts," *Englishwoman* 85 (January 1916): 13, 14–15.

44. Millicent Garrett Fawcett, "'An Immense and Significant Advance,'" *Englishwoman* 99 (March 1917): 195, 196.

45. C. Nina Boyle, "The Whipping Boy," *Vote*, 9 June 1916, p. 1066. C. Nina Boyle, "We Present Our Bill," *Vote*, 19 February 1915, p. 504.

CHAPTER 5
POSTWAR DISORDER AND THE SALVATION OF SEX

1. Sinclair, *The Tree of Heaven*, p. 368. The different attitudes about the relationship between war and sex demonstrated by Sinclair's various characters may well reflect the ambivalence she felt about her exposure to the war. On the one hand, she was in Belgium long enough to have shared the experiences—and to have expressed them in the same kind of language and imagery—of many other feminists at the front. On the other hand, she was not able to overcome her fear at the front, with the result that she was sent home by the head of the ambulance corps to which she belonged, fired, apparently, for incompetence. See Hynes, *A War Imagined*, pp. 93–94. Leed, *No Man's Land*, p. 8.

2. Hamilton, *Life Errant*, pp. 186, 187, 129. Gibbs, *Now It Can Be Told*, pp. 547–48.

3. Hynes, *A War Imagined*, p. 281; Leed, *No Man's Land*, pp. 202, 203. Rathbone, *We That Were Young*, p. 431. "Sex Rivalry or Sex Prejudice?" *Vote*, 30 May 1919, p. 203. "Child Assault," *Time and Tide*, 5 November 1920, p. 520.

4. "Child Assault," *Time and Tide*, 5 November 1920, p. 201; see Gibbs, *Now It Can Be Told*, p. 551. "Why Carriages Reserved for Women Are Needed," *Vote*, 24 October 1924, p. 342. Gibbs, *Now It Can Be Told*, pp. 551–52, 553.

5. Leed, *No Man's Land*, p. 21. Holtby, *Women and a Changing Civilization*, p. 5. Quoted in Braybon, *Women Workers*, p. 176.

6. Ray Strachey, *The Cause: A Short History of the Women's Movement* (1928; reprint, London, 1978), pp. 370–71. Clephane, *Towards Sex Freedom*, p. 201. C. Nina Boyle, "Signs of the Times—I," *Vote*, 22 September 1916, p. 1183.

7. Gibbs, *Now It Can Be Told*, p. 548. Quoted in Braybon, *Women Workers*, pp. 190, 189, 193–94. In 1911, 32.3 percent of British women reported themselves "gainfully employed." By 1921, the figure had fallen to 30.8 percent. Braybon, *Women Workers*, p. 210. Vera Brittain, *The Women at Oxford: A Fragment of History* (New York, 1960), p. 172.

8. Fussell, *The Great War and Modern Memory*, pp. 71, 73. Borden, *The Forbidden Zone*, p. 58. Hamilton, *Life Errant*, pp. 145, 149, 150.

9. Quoted in Alberti, *Beyond Suffrage*, p. 84.

10. Quoted in Fussell, *The Great War and Modern Memory*, pp. 73, 113. Rathbone, *We That Were Young*, p. 430. Christabel Pankhurst, *Pressing Problems of the Closing Age* (London, 1924), p. 13.

11. Leed, *No Man's Land*, p. 76; p. xi: "The cessation of hostilities did not mean the end of the war experience but rather the beginning of a process in which that experience was framed, institutionalized, given ideological content, and relived in political action as well as fiction." Fussell, *The Great War and Modern Memory*, p. 76. Hynes, *A War Imagined*, p. 337. Modris Eksteins, *Rites of Spring: The Great War and the Birth of the Modern Age* (Boston, 1989), pp. 252, 259, 255.

12. Fussell has claimed that until it became acceptable, in the 1960s and 1970s, to publish works that contained sexually explicit, often brutally obscene depictions, the war could not be fully portrayed. "It is the virtual disappearance during the sixties and seventies of the concept of prohibitive obscenity, a concept which has acted as a censor on earlier memories of 'war,' that has given the ritual of military memory a new dimension. And that new dimension is capable of revealing for the first time the full obscenity of the Great War. . . . it is only now . . . that the literary means for adequate remembering and interpreting are finally publicly accessible" (*The Great War and Modern Memory*, p. 334).

13. Sigmund Freud, "Reflections upon War and Death" (first published in *Imago*, 1915), in Philip Rieff, ed., *Character and Culture* (New York, 1963), pp. 113, 114, 117, 119.

14. Peter Gay, ed., in introduction to Sigmund Freud, *Beyond the Pleasure Principle* (1920), in *The Freud Reader* (New York, 1989), p. 594.

15. Freud, *Beyond the Pleasure Principle*, pp. 613, 615, 621.

16. Sigmund Freud, *The Ego and the Id* (1923; reprint, New York, 1960), pp. 31, 34, 34–35.

17. Sigmund Freud, *Civilization and Its Discontents* (1930; reprint, New York, 1961), pp. 65–66, 49, 104.

18. Sigmund Freud, *A General Introduction to Psychoanalysis* (London, 1922; New York, 1924), p. 153.

19. Quoted in Peter Gay, *Freud: A Life for Our Time* (New York, 1988), pp. 451, 452–53. Leed, *No Man's Land*, p. 6. Playne, *Society at War*, pp. 13, 16, 20, 28, 29.

20. Hirschfeld, *The Sexual History of the War*, pp. 22, 32. H. C. Fischer and Dr. E. X. Dubois, *Sexual Life during the World War* (London, 1937), pp. 47, 48, 48–49. I am indebted to Chris Waters for directing me to this source.

21. Hirschfeld, *The Sexual History of the War*, p. 34. Quoted in Brittain, *Testament of Friendship*, p. 52.

22. Fischer and Dubois, *Sexual Life during the World War*, p. 179. Hirschfeld, *The Sexual History of the War*, p. 52. I am indebted to Bonnie G. Smith for this insight.

23. Hirschfeld, *The Sexual History of the War*, pp. 34–35.

24. Fischer and Dubois, *Sexual Life during the World War*, pp. 53, 52, 66.

25. Havelock Ellis, *Psychology of Sex* (London, 1948), p. 124. Quoted in Jeffrey Weeks, *Sex, Politics and Society: The Regulation of Sexuality since 1800* (London, 1981), p. 149. Weeks, *Sex, Politics and Society*, p. 206. Dora Russell, *Hypatia, or Woman and Knowledge* (London, 1925), pp. 41–42. She continued, "What is man's part in sex but a perpetual waving of flags and blowing of trumpets and avoidance of the fighting?" See Jane Lewis, *The Politics of Motherhood: Child and Maternal Welfare in England, 1900–1939* (London, 1980), passim; Weeks, *Sex, Politics and Society*, pp. 127, 128.

26. Weeks, *Sex, Politics and Society*, pp. 200, 207. Th. H. Van de Velde, *Sex Hostility in Marriage: Its Origin, Prevention and Treatment* (London, 1931), p. 9; Hirschfeld, *The Sexual History of the War*, p. 17; Fischer and Dubois, *Sexual Life during the World War*, p. 179. Van de Velde, *Sex Hostility in Marriage*, pp. 13, 20, 22, 15–16, 17.

27. Van de Velde, *Sex Hostility in Mariage*, pp. 188, 206. See Isabel Emslie Hutton, *The Sex Technique in Marriage* (New York, 1932); Helena Wright, *The Sex Factor in Marriage* (New York); Van de Velde, *Sex Hostility in Marriage*. Mary Stocks, *Still More Commonplace* (London, 1973), p. 20. Richard Allen Soloway, *Birth Control and the Population Question in England, 1877–1930* (Chapel Hill, 1982), pp. 211–12. Van de Velde, *Sex Hostility in Marriage*, p. vi. My appreciation to Bonnie Smith for this insight into the role of sexologists and psychoanalysts in helping to create newly psychologized separate spheres for men and women.

28. Quoted in Weeks, *Sex, Politics and Society*, pp. 154–55. Sigmund Freud, "The Dissolution of the Oedipus Complex," quoted in Gay, *Freud*, p. 515. "There was nothing in the climate of the 1920s and nothing in Freud's psychological biography to prompt the revisions that would make him propound his controversial, at times scurrilous, views on woman" (Gay, *Freud*, p. 515). Sigmund Freud, "Some Psychological Consequences of the Anatomical Distinction between the Sexes" (1925), in Philip Rieff, ed., *Sexuality and the Psychology of Love* (New York, 1963), pp. 187, 188, 191, 193. Freud's original title was "Some Psychical Consequences of the Anatomical Distinction between the Sexes."

29. A. Costler et al., Norman Haire, gen. ed., *Encyclopaedia of Sexual Knowledge* (New York, 1940), pp. 288–89. (The English edition appeared in 1934.)

30. Van de Velde, *Sex Hostility in Marriage*, pp. 30, 43, 68–69, 120, 66. Karl Abraham, "Manifestations of the Female Castration Complex" (1920), in Jean Strouse, ed., *Women and Analysis: Dialogues on Psychoanalytic Views of Femininity* (New York, 1974), p. 139. Havelock Ellis, *Sex in Relation to Society*, vol. 6 of *Studies in the Psychology of Sex* (1946), quoted in Jeffreys, *The Spinster and Her Enemies*, p. 137.

31. Quoted in Sheila Jeffreys, "Sex Reform and Anti-feminism in the 1920s," in London Feminist History Group, *The Sexual Dynamics of History* (London, 1983), pp. 185, 190. K. A. Weith Knudsen, *Feminism—The Woman Question from Ancient Times to the Present Day* (London, 1928), quoted in Jeffreys, *The Spinster and Her Enemies*, p. 176. Quoted in Jeffreys, "Sex Reform and Anti-feminism," pp. 186, 199.

32. Van de Velde, *Sex Hostility in Marriage*, p. 67. Weith Knudsen, *The Woman Question*, quoted in Jeffreys, *The Spinster and Her Enemies*, p. 177. Arabella Kenealy, *Feminism and Sex-Extinction* (London, 1920), pp. vii, vi; "If women are to have scope and authority identical with men's, then they must forgo all privileges; must come out from their fence behind strong arms and chivalry to meet masculine blows in the face, economic and ethical—if not actual" (p. 108). Anthony M. Ludovici, *Lysistrata, or Woman's Future and Future Woman* (New York, 1925), pp. 92, 87, 78.

CHAPTER 6

POSTWAR FEMINISM: ESTABLISHING THE PEACE

1. Riley, *"Am I That Name?"*, pp. 59–60. Ray Strachey, ed., *Our Freedom and Its Results* (London, 1936), p. 10. Holtby, *Women and a Changing Civilization*, p. 96.

2. I am grateful to Bonnie Smith for this insight.

3. Holtby, *Women and a Changing Civilization*, p. 119. Hamilton, *Life Errant*, p. 251.

4. Fawcett, *Women's Victory*, p. 160.

5. A. Maude Royden, "The Woman's Movement of the Future," in Victor Gollancz, ed., *The Making of Women* (London, 1917), pp. 129, 130, 131, 132.

6. Eleanor Rathbone, "The Old and the New Feminism," *Woman's Leader*, 13 March 1925, p. 52. "What is Feminism?" *Woman's Leader*, 17 July 1925, p. 195.

7. Royden, "Woman's Movement of the Future," p. 143. Eleanor Rathbone, "Changes in Public Life," in Ray Strachey, ed., *Our Freedom and Its Results* (London, 1936), pp. 73–74, 76. Eleanor F. Rathbone, "What Is Equality?" pt. 1, *Woman's Leader*, 11 February 1927, p. 3.

8. "What Is Feminism?" *Woman's Leader*, 17 July 1925, p. 195.

9. Quoted in Holton, *Feminism and Democracy*, p. 143. Pat Thane, "The Women of the British Labour Party and Feminism, 1906–1945," in Harold L. Smith, ed., *British Feminism in the Twentieth Century* (Aldershot, 1990), pp. 128, 129.

10. K. D. Courtney et al., *Equal Pay and the Family: A Proposal for the National Endowment of Motherhood* (London, n.d. [1918]), p. 10. M. D. Stocks, *The Meaning of Family Endowment* (London, 1921), p. 8. Eleanor Rathbone, *The Disinherited Family: A Plea for the Endowment of the Family* (London, 1924), p. 82. Alberti, *Beyond Suffrage*, p. 130.

11. Review of *The Disinherited Family* in *Woman's Leader*, 28 March 1924, p. 72. Susan Pedersen, "The Failure of Feminism in the Making of the British Welfare State," *Radical History Review* 43 (Winter 1989): 90–91.

12. Eleanor Rathbone, "The Remuneration of Women's Services," *Economic Journal* 27, no. 105 (1917): 59. Millicent Garrett Fawcett, in response, challenged Rathbone's assumptions "that women are always industrially less advantageous to their employers than men and that their lower wages to a large extent merely reflect this lower value." The experience of the war, Fawcett argued, demonstrated that "a large proportion of supposed feminine disadvantages exist more in imagination than in reality. . . . No one knows what women or anyone else can do until they have had an opportunity of learning how and trying. . . . I am convinced that the best chance of women preserving, after peace returns, the industrial freedom which the war has

brought them lies in the earnestness and sincerity with which industrial women maintain the principle 'equal pay for equal work'" (Millicent Garrett Fawcett, "Equal Pay for Equal Work," *Economic Journal* 28, no. 109 [1918]: 2–3, 4, 5).

13. Olive Banks, *Faces of Feminism: A Study of Feminism as a Social Movement* (Oxford, 1986), p. 168. Royden, "Woman's Movement of the Future," p. 143.

14. Alberti, *Beyond Suffrage*, p. 130. Quoted in Lewis, *The Politics of Motherhood*, p. 170. Rathbone, "The Old and the New Feminism," *Woman's Leader*, 13 March 1925, p. 52. "What Is Feminism?" *Woman's Leader*, 17 July 1925, p. 195. Rathbone, "The Remuneration of Women's Services," p. 65. *Woman's Leader*, 28 March 1924, p. 72. Banks, *Faces of Feminism*, p. 178.

15. Elizabeth Abbott, "What Is Equality?" *Woman's Leader*, 11 February 1927, p. 4.

16. Alberti, *Beyond Suffrage*, p. 131. H. M. Swanwick, "Woman's Place III. The Married State," *Time and Tide*, 18 November 1927, p. 1031. Ray Strachey, "Changes in Employment," in Strachey, *Our Freedom and Its Results*, pp. 168, 170, 171–72.

17. A. Helen Ward, "What Is Equality?" *Woman's Leader*, 25 February 1927, p. 20. Dorothy Balfour of Burleigh, ibid., p. 21.

18. "To Officers and Members of the National Union of Societies for Equal Citizenship," *Woman's Leader*, 11 March 1927, pp. 36–38. "Statement by the Eleven Resigning Officers and Members of the National Union of Societies for Equal Citizenship Executive Committee," *Woman's Leader*, 11 March 1927, p. 38.

19. Rathbone, "Changes in Public Life," pp. 59–60.

20. "Equality of 'Protection' for Women?" *Vote*, 5 September 1924, p. 281. "An Effete Classification," *Time and Tide*, 13 August 1920, in Dale Spender, *Time and Tide Wait for No Man* (London, 1984), pp. 194, 195. Viscountess Rhondda, *Leisured Women* (London, 1928), pp. 59–60. Hamilton, *Life Errant*, pp. 208–9. Holtby, *Women and a Changing Civilization*, pp. 81–82, 168. Vera Brittain, "Men on Women," *Time and Tide*, 22 June 1928, quoted in Paul Berry and Alan Bishop, eds., *Testament of a Generation: The Journalism of Vera Brittain and Winifred Holtby* (London, 1985), pp. 118–19. Winifred Holtby, "Black Words for Women Only," *Clarion*, 24 March 1934, quoted in Berry and Bishop, *Testament of a Generation*, p. 86. Holtby, *Women and a Changing Civilization*, pp. 191, 192.

21. Editorial, *Time and Tide*, 14 May 1920, p. 4. Winifred Holtby, "'Feminism Divided,'" *Yorkshire Post*, 26 July 1926; reprinted in *Time and Tide*, 6 August 1926, pp. 714, 715.

22. Vera Brittain, "Why Feminism Lives," Six Point Group Pamphlet (1927), in Berry and Bishop, *Testament of a Generation*, pp. 98, 99. "Human Beings—and Females," *Time and Tide*, 3 February 1928, p. 97.

23. Riley, *"Am I That Name?"*, p. 63. My thanks to Susan Pedersen for reminding me of this dilemma. Holtby, "'Feminism Divided,'" *Time and Tide*, 6 August 1926, p. 714. See *Time and Tide*, 1930–1934, passim. I am grateful to David Doughan of the Fawcett Library, London, for pointing this out to me.

24. Sheila Jeffreys has argued that the sexology of the 1920s emphasizing sexually fulfilling motherhood was "absorbed into the 'new feminism' of Eleanor Rathbone and other women in the National Union for Equal Citizenship," successor to NUSEC, but she does not explain why, attributing to sexual discourse alone a power

it cannot claim and a lack of agency on the part of feminists that is belied by their pronouncements and activities. See Jeffreys, *The Spinster and Her Enemies*, p. 146.

25. Eleanor Rathbone, "What Is Equality?" *Woman's Leader*, 11 February 1927, p. 3. See Kent, *Sex and Suffrage*. "Our Common Humanity," *Common Cause*, 20 February 1914, p. 884. Royden, "Woman's Movement of the Future," p. 143.

26. Royden, "War and the Woman's Movement." A. Maude Royden, "Women and the League of Nations," *Englishwoman* 134 (February 1920): 88. A. Maude Royden, *Women at the World's Crossroads* (New York, 1923), pp. 116, 43, 79–80, 95.

27. F. W. Stella Browne, "The Sexual Variety and Variability among Women and Their Bearing upon Social Reconstruction," in Sheila Rowbotham, *A New World for Women: Stella Browne—Socialist Feminist* (London, 1977), p. 95. Elizabeth Robins, *Ancilla's Share: An Indictment of Sex Antagonism* (London, 1924), p. xxxix.

28. Sheila Jeffreys has argued that "during the years of the First World War the question of women's right to sexual pleasure was raised by some of the foremost proponents of sex reform," and that feminist sex reformers such as Stella Browne and Marie Stopes emphasized "care for the woman, both her right to sexual pleasure and her right to bodily integrity. . . . In contrast, the sexological literature of the 1920s locates women's frigidity as a problem, not for the woman herself, but for men, for marriage, for 'society' and 'civilization' in general. Woman's sexual pleasure becomes, for these writers, a means to an end rather than an end in itself" ("Sex Reform and Anti-feminism," pp. 181–82). I think Jeffreys is right about the different emphases, but she underestimates the extent to which sexual pleasure was also a means to an end for feminists, many of whom shared the belief that sexual pleasure promised rewards beyond the gratification of the immediate (heterosexual) couple.

29. Quoted in Clephane, *Towards Sex Freedom*, p. 204. Browne, "Sexual Variety and Variability among Women," p. 103. Rebecca West, "Six Point Group Supplement Point No. 3: Equality for Men and Women Teachers"; "Equal Pay for Men and Women Teachers," *Time and Tide*, 9 February 1923, p. 142. Russell, *Hypatia*, pp. 1, 12, 24–25.

30. Russell, *Hypatia*, p. 37. Dora Russell, "Marriage," delivered at the Guildhouse, 30 October 1927. In *Guildhouse Monthly* 13, no. 2 (1928): 53; Dora Russell, *The Right to Be Happy* (London, 1927), pp. 131–32.

31. As Alberti has noted, "the glimpses we have of the reception of the 'new morality' suggests that liberal feminists—Swanwick, Sharp, Rhondda, Stocks—welcomed freedom from censorship and control, but retained a distrust of promiscuity or 'excess'. . . . With the possible exception of Emmeline Pethick Lawrence and Maude Royden they did not consider that a greater recognition of her sexuality was a necessary part of women's emancipation" (Alberti, *Beyond Suffrage*, p. 112).

32. Swanwick, *War in Its Effect upon Women*, p. 21.

33. See A. Maude Royden, *A Threefold Cord* (London, 1948), passim. A. Maude Royden, *Sex and Common Sense* (London, 1921), pp. 4, 7–8, 36. A. Maude Royden, *The Moral Standards of the Rising Generation* (London, n.d.), pp. 7, 11, 13, 12.

34. "Cripicus," letter to editor, *Woman's Leader*, 11 January 1929, p. 383.

35. Quoted in Soloway, *Birth Control and the Population Question*, p. 233. F. W. Stella Browne, "The Feminine Aspect of Birth Control," in Raymond Pierpont, ed., *Report of the Fifth International Neo-Malthusian and Birth Control Conference* (London, 1922), p. 41. Russell, *Hypatia*, pp. 58, 63, 64.

36. Browne, "The Feminine Aspect of Birth Control," p. 40. See Hamilton, *Life Errant*, pp. 249, 251; Brittain, *Lady into Woman*, p. 163; Holtby, *Women and a Changing Civilization*, pp. 68, 169. Mrs. M. C. Crook, letter to editor, *Woman's Leader*, 4 May 1923, p. 111. Holtby, *Women and a Changing Civilization*, pp. 169–70, 190.

37. Marie Carmichael Stopes, *Wise Parenthood: The Treatise on Birth Control for Married People* (1918; reprint, London, 1933); *Queen's Hall Meeting on Constructive Birth Control* (London, 1921). See Soloway, *Birth Control and the Population Question*.

38. Quoted in *Malthusian* 40, no. 3 (1916): 32. *Vote*, 21 November 1924, p. 372. Quoted in Alberti, *Beyond Suffrage*, p. 168. For accounts of the struggle to assert the rights of women to birth control within the Labour party, see Soloway, *Birth Control and the Population Question*; Lewis, *The Politics of Motherhood*; Harold L. Smith, "Sex vs. Class: British Feminists and the Labour Movement, 1919–1929, *Historian* 47 (November 1984): 19–37.

39. "The Stopes Libel Action," *Woman's Leader*, 9 March 1923, p. 42. "Is Birth Control a Feminist Reform?" *Woman's Leader*, 2 October 1925, p. 283. "A Word with the Minister of Health," *Woman's Leader*, 20 March 1925, p. 59. Mary D. Stocks, *Family Limitation and Women's Organisations* (London, 1925), p. 3.

40. Alberti, *Beyond Suffrage*, pp. 120, 125. "Is Birth Control a Feminist Reform?" *Woman's Leader*, 2 October 1925, p. 283 (italics added). Banks, *Faces of Feminism*, pp. 190–91.

41. Royden, "Woman's Movement of the Future," p. 140.

42. Rathbone, "The Remuneration of Women's Services," p. 64. Courtney et al., *Equal Pay and the Family*, p. 7.

43. "What Is Feminism?" *Woman's Leader*, 17 July 1925, p. 195. "The 'New Feminism,'" *Woman's Leader*, 12 March 1926. Letter to *Woman's Leader*, 18 March 1927, p. 50. Rathbone, "Changes in Public Life," p. 76.

44. R. S., "Woman's Sphere Once More," *Woman's Leader*, 20 November 1925, p. 340. "Sex and Intelligence," *Time and Tide*, 2 February 1923, p. 109. John Beevers, review of Norman Haire's *Encyclopaedia of Sexual Knowledge*, *Time and Tide*, 21 July 1934, p. 934.

45. Holtby, *Women and a Changing Civilization*, pp. 192, 161, 131–32, 132–33, 161.

46. Vera Brittain, "Welfare for Middle-Class Mothers," *Time and Tide*, 30 March 1928, p. 305. Swanwick, *I Have Been Young*, pp. 272, 273. Holtby, *Women and a Changing Civilization*, p. 7.

47. Rebecca West, "Equal Pay for Men and Women Teachers," *Time and Tide*, 9 February 1923, p. 142. Quoted in Jeffreys, *The Spinster and Her Enemies*, p. 149. Riley, *"Am I That Name?"*, p. 59.

48. Robins, *Ancilla's Share*, pp. xxxvi, xliv, xxxix, 48.

49. Rebecca West, "On a Form of Nagging," *Time and Tide*, 31 October 1925, p. 1052.

50. Cicely Hamilton, "The Return to Femininity," *Time and Tide*, 12 August 1927, p. 737. Brittain, *Testament of Youth*, p. 582. Rathbone, *We That Were Young*, pp. 431–32. Borden, *The Forbidden Zone*, p. 48.

51. Catherine Gasquoine Hartley, *Motherhood and the Relationships of the Sexes* (London, 1917), pp. 14, 15, 18, 27, 31.

52. Pankhurst, *Pressing Problems of the Closing Age*, p. 38. See Kent, *Sex and Suffrage*, chaps. 6 and 7. Pankhurst, *Pressing Problems of the Closing Age*, p. 40. Robins, *Ancilla's Share*, p. xxxviii.

CONCLUSION

1. Joan W. Scott, "Rewriting History," in Margaret Randolph Higonnet et al., eds., *Behind the Lines: Gender and the Two World Wars* (New Haven, 1987), p. 27.

2. Michel Foucault, *The History of Sexuality*, vol. 1, *An Introduction* (New York, 1980), p. 123; Kent, *Sex and Suffrage*, pp. 15, 16.

3. Riley, *"Am I That Name?"*, pp. 59, 62.

4. Fussell, *The Great War and Modern Memory*, p. 79.

5. Holtby, *Women and a Changing Civilization*, p. 161.

6. Hamilton, *Life Errant*, p. 226; review of S. Dark's *The Jew Today* in *Time and Tide*, 3 March 1934, p. 289.

7. *Time and Tide*, 3 March 1934, p. 284.

8. Clephane, *Towards Sex Freedom*, pp. 227–28.

9. Hynes, *A War Imagined*, p. 467; Rathbone, "Changes in Public Life," p. 68.

BIBLIOGRAPHY

ARCHIVAL SOURCES

Margery Corbett Ashby Collection. Fawcett Library, London.
Elsie Bowerman Collection. Fawcett Library, London.
Marie Stopes Collection. British Library, London.
Minutes of the Executive Committee, National Union of Women's Suffrage Societies. Fawcett Library, London.
"Weekly Notes," National Union of Women's Suffrage Societies. Fawcett Library, London.

GOVERNMENT PAPERS

Committee on Alleged German Outrages. *Evidence and Documents Laid before the Committee on Alleged German Outrages*, 1915 (Appendix to Bryce Report).
House of Commons Parliamentary Debates, 1916, 1917, 1928.
House of Lords Parliamentary Debates, 1917, 1918.

PERIODICALS AND NEWSPAPERS

Britannia. London, 1915.
Common Cause. London, 1914–1917. Becomes *The Woman's Leader*, 1920.
Communist. London, 1922.
Englishwoman. London, 1914–1920.
Malthusian. London, 1914–1918.
Suffragette. London, 1914–1915. Becomes *Britannia*, 1915.
Time and Tide. London, 1920–1936.
Vote. London, 1914–1918.
Woman's Leader. London, 1922–1925.

PRIMARY SOURCES

Abraham, Karl. "Manifestations of the Female Castration Complex." In Jean Strouse, ed., *Women and Analysis: Dialogues on Psychoanalytic Views of Femininity*. New York, 1974.
Alec-Tweedie, Mrs. *Women and Soldiers*. London, 1918.
Bagnold, Enid. *A Diary without Dates*. New York, 1935.
Barnes, George N. "British Labour and the War." *Englishwoman* 71 (November 1914): 89–95.
Barton, Dorothea M. *Equal Pay for Equal Work*. London, 1919.
Blainey, J. *The Woman Worker and Restrictive Legislation*. London, 1928.
Blatch, Harriot Stanton. *Mobilizing Woman-Power*. New York, 1918.
Borden, Mary. *The Forbidden Zone*. London, 1929.

Brittain, Vera. "The Failure of Monogamy." In Norman Haire, ed., *Sexual Reform Congress*. London, 1930.

———. *Honourable Estate: A Novel of Transition*. New York, 1936.

———. *Lady into Woman*. London, 1953.

———. *Testament of Friendship*. London, 1940.

———. *Testament of Youth*. 1933. Reprint. London, 1978.

———. *War Diary, 1913–1917: Chronicle of Youth*. Edited by Alan Bishop with Terry Smart. London, 1981.

———. *The Women at Oxford: A Fragment of History*. New York, 1960.

Browne, F. W. Stella. "The Feminine Aspect of Birth Control." In Raymond Pierpont, ed., *Report of the Fifth International Neo-Malthusian and Birth Control Conference*. London, 1922.

———. "The Right to Abortion." In Norman Haire, ed., *Sexual Reform Congress*. London, 1930.

———. "The Sexual Variety and Variability among Women and Their Bearing upon Social Reconstruction." In Sheila Rowbotham, *A New World for Women: Stella Browne—Socialist Feminist*. London, 1977.

———. "The 'Women's Question.'" *Communist* 84 (11 March 1922): 7.

Bulan, S. "The Untrained Nurse in National Emergency." *Englishwoman* 69 (September 1914): 267–72.

Chesser, Elizabeth Sloan, M.D. *The Woman Who Knows Herself*. London, 1926.

Churchill, Lady Randolph, ed. *Women's War Work*. London, 1916.

Clephane, Irene. *Towards Sex Freedom*. London, 1935.

Costler, A., et al. Norman Haire, gen. ed. *Encyclopaedia of Sexual Knowledge*. New York, 1940.

Courtney, Kate. *Extracts from a Diary during the War*. Privately printed, 1927.

Courtney, K. D., et al. *Equal Pay and the Family: A Proposal for the National Endowment of Motherhood*. London, n.d. [1918].

Craig, Grace Morris. *But This Is Our War*. Toronto, 1981.

Daggett, Mabel Potter. *Women Wanted: The Story Written in Blood Red Letters on the Horizon of the Great War*. London, 1918.

The Deportation of Women and Girls from Lille. New York, n.d.

Dexter, Mary. *In The Soldier's Service: War Experiences of Mary Dexter, 1914–1918*. Boston, 1918.

Ellis, Edith Lees. *The New Horizon in Love and Life*. London, 1921.

Ellis, Havelock. *Psychology of Sex*. London, 1948.

A F.A.N.Y. in France. Nursing Adventures. London, 1917.

Fawcett, Millicent Garrett. "Equal Pay for Equal Work." *Economic Journal* 28, no. 109 (1918): 1–6.

———. "'An Immense and Significant Advance.'" *Englishwoman* 99 (March 1917): 193–97.

———. "Lift Up Your Hearts." *Englishwoman* 85 (January 1916): 5–15.

———. "The National Union of Women's Suffrage Societies and the Hague Congress." *Englishwoman* 78 (June 1915): 193–200.

———. "'Peace Hath Her Victories No Less Renowned Than War.'" *Englishwoman* 111 (March 1918): 163–68.

———. "The War Conscience in Time of Peace." *Englishwoman* 96 (December 1916): 196–209.

_____. *What I Remember*. 1925. Reprint. Westport, Conn., 1976.

_____. *The Women's Victory—and After: Personal Reminiscences, 1911–1918*. London, 1920.

Fischer, H. C., and Dr. E. X. Dubois. *Sexual Life during the World War*. London, 1937.

Ford, Ford Madox. *Parade's End*. New York, 1979.

Fraser, Helen. "Men, Women, and War." *Englishwoman* 75 (March 1915): 239–45.

_____. *Women and War Work*. 1917. New York, 1918.

Freud, Sigmund. *Beyond the Pleasure Principle*. 1920. In Peter Gay, ed., *The Freud Reader*. New York, 1989.

_____. *Civilization and Its Discontents*. 1930. Reprint. New York, 1961.

_____. *The Ego and the Id*. 1923. Reprint. New York, 1960.

_____. "Female Sexuality." 1931. In Philip Rieff, ed., *Sexuality and the Psychology of Love*. New York, 1963.

_____. *A General Introduction to Psychoanalysis*. London, 1922. New York, 1924.

_____. *Group Psychology and the Analysis of the Ego*. 1921. Reprint. New York, 1959.

_____. "Reflections upon War and Death." 1915. In Philip Rieff, ed., *Character and Culture*. New York, 1963.

_____. "Some Psychological Consequences of the Anatomical Distinction between the Sexes." 1925. In Philip Rieff, ed., *Sexuality and the Psychology of Love*. New York, 1963.

Gasquoine Hartley, C. *Divorce (To-day and To-morrow)*. London, 1921.

_____. *Motherhood and the Relationships of the Sexes*. London, 1917.

_____. *The Truth About Women*. London, 1913.

_____. *Women, Children, Love and Marriage*. London, 1924.

_____. *Women's Wild Oats: Essays on the Re-Fixing of Moral Standards*. London, 1919.

Gibbs, Philip. *Now It Can Be Told*. New York, 1920.

Graves, Robert. *Good-bye to All That*. 1929. 2d ed. New York, 1957.

Haldane, Charlotte. *Motherhood and Its Enemies*. London, 1927.

Hall, Ruth, ed. *Dear Dr. Stopes: Sex in the 1920s*. London, 1978.

Hamilton, Cicely. *The Englishwoman*. London, 1940.

_____. *Life Errant*. London, 1935.

_____. *William—An Englishman*. London, 1919.

_____. "The Women's Congress and the Peace Problem." *Englishwoman* 140 (August 1920): 81–86.

Hamilton, Mary Agnes. "Changes in Social Life." In Ray Strachey, ed., *Our Freedom and Its Results*. London, 1936.

Harraden, Beatrice. *Our Warrior Women*. London, 1916.

Hay, Ian. *The First Hundred Thousand: Being the Unofficial Chronicle of a Unit "K(I)."* New York, n.d.

Hirschfeld, Magnus. *The Sexual History of the World War*. New York, 1937.

Holtby, Winifred. *Letters to a Friend*. London, 1937.

_____. *Women and a Changing Civilization*. 1935. Reprint. Chicago, 1978.

How-Martyn, Edith, and Mary Breed. *The Birth Control Movement in England*. London, 1930.

Hutton, Isabel Emslie, M.D. *The Hygiene of Marriage*. London, 1923.

Kenealy, Arabella. *Feminism and Sex-Extinction*. London, 1920.

LaMotte, Ellen N. *The Backwash of War*. New York, 1934.

Lawrence, D. H. "Tickets, Please." In *England, My England*. London, 1924.

Llewelyn Davies, Margaret, ed. *Maternity: Letters from Working Women*. 1915. Reprint. New York, 1978.

Lowndes, Mary. "The Recrudescence of Barbarism." *Englishwoman* 70 (October 1914): 20–27.

Ludovici, Anthony M. *Lysistrata, or Woman's Future and Future Woman*. New York, 1925.

Macaulay, Rose. *Non-Combatants and Others*. London, 1916.

Manning, Frederic. *Her Privates We*. London, 1986. Originally published as *The Middle Parts of Fortune*, 1929.

Marshall, Catherine E. "The Future of Women in Politics." In Margaret Kamester and Jo Vellacott, eds., *Militarism versus Feminism: Writings on Women and War*. London, 1987.

———. "Women and War." In Margaret Kamester and Jo Vellacott, eds., *Militarism versus Feminism: Writings on Women and War*. London, 1987.

Mathews, Vera Laughton, M.B.E. *The Woman's Movement and Birth Control*. London, n.d.

Meikle, Wilma. *Towards a Sane Feminism*. London, 1916.

Millicent, duchess of Sutherland. *Six Weeks at the War*. Chicago, 1915.

Mills, Ernestine. "Mothers in Factories." *Englishwoman* 121 (January 1919): 9–11.

Montefiore, Dora. *From a Victorian to a Modern*. London, 1927.

———. *Race Motherhood: Is Woman the Race?* London, 1920.

Neilans, Alison. "Changes in Sex Morality." In Ray Strachey, ed., *Our Freedom and Its Results*. London, 1936.

Open Door Council. *Economic Emancipation Next*. London, 1929.

———. *Fallacies in Factory Legislation*. London, 1927.

———. *First Annual Report*. Leicester, 1927.

———. *The Married Woman: Is She a Person?* London, n.d.

———. *Maternity and Childbirth*. London, 1929.

———. *The Real Protection of the Woman Worker*. London, 1926.

———. *Restrictive Legislation and the Industrial Woman Worker: A Reply by the Open Door Council to the Statement by the Standing Joint Committee of Women's Industrial Organisations*. London, 1928.

———. *Should There Be Special Restrictions on Women's Work?* London, n.d.

Pankhurst, Christabel. *America and the Great War: A Speech Delivered at Carnegie Hall, New York, October 24, 1914*. London, 1914.

———. *International Militancy: A Speech Delivered at Carnegie Hall, New York, January 13, 1915*. London, 1915.

———. *Pressing Problems of the Closing Age*. London, 1924.

———. *Unshackled: The Story of How We Won the Vote*. 1959. Reprint. London, 1987.

———. *The War: A Speech Delivered at the London Opera House, September 8, 1914*. London, 1914.

Pankhurst, E. Sylvia. *The Home Front: A Mirror to Life in England during the First World War*. 1932. Reprint. London, 1987.

Parr, Olive Katharine. *Woman's "Emancipation."* Devon, n.d.

Peel, Mrs. C. S. *How We Lived Then, 1914–1918: A Sketch of Social and Domestic Life in England during the War*. London, 1929.

Pethick Lawrence, Emmeline. *My Part in a Changing World*. London, 1938.

Playne, C. E. *The Neurosis of the Nations*. New York, 1925.

——. *Society at War, 1914–1916*. Boston, 1931.

Rathbone, Eleanor. "Changes in Public Life." In Ray Strachey, ed., *Our Freedom and Its Results*. London, 1936.

——. *The Disinherited Family: A Plea for the Endowment of the Family*. London, 1924.

——. "The Remuneration of Women's Services." *Economic Journal* 27, no. 105 (1917): 55–68.

Rathbone, Irene. *We That Were Young*. 1932. Reprint. New York, 1989.

Rhondda, Viscountess. *Leisured Women*. London, 1928.

——. *This Was My World*. London, 1933.

Robins, Elizabeth. *Ancilla's Share: An Indictment of Sex Antagonism*. London, 1924.

Royden, A. Maude. "Introduction." In Johann Ferch, *Birth Control*. London, 1932.

——. "Modern Love." In Victor Gollancz, ed., *The Making of Women*. London, 1917.

——. *The Moral Standards of the Rising Generation*. London, n.d.

——. *Sex and Common Sense*. London, 1921.

——. "War and the Woman's Movement." In Charles Roden Buxton, ed., *Towards a Lasting Settlement*. London, n.d.

——. "The Woman's Movement of the Future." In Victor Gollancz, ed., *The Making of Women*. London, 1917.

——. "Women and the League of Nations." *Englishwoman* 134 (February 1920): 81–88.

——. *Women and the Sovereign State*. London, 1917.

——. *Women at the World's Crossroads*. New York, 1923.

Russell, Dora. *Hypatia, or Woman and Knowledge*. London, 1925.

——. "Marriage." *Guildhouse Monthly* 13, no. 2 (1928): 46–53.

——. "Marriage and Freedom." In Norman Haire, ed., *Sexual Reform Congress*. London, 1929.

——. *The Right to Be Happy*. London, 1927.

——. *The Tamarisk Tree*. Vol. 1. London, 1977.

Sassoon, Siegfried. "Glory of Women." In John Silken, ed., *The Penguin Book of First World War Poetry*. 2d ed. Harmondsworth, 1981.

——. *Memoirs of a Fox-Hunting Man*. London, 1928.

——. *Memoirs of an Infantry Officer*. New York, 1930.

——. *Sherston's Progress*. London, 1936.

Scharlieb, Mary. *Artificial Limitation of the Birth-Rate: Social and Religious Aspects*. Maidstone, n.d.

——. *The Bachelor Woman and Her Problems*. London, 1929.

——. "The Medical Aspects of Conception Control." In James Marchant, ed., *Medical Views on Birth Control*. London, 1926.

——. "The Moral Training of Modern Girls." In James Marchant, ed., *The Claims of the Coming Generation*. London, 1923.

Scharlieb, Mary. *Reminiscences*. London, 1924.

———. *Straight Talks to Women*. London, 1923.

———. *What It Means to Marry*. London, 1914.

Selborne, Maud. "The Suffrage Compromise." *Englishwoman* 103 (July 1917): 13–15.

Sinclair, May. *A Journal of Impressions in Belgium*. New York, 1915.

———. *The Romantic*. New York, 1920.

———. *The Tree of Heaven*. New York, 1917.

Six Point Group. *Annual Report, 1931–1932, and News Sheet*. London, 1932.

Smart, Fanny. "Open Letter: Women and Defence." *Englishwoman* 73 (January 1915): 76–80.

Smith, Helen Zenna. *Not So Quiet . . . Stepdaughters of War*. 1930. Reprint. New York, 1989.

Smyth, Ethel. *A Final Burning of Boats*. London, 1928.

———. *Streaks of Life*. London, 1921.

Society of Friends. *Marriage and Parenthood: The Problem of Birth control*. London, n.d.

Stocks, Mary. *The Case for Family Endowment*. London, 1927.

———. *Eleanor Rathbone: A Biography*. London, 1950.

———. *Family Limitation and Women's Organisations*. London, 1925.

———. *The Meaning of Family Endowment*. London, 1921.

———. *Still More Commonplace*. London, 1973.

Stopes, Marie Carmichael. *Enduring Passion*. New York, 1931.

———. *Married Love: A New Contribution to the Solution of Sex Difficulties*. 1918. Reprint. London, 1923.

———. *A New Gospel to All Peoples*. London, 1922.

———. *Wise Parenthood: The Treatise on Birth Control for Married People*. London, 1933.

Stopes, Marie Carmichael, and Humphrey Vernon Roe. *The Mothers' Clinic for Birth Control*. London, 1921.

Strachey, Oliver. "The Implications of the Women's Suffrage Movement." *Englishwoman* 76 (April 1915): 1–10.

Strachey, Ray. *The Cause: A Short History of the Women's Movement*. 1928. Reprint. London, 1978.

———, ed. *Our Freedom and Its Results*. London, 1936.

Swanwick, H. M. *I Have Been Young*. London, 1935.

———. "The Implications of the Women's Suffrage Movement—A Reply." *Englishwoman* 77 (May 1915): 175–78.

———. *The Roots of Peace*. London, 1938.

———. *The War in Its Effect upon Women*. 1916. Reprint. New York, 1971.

———. *Women and War*. 1915. Reprint. New York, 1971.

Tawney, R. H. "Some Reflections of a Soldier." *Nation*, 21 October 1916, 104–6.

The Times History of the World War, 1914–1918. 18 vols. London, 1914–1918.

Toynbee, Arnold J. *The German Terror in Belgium: An Historical Record*. New York, 1917.

Van de Velde, Th. H. *Sex Hostility in Marriage: Its Origin, Prevention and Treatment*. London, 1931.

WAAC: The Woman's Story of the War. London, 1930.

Ward, Mrs. Humphry. *England's Effort*. New York, 1919.

———. *Towards the Goal*. New York, 1917.

A War Nurse's Diary: Sketches from a Belgian Field Hospital. New York, 1918.

Wells, H. G. *Mr. Britling Sees It Through*. New York, 1916.

West, Rebecca. "Hands That War: The Cordite Makers." *Daily Chronicle*, 1916. In Jane Marcus, ed., *The Young Rebecca: Writings of Rebecca West, 1911–1917*. New York, 1982.

———. "Socialism in the Searchlight." *Daily Chronicle*, 6 November 1916. In Jane Marcus, ed., *The Young Rebecca: Writings of Rebecca West, 1911–1917*. New York, 1982.

A Woman at War, Being Experiences of an Army Signaller in France in 1917–1919. Liverpool, n.d.

Wright, Helena. *Marriage*. Kent, n.d.

SECONDARY SOURCES

Adams, Parveen, and Jeff Minson. "The 'Subject' of Feminism." *m/f* 2 (1978): 43–61.

Alberti, Johanna. *Beyond Suffrage: Feminists in War and Peace, 1914–1928*. New York, 1989.

Banks, Olive. *Faces of Feminism: A Study of Feminism as a Social Movement*. Oxford, 1986.

Berry, Paul, and Alan Bishop, eds. *Testament of a Generation: The Journalism of Vera Brittain and Winifred Holtby*. London, 1985.

Bland, Lucy. "In the Name of Protection: The Policing of Women in the First World War." In Julia Brophy and Carol Smart, eds., *Women-in-Law: Explorations in Law, Family and Sexuality*. London, 1985.

Bogacz, Ted. "'A Tyranny of Words': Language, Poetry, and Antimodernism in England in the First World War." *Journal of Modern History* 58 (September 1986): 643–68.

Box, Muriel. *The Trial of Marie Stopes*. London, 1967.

Braybon, Gail. *Women Workers in the First World War: The British Experience*. London, 1981.

Braybon, Gail, and Penny Summerfield. *Out of the Cage: Women's Experiences in Two World Wars*. London, 1987.

Briant, Keith. *Marie Stopes: A Biography*. London, 1962.

Brookes, Barbara. "The Illegal Operation: Abortion, 1919–39." In The London Feminist History Group, *The Sexual Dynamics of History*. London, 1983.

Buitenhuis, Peter. *The Great War of Words: Literature as Propaganda, 1914–18 and After*. London, 1989.

Burton, Antoinette, "The Feminist Quest for Identity: British Imperial Suffragism and 'Global Sisterhood,' 1900–1915." *Journal of Women's History* 3, no. 2 (1991): 46–81.

Byles, Joan Montgomery. "Women's Experience of World War One: Suffragists, Pacifists and Poets." *Women's Studies International Forum* 8, no. 5 (1985): 473–87.

Cook, Blanche Wiesen, ed. *Crystal Eastman on Women and Revolution*. New York, 1978.

Dangerfield, George. *The Strange Death of Liberal England, 1910–1914*. New York, 1961.

Eksteins, Modris. *Rites of Spring: The Great War and the Birth of the Modern Age*. Boston, 1989.

Eoff, Shirley M. *Viscountess Rhondda, Equalitarian Feminist*. Columbus, Ohio, 1991.

First, Ruth, and Ann Scott. *Olive Schreiner*. London, 1980.

Foster, Jeannette H. *Sex Variant Women in Literature*. New York, 1956.

Fussell, Paul. *The Great War and Modern Memory*. New York, 1975.

Garner, Les. *Stepping Stones to Women's Liberty: Feminist Ideas in the Women's Suffrage Movement, 1900–1918*. Rutherford, N.J., 1984.

Gay, Peter. *Freud: A Life for Our Time*. New York, 1988.

———, ed. *The Freud Reader*. New York, 1989.

Gilbert, Sandra. "Soldier's Heart: Literary Men, Literary Women, and the Great War." *Signs* 8, no. 3 (1983): 422–50.

Gould, Jenny. "Women's Military Services in First World War Britain." In Margaret Randolph Higonnet et al., eds., *Behind the Lines: Gender and the Two World Wars*. New Haven, 1987.

Graves, Robert, and Alan Hodge. *The Long Weekend: A Social History of Great Britain, 1918–1939*. New York, 1963.

Harrison, Brian. *Prudent Revolutionaries: Portraits of British Feminists between the Wars*. Oxford, 1987.

———. *Separate Spheres: The Opposition to Women's Suffrage in Britain*. London, 1978.

———. "Women's Suffrage at Westminster, 1866–1928." In Michael Bentley and John Stevenson, eds., *High and Low Politics in Modern Britain*. Oxford, 1983.

Haste, Cate. *Keep the Home Fires Burning: Propaganda in the First World War*. London, 1977.

Higonnet, Margaret Randolph, Jane Jenson, Sonya Michel, and Margaret Collins Weitz, eds. *Behind the Lines: Gender and the Two World Wars*. New Haven, 1987.

Holton, Sandra Stanley. *Feminism and Democracy: Women's Suffrage and Reform Politics in Britain, 1900–1918*. Cambridge, 1986.

Hynes, Samuel. *A War Imagined: The First World War and English Culture*. New York, 1991.

Jeffreys, Sheila. "Sex Reform and Anti-feminism in the 1920s." In London Feminist History Group, *The Sexual Dynamics of History*. London, 1983.

———. *The Spinster and Her Enemies: Feminism and Sexuality, 1880–1930*. London, 1985.

Kamester, Margaret, and Jo Vellacott, eds. *Militarism versus Feminism: Writings on Women and War*. London, 1987.

Kent, Susan Kingsley. "Gender Reconstruction after the Great War." In Harold L. Smith, ed., *British Feminism in the Twentieth Century*. London, 1989.

———. "The Politics of Sexual Difference: World War I and the Demise of British Feminism." *Journal of British Studies* 27 (July 1988): 232–53.

———. *Sex and Suffrage in Britain, 1860–1914*. Princeton, 1987.

Leathard, Audrey. *The Fight for Family Planning: The Development of Family Planning Services in Britain, 1921–74*. London, 1980.

Leed, Eric J. *No Man's Land: Combat and Identity in World War I*. Cambridge, 1979.

Lewis, Jane. "Feminism and Welfare." In Juliet Mitchell and Ann Oakley, eds., *What Is Feminism?* New York, 1986.

———. "In Search of a Real Equality: Women between the Wars." In Frank Gloversmith, ed., *Class, Culture and Social Change: A New View of the 1930s*. Brighton, N.J., 1980.

———. *The Politics of Motherhood: Child and Maternal Welfare in England, 1900–1939*. London, 1980.

———. *Women in England, 1870–1950: Sexual Divisions and Social Change*. Bloomington, 1984.

Liddington, Jill. *The Life and Times of a Respectable Rebel: Selina Cooper, 1864–1946*. London, 1984.

Liddington, Jill, and Jill Norris. *One Hand Tied behind Us: The Rise of the Women's Suffrage Movement*. London, 1978.

Lock, Joan. *The British Policewoman: Her Story*. London, 1979.

Longenbach, James. "The Women and Men of 1914." In Helen M. Cooper et al., eds., *Arms and the Woman: War, Gender, and Literary Representation*. Chapel Hill, 1989.

MacKenzie, Midge. *Shoulder to Shoulder*. New York, 1988.

Marwick, Arthur. *The Deluge: British Society and the First World War*. New York, 1965.

———. *Women at War, 1914–1918*. London, 1977.

Mitchell, David. *Monstrous Regiment: The Story of the Women of the First World War*. New York, 1965.

Morgan, David. *Suffragist and Liberals: The Politics of Woman Suffrage in England*. Totowa, N.J., 1975.

Pedersen, Susan. "The Failure of Feminism in the Making of the British Welfare State." *Radical History Review* 43 (Winter 1989): 86–110.

———. "Gender, Welfare, and Citizenship in Britain during the Great War." *American Historical Review* 95, no. 4 (1990): 983–1006.

Poovey, Mary. *Uneven Developments: The Ideological Work of Gender in Mid-Victorian England*. Chicago, 1988.

Pugh, Martin. *Electoral Reform in War and Peace, 1906–18*. London, 1978.

———. "Politicians and the Woman's Vote, 1914–1918." *History* 59, no. 197 (974): 358–74.

———. *The Tories and the People, 1880–1935*. Oxford, 1985.

———. *Women and the Women's Movement in Britain, 1914–1959*. London, 1992.

Read, James Morgan. *Atrocity Propaganda, 1914–1919*. New Haven, 1941.

Rickards, Maurice, and Michael Moody, eds. *The First World War: Ephemera, Mementoes, Documents*. London, 1975.

Riley, Denise. *"Am I That Name?" Feminism and the Category of "Women" in History*. London, 1988.

———. " 'The Free Mothers': Pronatalism and Working Women in Industry at the End of the Last War in Britain." *History Workshop Journal* 11 (Spring 1981): 59–83.

———. *War in the Nursery: Theories of the Child and Mother*. London, 1983.

Roberts, Mary Louise. *The Reconstruction of Gender in Postwar France, 1917–1927*. Chicago, forthcoming.

—————. " 'This Civilization No Longer Has Sexes': *La Garçonne* and Cultural Crisis in France after World War I." *Gender and History* 4, no. 1 (1992): 49–69.

Rosen, Andrew. *Rise Up, Women! The Militant Campaign of the Women's Social and Political Union, 1903–1914*. London, 1974.

Rowbotham, Sheila. *A New World for Women: Stella Browne—Socialist Feminist*. London, 1977.

Sanders, M. L., and Philip M. Taylor. *British Propaganda during the First World War, 1914–1918*. London, 1982.

Scott, Joan W. "Deconstructing Equality-Versus-Difference: or, the Uses of Poststructuralist Theory for Feminism." *Feminist Studies* 14, no. 1 (1988): 33–50.

—————. "The Evidence of Experience." *Critical Inquiry* 17, no. 4 (1991): 773–97.

—————. *Gender and the Politics of History*. New York, 1988.

—————. "Rewriting History." In Margaret Randolph Higonnet et al., eds. *Behind the Lines: Gender and the Two World Wars*. New Haven, 1987.

Showalter, Elaine. *The Female Malady: Women, Madness, and English Culture, 1830–1980*. New York, 1985.

Smith, Bonnie G. *Changing Lives: Women in European History since 1700*. Lexington, Mass., 1989.

Smith, Harold L. "British Feminism in the 1920s." In Harold L. Smith, ed., *British Feminism in the Twentieth Century*. Aldershot, 1990.

—————. "Gender and Pay: The Equal Pay for Equal Work Issue in Britain in the 1920s." Unpublished manuscript, 1991.

—————. "The Problem of Equal Pay for Equal Work in Great Britain during World War II." *Journal of Modern History* 53 (December 1981): 652–72.

—————. "Sex vs. Class: British Feminists and the Labour Movement, 1919–1929." *Historian* 47 (November 1984): 19–37.

Soloway, Richard Allen. *Birth Control and the Population Question in England, 1877–1930*. Chapel Hill, 1982.

Spender, Dale. *Time and Tide Wait for No Man*. London, 1984.

Stromberg, Roland, N. *Redemption by War: The Intellectual and 1914*. Lawrence, Kans., 1982.

Summers, Anne. *Angels and Citizens: British Women as Military Nurses, 1854–1914*. London, 1988.

Thane, Pat. "The Women of the British Labour Party and Feminism, 1906–1945." In Harold L. Smith, ed., *British Feminism in the Twentieth Century*. Aldershot, 1990.

Thom, Deborah. "Women and Work in Wartime Britain." In Richard Wall and Jay Winter, eds., *The Upheaval of War: Family, Work and Welfare in Europe, 1914–1918*. Cambridge, 1988.

Tickner, Lisa. *The Spectacle of Women: Imagery of the Suffrage Campaign, 1907–14*. Chicago, 1988.

Tylee, Claire M. " 'Maleness Run Riot'—The Great War and Women's Resistance to Militarism." *Women's Studies International Forum* 11, no. 3 (1988): 199–210.

Vellacott, Jo. "Feminist Consciousness and the First World War." *History Workshop Journal* 23 (Spring 1987): 81–101.

Ware, Vron. *Beyond the Pale: White Women, Racism and History*. London, 1992.

Weeks, Jeffrey. *Sex, Politics and Society: The Regulation of Sexuality since 1800.* London, 1981.

Wilson, Trevor. *The Myriad Faces of War: Britain and the Great War, 1914–1918.* Cambridge, 1986.

Wiltsher, Anne. *Most Dangerous Women: Feminist Peace Campaigners of the Great War.* London, 1985.

Wohl, Robert. *The Generation of 1914.* Cambridge, Mass., 1979.

Woollacott, Angela Mary. *"Mad on Munitions": The Lives of Women Munitions Workers in World War I.* Ph.D. diss., University of California, Santa Barbara, 1988.

INDEX

Abbott, Elizabeth, 117, 120–22
Abraham, Karl, 111
Active Service Cadet Corps, 29
Adams, Parveen, 7
agricultural laborers: women as, 35
air raids, 52, 65
Alberti, Johanna, 4, 5, 7, 16, 119–21, 132, 162n.31
Alec-Tweedie, Mrs., 36, 39, 44, 46
"Am I That Name?" Feminism and the Category of "Women" in History, 7
ambulance drivers, 10, 17, 35, 52, 61–62, 64, 67
Ampthill, Lord, 118
Antidote, 42
antifeminism, 4, 113, 117–18, 120, 137
Anti-Suffrage Review, 87
antisuffragism, 6, 18, 75, 80, 82, 84–85, 87, 91, 121–22, 125
Ashby, Brian, 53
Ashby, Margaret, 53
Ashton, Margaret, 77–78, 80, 118
Asquith, Herbert H., 82, 88–89, 94
atrocities, German, 23–26, 30, 47, 50, 75, 77, 96, 115. *See also* propaganda, atrocity
auxiliary soldiers: women as, 10, 35

Bagnold, Enid, 67
Balfour, Lady Dorothy, 122
Balfour, Lady Frances, 78, 80–81
Banks, Olive, 120, 132
Barclay, Florence L., 43
Bartlett, F. C., 46
Battle of the Somme, The (film), 48
Belgian atrocities. *See* atrocities, German
Belgian deportees, 26
Belgian women, 24, 26, 30, 77, 96
Belgium, 9, 22–24, 32–34, 47, 55, 59–60, 68, 74–76, 79–80
Bellairs, Commander, 89
Beyond the Pleasure Principle, 103, 106
Billing, Noel Pemberton, 42
biology: as determinant of sex roles, 110–12, 139–40
birth control, 117, 123–24, 129–31, 132
Bland, Lucy, 28

Blatch, Harriot Stanton, 35–37, 42–43
Blunden, Edward, 101
Board of Trade, 33
Bolshevik Revolution. *See* Russia: revolution in
Bonar Law, Andrew, 84, 90–91
Borden, Mary, 62, 66–67, 71, 101, 137
Bowerman, Elsie, 48, 51, 59
Boyle, Nina, 20–21, 35, 47, 75, 95–96, 100
Britannia, 89, 156n.31
British Expeditionary Force, 14
Brittain, Edward, 53, 63
Brittain, Vera, 14, 53–55, 58–60, 62–71, 116, 118, 124–25, 130, 134–37, 141
Brooke, Rupert, 13, 48
Browne, F. W. Stella, 126–28, 130–32
Bryce, Lord, 23, 85
Bryce Report, 23–26
Bulan, S., 17
Burton, Antoinette, 93

Canetti, Elias, 105
Carson, Sir Edward, 89
castration, 41, 71
Catt, Carrie Chapman, 79
Cavell, Edith, 87, 156n.28
Cecil, Lord Hugh, 90
Cecil, Lord Robert, 76, 84
Chance, Janet, 112
Chesterton, G. K., 108
Chew, Ada Nield, 10
Church of England, 130
Churchill, Lady Randolph, 27
Churchill, Winston, 82
Civilization and Its Discontents, 104
Clephane, Irene, 28, 40–41, 100, 142
Clynes, J. R., 90
Committee on War Films, 48
Common Cause, 15–19, 21, 28–29, 31, 33, 79, 125
Conan Doyle, Arthur, 39
conscientious objectors, 45, 82
conscription, 43, 87
Conservative party, 82
Contagious Diseases Act, 9, 28
Cooper, Selina, 10

Star, 23

Stekel, William, 106–8, 112

Stocks, Mary, 83, 109, 117, 119–20, 132, 152n.6

Stopes, Marie, 109, 127, 130

Strachey, J. M., 81

Strachey, Oliver, 80

Strachey, Ray, 21, 77–78, 100–101, 114, 122, 134–35

Subjection of Women, The, 120

suffrage. *See* vote, the

Suffrage Sewing Guilds, 17

Suffragette, 26, 34, 74–75, 89

suffragette prisoners, 20

suffragists, 3, 9, 16, 18, 20, 28, 34, 64, 80, 96; constitutional, 83; militant, 13–14, 20, 32, 47, 74–75, 82–84, 96, 136

Swanwick, Helena, 18–20, 40, 48, 77, 79, 121, 128–29, 134–35

Sydenham, Lord, 14, 85

Tatler, 44

Tawney, R. H., 47

Territorial Force, 18

Thane, Pat, 118

Thompson, Helen, 134

Tickner, Lisa, 34

Time and Tide, 56, 73, 98, 123–25, 131, 133–34, 142

Times, 23, 34, 39, 48, 105

Times History of the World War, 28

tram conductors: women as, 35

Tree of Heaven, The, 63, 71, 97

trench warfare, 48, 50, 58, 63, 65, 87, 89, 95, 101

Tuke, Mrs., 80

U-boats, 31, 52, 57

Van de Velde, Theodore, 108–9, 111–12

Vellacott, Jo, 147n.15

venereal disease, 9, 39, 41, 99

Voluntary Aid Detachment (VAD), 10, 17, 52–53, 60, 62, 65–67, 71

Vote, 47, 76, 98, 123

vote, the, 3–4, 18, 47, 73, 127; age restriction on, 91–93, 96; as linked to debates over war, 74–96. *See also* antisuffragism; Representation of the People Act; suffragists

war: memoirs and novels of women during, 9; romantic vision of, 48–49, 51; sexual im-

agery of, 25–27, 29, 30, 52, 68, 72, 97, 102–6, 111, 115, 126, 140–41

war babies, 28, 30, 33, 39

War Pensions Committee, 98

Ward, Arnold, 87, 91

Ward, Helen, 122

Ware, Vron, 93

We That Were Young, 54, 66, 69

Wells, H. G., 13, 41–42, 46, 53

West, Rebecca, 14, 35, 36, 75, 118, 127, 135–37

Westminster Gazette, 23

Wilde, Oscar, 42

Wilkinson, Ellen, 142

William II, 75

Wilson, Dr. Helen, 17

Wilson, Trevor, 25, 31, 39–40, 42–43

Wiltsher, Anne, 20, 81

Woman's Leader, 118–20, 129–31, 133–34

women: as a constructed category, 7–8, 18; as defined against "the social," 8–9, 18, 22, 141; as life-givers, 21; passionlessness of, 110; passivity in, 19–20; protection of, 6, 23, 26, 33, 47; responsibilities of in wartime, 16–18; as sexual property, 26; traditional roles of, 14, 16–18, 22, 30, 112, 115, 120; as victims of atrocities, 23–26, 30; violence against, 95–96, 98; as warriors, 115. *See also* femininity

Women and War, 19

Women of England's Active Service League, 26–27

Women Volunteer Police, 21

Women's Army, 17–18

Women's Auxiliary Army Corps (WAAC), 40, 42, 59, 61–62, 65, 68–71

Women's Freedom League (WFL), 20–21, 35, 75, 123, 130–31

Women's Interest Committee of NUWSS, 21

Women's Liberal Review, 35

Women's Social and Political Union (WSPU), 20, 26, 33, 48, 51, 59, 74, 84, 89

Women's Suffrage National Aid Corps, 21

Women's Volunteer Reserve Army, 32

working-class women, 4, 9, 21, 29, 92, 118–19, 123, 130

Wright, Helena, 109

Young, Sir George, 27

Young, Winifred, 61